Art, Community and Environment
Educational Perspectives

Art, Community and Environment
Educational Perspectives

Edited by Glen Coutts and Timo Jokela

Series Editor: John Steers

intellect Bristol, UK / Chicago, USA

First Published in the UK in 2008 by
Intellect Books, The Mill, Parnall Road, Fishponds, Bristol, BS16 3JG, UK

First published in the USA in 2008 by
Intellect Books, The University of Chicago Press, 1427 E. 60th Street, Chicago,
IL 60637, USA

Series: Readings in Art and Design Education
Series Editor: John Steers

A catalogue record for this book is available from the British Library.

Cover Design: Gabriel Solomons
Copy Editor: Holly Spradling
Typesetting: Mac Style, Beverley, E. Yorkshire

ISSN 1747-6208
Paperback ISBN 978-1-84150-257-1
Hardback ISBN 978-1-84150-189-5

Printed and bound by Gutenberg Press, Malta.

CONTENTS

ACKNOWLEDGEMENTS

First, we are grateful to the authors, those who have allowed their papers to be reprinted and to those who have revised papers or written a chapter specifically for this collection.

Second, our thanks to Intellect Books, Blackwell Publishing, the NSEAD, John Steers in particular and the Editorial Board of the International Journal of Art and Design Education that collectively made this publication possible. Third, we would like to thank Donald Gunn for his critical readings of new material, insightful suggestions and patience.

Finally we would like to thank our colleagues in the Department of Sport, Culture and the Arts, University of Strathclyde and the University of Lapland; without their support, encouragement and patience this book would not have appeared.

Glen Coutts and Timo Jokela

PREFACE

This book is the seventh in a planned series of anthologies dealing with a range of issues in art and design education. The previously published titles in the Intellect 'Readings in Art and Design Education' series are:

Critical Studies In Art & Design Education
Postmodernism and Art and Design Education: Collected Essays
Histories of Art and Design Education
The Problem of Assessment in Art & Design
Research in Art & Design Education: Issues and Exemplars
Writing on Drawing: Essays on Drawing Practice and Research

Further titles are in preparation.

The primary, but not exclusive source of chapters are papers previously published in the *International Journal of Art & Design Education* and where appropriate these have been updated. It should be noted that any reference to the English National Curriculum statutory Orders, the Scottish National Guidelines etc. are to the versions of curriculum current at the time of original publication.

The *National Society for Education in Art and Design* is the leading national authority in the United Kingdom, combining professional association and trade union functions, which represents every facet of art, craft and design in education. Its authority is partly based upon 120 years concern for the subject, established contacts within government and local authority departments, and a breadth of membership drawn from every sector of education from the primary school to universities.

More information about the Society and its range of publications is available at www.nsead.org or from NSEAD, The Gatehouse, Corsham Court, Corsham, Wiltshire SN13 0BZ, United Kingdom. (Tel: +44 (0)1249 714825)

John Steers
Series Editor

INTRODUCTION

The sixteen chapters in this book explore the complex relationship between art practice, community participation and the environment, built or natural. Five of the papers have been previously published in the *International Journal of Art and Design Education* (iJADE). The other eleven chapters were commissioned specifically for this edition.

The *Readings in Art and Design Education* series sets out to promote debate about a range of issues in art and design education, and other volumes have dealt with issues ranging from the assessment and history of art education to the impact of postmodernism. The theme of this volume is the broad educational potential of environmental and community art, explored from the personal perspectives of authors from the UK, Finland and Australia.

To fully explore these emergent dimensions in art education would require at least two volumes, one on the environment and the other on community. The formal sector of education in art and design, in the UK at any rate, has been subject to constant review and reform, but informal contexts such as community centres and local projects have managed to escape the levels of prescription bemoaned by art educators in schools. Because many of the projects discussed in this book are community driven, happening outside of school, college or university walls, they occupy an educational 'twilight zone' free of attainment targets, league tables, national tests and other such constraints.

We have chosen to take a broad view of art and design education, embracing the more informal sectors of society and the tricky and often elusive concept of community art. What is going on in different countries and in the different sectors of education there? When does art practice cross the line into pedagogy? What do artists and art educators mean when they talk about 'ownership', 'empowerment' or 'agency'? What can school-based art educators learn from people working with community groups outside the school curriculum and vice versa? What are the particular training needs of community artists? These are just some of the questions addressed by contributors to this edition. Readers reflecting on their own experiences will no doubt think of many more.

The book is divided into three sections, with the general themes of 'Environments', 'Communities' and 'Education', which the contributors explore from their personal perspectives as artists, academics or authors. Inevitably, however, there are many points of overlap. Making connections is a key dimension of practice in the field of community and environmental art and research, and debate in these areas does not lend itself to neat categorization.

In the first section, Environments, three authors focus on arts practice and its implications for education. Jokela offers an account of his background as an artist and art educator, explaining how his art is inextricably linked with his identity as a Laplander, and with the wilderness environment of Finnish Lapland. McWilliam outlines an ongoing project with outdoor education and community art students at the University of Strathclyde, using a vignette of the students' own reflective writing to describe how they are challenged to consider the relationship between art, environment and aesthetics. Miles shifts the focus from wilderness and rural to urban environments, arguing that education has a responsibility to investigate the problems of urban sustainability and changing notions of 'the city'.

The next section, Communities, contains four chapters with the recurrent themes of participation, ownership and empowerment. Using examples of local projects directly involving community participants, Dawes, like Miles but from a slightly different perspective, considers the changing role of the artist in the light of the impact recent political shifts in Scotland have had on community and cultural policy. Huhmarniemi takes us on a very different journey. Teachers and students in Finland are engaged in various community art projects in towns and villages all over the country, but are often unable to meet face to face for debate or tutorial support. This chapter describes how virtual learning environments might lead to the creation of effective communities of learning. Another Finnish author, Hiltunen, argues that community art enlivens and energizes through the notion of 'agency'. She describes the inclusive approach of some remarkable projects, in which representatives of every sector of even the most isolated village populations were encouraged to participate. Bennett, in the final chapter in this section, describes a collaborative project called 'Window Sills', which explores the notion of 'territories' and the interface of public and private space within a specific community.

The third and largest section contains nine chapters. In both chapters, in her own right, Adams examines the potential educational benefits of study in, and through, the built environment. Her collaboration with Chisholm describes a small-scale project where student-teachers focus on the built environment as a formal educational resource. By contrast, Austin succinctly outlines a unique undergraduate programme for community artists training to work in the informal sector. She considers the essential ingredients of a four-year-degree programme, asking what areas need to be addressed to provide graduates with the range of skills necessary to work in community arts. Coutts examines the relationship between 'public' and 'community' art in Glasgow, asking where there might be points of overlap, distinction or tension. He raises questions not only about the purpose of community art, but also about how we know when it is effective. Jokela offers a similar account of a programme for trainee art teachers in Lapland, arguing that a 'project-based' approach has much to commend it. McKenzie takes a fascinating look at whether public sculpture might have played a didactic role in the nineteenth-century Glaswegian education system, while from Australia, Hooper and Boyle outline a project entitled *Living City*. Inviting young people to work with artists, designers and planners on urban design projects, they argue that the project's 'workshop' approach can be seen as 'laboratories of urban literacy and empowerment for young people'. In the final chapter, Coutts looks back at a project that used multimedia techniques to encourage students in Glasgow's schools to consider the role and function of public art and urban design.

The chapters in this book range from descriptions of specific projects to polemics on the purposes and efficacy of art in public and community contexts. We hope that the personal and theoretical perspectives of the artists, writers and academics who have contributed will play a fruitful part in the debate about the educational potential of environmental and community art.

Glen Coutts and Timo Jokela

Part One
Environments

1

A Wanderer in the Landscape: Reflections on the Relationship between Art and the Northern Environment

Timo Jokela

The landscape of identity

I am an environmental artist and places affect me perhaps more than people do. I was born and have lived most of my life in northern Finland. Being a Laplander is one of the stronger aspects of my identity. This identity is not static; I consider it a dynamic whole that is constantly being reconstructed and comprises many other identities.[1] Identities are located in symbolic time and space – in an 'imaginary geography'. They always incorporate a feeling of home, the 'landscape of the identity'.[2] It is precisely in the landscape that my art and my identity as a Laplander converge and form a leitmotif for my most salient work as an artist.[3] I recognize myself in the following text, where Tournier describes the bond between person and place at its strongest:

> ...individuals become attached to their place and merge with it; they associate their place with their image of themselves; they locate themselves there wholly, so that no one can touch the place without touching them.[4]

In territorial terms, the landscape of my identity is extensive indeed. It ranges from the forests and rivers of Lapland to its fells and the shores of the Arctic Ocean. I have worked in this landscape since the mid-1970s. Before starting my formal education as an artist, I made drawings and paintings. What interested me were the marks people left on the landscape: reindeer fences, lumberjacks' cabins, villages along a river and fishery buildings on the Arctic Ocean. I could experience the narratives infused in these objects and feel how people had found their place amid nature, on this planet, and under this sky. In my eyes, these structures erected as part of the workaday world were manifestations

Snow installation in Kirkenes at the Barents Sea, Timo Jokela. 2005. Norway. *Photograph by Timo Jokela*

of commercial history and of a material cultural heritage, and, yet, at the same time, reflections of how people conceived of themselves as part of the universe. Later, on reading the work of Norberg-Schulz, I came upon the name for this aesthetically and cultural-historically coloured experience, a term familiar in the phenomenology of landscape and architecture, *genius loci*.[5] I also came across the concept later when I became involved in environmental art.[6]

I received a modernist art education. This dislodged my local identity, questioning its significance. At that time, art was seen as a universal phenomenon, with no real place for the voice of local people. Good art was independent of its surroundings. The basic tenets of modernism – the individuality of the artist, the autonomy of art and its emanation from centres towards peripheries – now, seen from a postmodern perspective, smack of colonialism. Modernism subjugated art to the point where landscape art, as a tradition for depicting 'localness', came to be seen as the preserve of the dilettante. When I was a student, and for some time afterwards, I felt doubly marginalized by modernism. I had taken an interest not only in the Northern periphery, but in landscape as well.

The way back to the Northern landscape and its essential elements revealed itself to me during my travels in Europe. People's natural and everyday links to the landscape had been broken in the big cities. The exposition in Paris of the Italian *Arte Povera*[7] movement opened the way for me to go back to the materials and traditional methods of my own environment. When I returned from my journey, the fish dams, hayricks and woodpiles where I lived took on a new aesthetic significance. I began to think about making the work, the methods and the skills which these objects embodied, and which I knew well, part of my art. The *MA space-time*[8] exhibition, which illustrated the influence of Zen on the arts in Japan, provided me with a new perspective on how I might work in the landscape. The way I experienced space and time and my interaction with nature – fishing, hunting, picking berries and cutting firewood – found their counterparts in the meditative and holistic sensitivity to the landscape found in Zen art. The coordination of body and mind, and the aesthetics and essence of moving around in a landscape, began to coalesce into artistic activity. It was only later that the examples of American and English environmental art signposted and reinforced a strategy which enabled me to approach my own environment as art. A common basis for making and conceptualizing art began to take shape and became a permanent facet of my existence.

Since finishing my formal education as an artist, in addition to making my own art, I have worked at the University where I have focused on developing art education and teaching in that field. Today we have rediscovered the bond between art and the environment in which it is realized, and marginality now has a place of its own in discussions about art.[9] For me, the way my art addresses the North has become something which I use to model and develop not only my art itself, but also pedagogy dealing with the relationship between art and the environment.[10] The fact that I know the North from within helps me to assess the impact my art has on the environment where it is located and created.

There are many issues connected with the interaction between art and environment. Firstly, the relationship between localness and being an artist always entails the dilemma of colonialism and emancipation.[11] Secondly, I must ask myself what makes me think I can offer something through my art that surpasses the local people's everyday experience and knowledge of a place, and how I can incorporate into my art my own life experience, conception of art and what I think is of value in art without colonializing local people and places. Thirdly, how can I give my work a form that will allow the environment and community to be a productive and constructive element of its artistic content? And, fourthly, how might I guide future art educators to plan and realize emancipatory processes without colonializing the communities in which they will work? These questions are basic methodological and philosophical considerations in environmental and community art – choices about the way art is done. They also underscore the relationship of art to our cultural heritage and the values it embraces.

The ways of art and science
Artists often find it difficult to talk about their works and the experiences associated with creating them. The creative process is an intense, experience-directed and often confused one. Art involves a great deal of tacit knowledge.[12] Making art does not require the same verbally articulated basis as academic research does. Researchers follow a particular path, which they define in theoretical terms and try to adhere to in the hope of reaching their goal. Artists fumble about and do not always know what their goal is; when they reach it, they cannot necessarily describe the path they took to get there. However, I can try to understand my art by assuming the position of a researcher and observing my work as a product of the culture to which I belong. I can also toy with different perspectives by venturing into the no-man's-land between art and science. This liminal space is very often the site where concepts and experiences exert complementary influences on each other, and this is what interests me most.

This path leads into the realm of phenomenology and to an attempt to understand phenomenal experiences, of which the works I create and their sites are examples. According to Arnold Berleant,[13] a phenomenological description produces an effective and direct presentation. Description of the environment requires the same sensitivity as the description of art, because as well as the outward appearance of the landscape, it must depict the actions and reactions that are connected to it and the meanings associated with them.

Common filters for studying landscape and art
The basis for my art and for my understanding of it is an intertextual weave comprising a discourse born of localness, 'differentness', marginality and otherness in the postmodern sense, rather than an account of my art in theoretical terms or a practical description of my work. Moving away from the conventional modernist perspective, I am looking outside the world of art for appropriate interpretative models. Taking my lead from environmental aesthetics, I have made a close study of phenomenal, culturally bound environmental experience,[14] and my guide to the textuality of landscape and a multidimensional reading and interpretation of it has been the tradition of humanist geography.[15] A search for beauty is central to the humanistic study of landscape and is something it has in common with the world of art.[16] My approach has also

Litus Repromissiosis – The Promised Shore, Timo Jokela. 2001. Snow installation at Arctic Ocean waiting for the tide.
Signs are from the door of an old church cabin. Northern Norway. *Photograph by Timo Jokela*

Sinus Varanger. Timo Jokela. 2001. Detail of the snow installation at Varangerfjorden, Northern Norway. *Photograph by Timo Jokela*

been greatly influenced by Yi-Fu Tuan's[17] study of topophilia (the feeling of belonging to a place, love for a place) and Edward Relph's[18] studies of place, which look at the bond between person and place, local identity and its converse, placelessness. 'Landscape' and 'place' are, in fact, often used as overlapping concepts, although 'place' has wider social implications.[19] I have also drawn on postmodern art research, including the work of Lucy Lippard[20] and Suzanne Lacy,[21] which reflects a shift of interest away from modernist thought towards the relationship of individuals and communities to the environment, landscapes, places, localness and their own lifeworlds. Similarly, in their environmental and community art, Suzi Gablik[22] and Irit Rogoff[23] offer new interpretations of the relationship of art to place, to landscape and to the work and leisure activities that are carried out in them.

Intelligent embodiment

One of the principal challenges of postmodernism has been to question the long-standing convention of emphasizing the separation of people's everyday activities, such as their work, from their aesthetic experience. As Esa Sironen puts it:

> The subject of a landscape is not the farmer, just as the subject of water is not a fish swimming in it. To be such a subject, a person may not naively be part of nature but must comprehend him – or herself as standing opposite to nature, distinguished from it. Landscape is a relational concept. It requires mowing hay, cutting down trees, stopping one's mushroom picking, straightening one's back and putting oneself for only a moment beyond the confines of work and productivity – looking at things as a child, artist, philosopher.[24]

The background to this is the assumption by Kantian aesthetics that when we are inside a landscape we are unable to recognize its aesthetic aspects.[25] As Kari Väyrynen explains, Kant sought to demonstrate the superiority of moral consciousness to sensuality and physical human frailty.[26] This, in turn, is underlain by a Cartesian dualism which divides the world into reason and feeling, subject and object. But it is precisely corporeality, and, in particular, the relationship between the work that human beings do and aesthetic experience, that underpins the new paradigm of art and the environment and provides a direction for my personal art practice. In striving for experience that is not divided crudely into subject and object, I am adopting the existential-phenomenological position of Merleau-Ponty, who believed that embodiment in the environment is the elemental condition for all thought, and that no thought can originate from pure consciousness.[27]

Our bodily relationship to the environment has changed since the times of Descartes and Kant. In general, the amount of physical work we do has decreased dramatically, and it is to counterbalance this that I have made an effort in my art to transform traditional working methods into methods for experiencing the environment and creating environmental and community art. This turns upside down the Kantian relationship between acting in and aesthetically experiencing the environment. What was previously referred to as 'work' (routine activity that stifled creative thought and aesthetic experience) now becomes 'stopping in the landscape' (a physical experience which makes thought possible). Physical work becomes a type of meditation in which the body opens pathways to sensation, to the environment's stream of consciousness,

Pallas – *Fathers' Signs*. Timo Jokela. 2005. Snow installation on Pallas Fell, Finland. Patterns based on earmarks of reindeers, realization made in cooperation with locals. *Photograph by Timo Jokela*

and disengages for a moment our dualist Cartesian brains. This releases creative potential, engenders aesthetic experience and restores the link between body and mind in a way that resonates with the fundamental Heideggerian concept of 'beginning thought from the beginning'.[28]

Lived landscape

When I work in the Northern landscape, I would argue that I am continuing the tradition of landscape painting. As active subject, I am not the ideal, free individual, but a social being conditioned by culture.[29] Clearly, the landscapes that form the starting point for landscape art, whether in their natural state or shaped by people, are always products of a culture and defined by it before they become themes for a work of art.[30] The way I conceive of the Northern landscape is simultaneously guided by two models: the relationship to nature[31] that forms part of my Northern identity and the tradition of visual art. I have, however, moved a long way from landscape painting, the traditional means of depicting and imparting value to the association between environment and culture.[32] I do not place myself before a landscape as a visual observer, nor do I frame what I see; rather, I try to discover the landscape from within, using all the senses that enable me to experience it. I try to work with the materials of the place and with the stimuli and content it offers. I call myself not a landscape artist but an environmental artist.[33]

In making this statement I want to shift the focus from an external view of the landscape to its 'flow', which goes through me in the form of material, observations, experiences, meanings and values. The environment flows not only through me but through the entire community in which I am working at a particular time. My observations and experiences are my own as an individual, but I interpret and understand them as a member of the culture of which I am a part. It becomes difficult to distinguish the environment and the community from one another – the concept 'North', for example, defines both location and community simultaneously. The North is a network of different places and the communities living and working in them. Looked at in this way, my environmental art has affinities with Suzanne Lacy's[34] 'new genre public art', in which public participation and commitment are the basis for and the objective of making art. New genre public art is defined not only by its environment but, also, by its public. The focus is not merely the specific place or area where the art is located, but also the aesthetic expression of the values it activates in its human participants.

My aim is that my art should form part of the cultural practice in which landscapes and the values they incorporate are produced and renewed. My works reflect the concept of landscape in Lapland by being at the same time products and constituents of it. My preference for the term 'environmental art' over 'landscape art' can be attributed not only to the fact that my art emphasizes community and ecological values but, also, to my interest in detaching it from a historical tradition with unwanted overtones. There is nothing revolutionary about this, it is more a subtle shift of perspective, or even a shuttling between mainstream 'high art' and local art culture – a moving about in the reality which I am constructing for myself and in which I construct my identity. As a product of a western artistic education and a native of a northern village, I

Arjeplog – at the Border. Stone installation at the border of Sweden and Norway. Realization by Timo Jokela and the artists of The Trans Barents Highway Workshop. 2004. *Photograph by Timo Jokela*

try to place myself between the two, looking in two directions at the same time from a single point. I try to examine the North – my own phenomenal world – as an intertextual narrative in which western art and science are interwoven with the stories, meanings and truths of the local people.

Dimensions of the environment and making art

Environment is in itself a multidimensional concept, and there is some disagreement on how it should be defined. When working in the environment, one must nevertheless start with something concrete; as an artist, one cannot engage in indefinite ontological reflection. In picking up a snow shovel, video recorder, chainsaw or camera, I come into contact with different dimensions of the environment, which can be examined by analysing it in terms of the levels of its objective, emotional and textual meaning.[35] This opens up different, but simultaneous, perspectives on the environment, the works of art being constructed in it and the interpretation of these works. My aim is to create in my works a relationship to the environment that interacts with each of its levels.

First of all, the objective environment and its visible landscape elements, such as rivers, forests, fells, the sea, the darkness of winter and light summer nights, determine the physical form of the work I create – its material, scale and way of being. There are also less visible dimensions related to the flow of the environment: growing, withering, the melting of snow, the freezing of water. Secondly, landscapes open up views into the emotions and the subjective level of the world of experience: work, free time, trekking or simply living. As well as bringing my tools to the sites where I work, I take along my sensing, observing and feeling self. My phenomenal environment is always shaped by my world of experience, my emotions and personal history. On the third, or textual, level the cultural context of my art comes to light. The works become attached to issues and values manifested by a range of interests – the local community, tourism, commerce, ecology, artistic institutions and schemes for social inclusiveness.

On the textual level, my approach has much in common with iconographic studies which look at landscapes through the meanings and cultural messages they contain. Of particular interest in such research are meanings associated with the landscape and its elements that are shared by particular groups of people and the deeper cultural, historical and ideological factors underlying these meanings.[36] The discourse involving the landscape itself, the artist interpreting it, the work of art and the recipient who interprets it is not stable or enduring. A landscape is not a static mental image, but a mood that lives and changes along with the life history of the person experiencing it.[37] In my case, the path has led from the gaze of a hunter and fisher to that of an artist. In my art, I often relive the processes of change that have affected the cultural heritage of the places where I work and my own personal interaction with the landscape. At a very early stage, art became a means of reconstructing my relationship to the Northern environment and its communities.

Timo Jokela working with snow installation at Levi Fell. 2000.
Photograph by Mirja Hiltunen

Daughters of Päiviö. Timo Jokela. 1998. Detail of the snow installation on the top of Levi Fell. Finland. *Photograph by Timo Jokela*

Traditional images of the landscape in the North – constraint or opportunity?

Tarasti points out that the reality of a landscape – as a culture or community conceives of it – can be grasped only if it is manifest as images in the different texts of that culture.[38] It has been typical of both literature and the visual arts in Lapland that earlier works have provided impetus and models for later descriptions of the region.[39] The body of images of the landscape that art has created programmes the way in which we look at the environment, and in the case of Lapland has ideologized this perspective as a provincial 'album'.[40] It would merit a study in its own right to investigate whether the album prevailing at any given time is a product of the general mentality of the times, of an iconological drift, or of conscious ideological-political activity. How we understand the landscape in Lapland depends on whose descriptions and texts we are interpreting,[41] and it is this 'who' that has become the crucial question in postmodern discussion of the aesthetic aspects of art and nature.[42]

Landscape art in Lapland has in the past been treated as little more than a peripheral afterthought of the German Romantic tradition. In the 1950s and 1960s, in particular, it was approached as a kind of outdoor realism seen through an Impressionist-tinged interpretative filter – landscape artists were called depicters of lights and of the colours of water and air,[43] and discussion of landscape art became fixated on the perspectives offered by two fundamentally very different concepts. But whereas nature with its grand 'abstract' phenomena – including light, shadow, colour and rhythm – to a certain extent remained an object of formal attention in the study of art, in keeping with the traditions of Impressionism and Expressionism, the meanings of the landscape and their regional, local and textual levels did not interest researchers in visual art, in thrall as they were to the god of Modernism.

More than this, discussion of landscape art in Finland was circumscribed by a climate of national guilt, and Lapland was no exception. Interest in its landscapes was seen partly as a post-war phenomenon: Lapland was portrayed as something lost, the type of 'primeval landscape' associated with Karelia, onto which a negative reaction to modernization could be projected.[44] Attempts to understand the landscapes of Lapland proceeded via written art history, and the voice of the local population was not taken into consideration.

This mentality detached the interpretation of art from its natural context and anchored it beyond where the local people could give it meaning. Nature was divorced from culture, and those who lived amid nature, along with ideas associated with it, were exiled to the margins. This utilitarian view of nature applies no less to landscape than to any other area of art and art research. Porteous[45] reminds us that when landscape lost its significance as a focus of interest in art, science and philosophy, its bond to the romantic tradition was also severed. It did, however, live on in the public consciousness, and an undercurrent of Romanticism still plays a major role in the perception of the North, particularly in the area of tourism. A knowledge of all the factors that have contributed to the creation of the landscape album of the North is important to me. It is only against this historical background that I am able to assess the innovative quality of my art, and what and whose 'North' is speaking in my work at any given time.

Makreeta of Kurtakko. 2005. Willow installation. A community art work made by villagers of Kurtakko and Timo Jokela. Photograph by Timo Jokela

The wanderer in the landscape

The snow, ice, hay or wood installations I create form part of the northern landscape. Often, they are located in places that can be described as edges, boundaries or extremes. This may be the top of a fell, an outlying crag on the Arctic Ocean coast or a forested 'middle of nowhere'. Within the tradition of landscape art, the North has its own distinctive place. 'North' carries associations of loneliness, barrenness, wilderness, emptiness and extremity. The spreading wilderness that shimmers before our mind's eye represents the promise of a cleansing of mind and soul, a chance to get closer to something which is threatening to disappear from our modern world. The tradition of German Romanticism that underlies this mindset draws on Kantian philosophy and is grounded in the concept of 'grandeur'. Carl Gustav Carus has this to say:

> Before the grandeur of nature human beings become aware of their insignificance, but through this realisation rise above nature – or their own nature.[46]

The idea of the wanderer, traveller or artist seeking a sublime natural experience has surfaced in Lappish travel literature, as can be seen in the work of Kullervo Kemppainen:

> Hurry and anxiety, those nightmarish companions of modern life, cannot extend their influence that far. Embraced in nature's grandeur, we experience our insignificance, see the triviality of our concerns. There, the mind is quickened, the body toughened and the soul cleansed.[47]

This echoes the concept of the spiritually sublime in German Romanticism, of the 'divine wilderness', or in the American wilderness tradition, of the frontier as a site of a heroic encounter between noble savage and pioneer. The perception of the North as a land of fells and scenic outlooks is common throughout Europe, and its origins go back to the 1700s. As Esa Sironen writes:

> Thus, rising to the mountaintop became a ritual of the new, modern world and a rite of passage which here in Finland, for historical reasons, took on the added facet of the gilt frame of the National Awakening.[48]

The motif of wandering in my work can be seen as a seeking out of barren extremes. There is a parallel to the literature of Lapland in which, according to Lehtola,[49] the protagonists often relinquish security and set out for the unknown, where they can test their manhood. This way of combining time and place is typical of Lappish literature. The main characters work outdoors, are constantly on the move, hunt and camp in the wilds and travel both by night and by day in all kinds of weather conditions. Their dwellings are temporary shelters with the open world just beyond their doors. Being on the road and working in the landscape involve movement in both a physical and an abstract or psychological

Sagadi Sign. Timo Jokela. 2002. Wood installation at Sagadi Manor, Estonia. Realization in cooperation with locals. *Photograph by Timo Jokela*

Isghl – on the Alps. Timo Jokela. 2002. Hay installation. *Photograph by Timo Jokela*

space. A journey and the route it takes can act as a spatial metaphor in everyday speech as well as in art: life is often compared to a road, and travel seen as a journey of the mind, something more than simply physical movement from one point to another.[50]

This physical movement is, however, important – it is the constant change of place that is crucial, not the destination. The journey to the physical sites where my works are located is an essential part of the process of creating the work and, also, perhaps of the ontological manifestation of my art.

Landscape art emphasizes information about the landscape that is conveyed by visual observation; but when the artist inhabits an environment and moves around within it, all the senses are involved and contact is made with the landscape through a feeling body. This invests my art with an aspect of pilgrimage, which is often interpreted as proof that I have been face to face with natural aesthetics. A work of art in a lonely location, on a barren shore or next to a wilderness trail can seem to represent silence and purity, but also a Biblical landscape of rivalry and suffering.[51] To the casual observer, therefore, my artworks appear to be to have clear roots in Kantian natural aesthetics.

Community landscapes

On the textual level of my works, the Kantian aesthetic paradigm whereby the lonely romantic artist comes into contact with nature is turned on its head. The wilderness and the Arctic Ocean are not 'nature' to the residents of those areas, but places that are created and constructed by culture.[52] They are the meeting points of the mind and the language in which the culture of the region and the identity of its inhabitants find expression. Being alone in a landscape becomes communally understood in the experience of people in the North, and the activities embraced there are shared and given communal meaning. Accordingly, my artworks, although things made by someone who travels alone in the landscape, are paradoxically communal at the same time. My art is not about the mercilessness of the wilds, a masculine occupation of the landscape, but more about a social connection, a reflection of the communal discourse of a way of life in the landscape.

I often encourage the people in the area where I am making a work of art to commit themselves to the creative process. I strive for communication in my art, and this takes the form of traditional work amid the landscape rather than an external aesthetic appraisal of it. In this way, my art stimulates, transmits and brings an awareness of the culture's own way of looking at the landscape and experiencing it. It refines what already exists and does not import a model of aesthetic experience from outside the community or act as 'the centre rushing in to rescue the periphery'. My art often starts with an analysis of the environment, where I survey the opportunities offered by the site where I plan to work. The point of departure is usually the sociocultural circumstances of the place, and I begin by exploring its cultural heritage and history. Most essential, however, is communication with the site, its history, the names of people and places and the narratives of the people in the area. In other words, I build a foundation for my works by gathering an intertextual account of the place and the community who ideally take an active interest in this process.

The Northern landscape that forms the basis of my art is not devoid of cultural meanings; it is not pristine nature. It acquires its meaning through a network of social narratives and local history. Its communally produced textual meanings are often veiled in everyday activities, and in order to uncover them, I often transform the process of creating art into work physically done *in situ*. This puts me in touch with the feelings that the local community projects onto the site. It stimulates memories, which then prompt activity that encourages the recognition and construction of identity and acts to restore the link between the body and reason in the manner suggested by Merleau-Ponty. The origin of my works lies in the movements of my body or of the bodies of my colleagues, in an encounter with the environment, in a process that binds our work concretely to the site and the landscape.

The intermediate level of my art is often the local community, who give the works meaning by taking part in their creation and presenting its interpretations of the processes and the outcome. These interpretations, particularly in the case of local men, fit into the general pattern of how aesthetic experience is discussed. The language of aesthetics is common in everyday speech in the North, but aesthetic experiences and preferences are not expressed directly – this is socially unacceptable or even forbidden. Both subjective and textual aesthetic experience, whether related to the landscape itself or to works located in it, are almost always expressed obliquely, in descriptions of what is happening in the landscape: stories of fishing, hunting, reindeer herding, hay-making trips, berry picking, forestry. Aesthetic experience of the landscape or a work of art referring to it is represented and passed on when people talk about what they do amid nature. I feel that I have succeeded in my art if my works function as catalysts for, and expressions of, this communal discussion. According Pauli Tapani Karjalainen, this is what is happening:

> At the nexus of time and place what also materialises is that which we call the ego – every person's unique being here and now.[53]

At its best, art taps into and nurtures this process on both an individual and a community level.

Sometimes the sites of my works become forums for individuals and groups whose voices would not otherwise be heard. In this respect, my art can be seen as a type of plough that turns the soil and unearths fresh textual elements of the local culture, and this material serves as a basis for changes in and reconstruction of the local identity. At present, the principal force transforming the concept of the North is tourism.[54] I do not wish to deny the importance of tourism as a factor in Lapland's socio-economic well-being, and I believe that my art has a part to play in the development of a socially responsible model of cultural tourism. In other words, I see no clash between my art and pragmatic aesthetics, whose goals include the linking of art and aesthetic experience to the practical and social needs of the community.[55] If one of these needs is the Kantian aesthetic experience of the innocent wanderer, I am more than happy for anyone who chooses to do so to walk in this Northern wilderness of the imagination, where nature's grandeur cleanses the mind.

The final phase in the creation of my art generally involves the artistic communities who have contact with the documents relating to my works and the representations of them that are realized in the art world. Hopefully this completes a continuum accommodating a conceptual dialogue that is an extension of the bodily movements in the landscape and work in the local community occurring earlier in the process. In this way it contributes to the construction of the concepts of the environment, the public and identity in Lapland. Anything that arises from the reworking of tradition can ultimately survive only on the terms set by the means of communication and technology of the dominant culture, but if it is successful in finding its place in this global process, the margin may be emboldened. My art by no means seeks to effect a return to traditional roots and is, I hope, more informed by Stuart Hall's insight that all new discourses in a culture are always located somewhere and always come from somewhere:

They come from some area, some history, some language, some cultural tradition; it is from these that they gain their shape.[56]

Conclusion

It seems that like western science, western art has taken on an obsessive need for conquest. The creation of a work of art and doing research both entail a constant process of surveying and taming, which always destroy something original. Though we may be able to convey through science or art something that we feel is valuable, there is also always something associated with the real world of experience that remains beyond the scope of our representations. Does the grip of art and science mean that the North I love must ultimately escape my grasp? Will the artistic or scientific representation of the North turn out to be impossible? Does anything new and identifiable disappear as soon as it is attained? Perhaps what escapes us is, in the end, precisely the intriguing secret of the unknown and indefinable – the very thing that prompts artists and scientists to go in search of new discoveries and new territories.

Notes

1. See, for example, Berger, P. & Luckman, T. (1994). *Todellisuuden sosiaalinen rakentuminen. Tiedonsosiologinen tutkielma.* Helsinki: Gaudeamus, pp. 149–179. Berger and Luckman stress that both personal and collective identities are ongoing processes of definition and that the identity of an individual or group takes shape through interaction with the environment. See also Pulkkinen, T. (1998) Naisyhteisö: subjektius, identiteetti ja toimijuus. In Kotkavirta, J. & Laitinen, A. (Eds.) *Filosofian näkökulmia yhteisöllisyyteen.* SoPhi. Yhteiskuntatieteiden, valtio-opin ja filosofian julkaisuja 16. Jyväskylän yliopisto. Jyväskylä: Jyväskylän yliopistopaino, p. 248. Pulkkinen emphasizes the constant construction of the postmodern conception of identity as well as the political nature of this process.
2. Hall, S. (1999). *Identiteetti.* Tampere: Vastapaino, pp. 59–60.
3. Ronkainen, S. (1997). *Ajan ja paikan merkitsemät. Subjektiviteetti, tieto ja toimijuus.* Helsinki: Gaudeamus, p. 37. According to Ronkainen, some subjectivities, i.e., a subject position (identity), may become the leitmotif of a first-person narrative – at least in certain discourses and situations.
4. Tournier, I. (1971). *Ihmisen paikka.* Porvoo: WSOY, p. 60.

5. Norberg-Schulz. C. (1980). *Genius Loci. Towards a Phenomenology of Architecture*. London: Academy Edition, p. x.

6. See, e.g., Davies, P., Knipe, T. (1994). *A Sense of Place. Sculpture in Landscape*. Suderland Arts Centre. Sunderland: Ceolfith Press.

7. See, for example, Christov-Bakargiev, C. (Ed.) (1999). Arte Povera. London: Phaidon Press.

8. "MA" tila-aika Japanissa. (1981). Exhibition catalogue. Helsinki: Helsingin kaupungin taidemuseo.

9. See, for example, Lacy, S. (1995). Cultural Pilgrimages and Metaphoric Journeys. Lacy, S. (Ed.). In Lacy, S. Mapping *the Terrain. New Genre Public Art*. Bay Press, Seattle.Washington, pp. 19–47. Gablik, S. (1991). *The Reenchantment of Art*. New York: Thames and Hudson. Lippart, L. R. (1995). Looking Around: Where We Are, Where We Could Be. In Lacy, S. (Ed.) *Mapping the Terrain. New Genre Public Art*. Seattle.Washington: Bay Press, pp. 114–130. Lippard, L. R. (1997). *The Lure of the Local. Senses of Place in a Multicentered Society*. New York: The New Press.

10. See Hiltunen, M. & Jokela. T. (2001). *Täälläkö taidetta? Johdatus yhteisölliseen taidekasvatukseen*. Lapin yliopisto. Taiteiden tiedekunnan julkaisuja D 4. VSL-opintokeskus. Rovaniemi: Lapin yliopistopaino and Jokela, T. (1996). Ympäristöstä paikaksi – paikasta taiteeksi. In Huhtala, Anni (Ed.) *Ympäristö – arvot? Heijastuksia pohjoiseen*. Rovaniemi: Lapin Yliopisto, pp. 161–178.

11. See Koskela, H. (1994). *Tilan voima ja paikan henki – yhteiskuntateoria ja humanismi uudessa aluemaantieteessä*. Helsingin yliopiston maantieteen laitoksen julkaisuja. Helsinki: Helsingin yliopisto. Koskela reflects on this same issue in her study of local communities from the perspective of cultural geography.

12. Koivunen, H. (2000). *Hiljainen tieto*. Keuruu: Otavan kirjapaino Oy. Koivunen, citing Polanyi (1973), draws a distinction between explicit and tacit knowledge, pp. 75–93.

13. Berleant, A. (1994). Ympäristökritiikki. In Sepänmaa, Yrjö (Eds.) *Alligaattorin hymy. Ympäristöestetiikan uusi aalto*. Helsingin yliopisto. Lahden tutkimus – ja koulutuskeskus. Jyväskylä: Gummerus, p. 159.

14. See Porteous, J. D. (1996). *Environmental Aesthetics. Ideas, politics and planning*. London and New York: Routledge. See also Berleant, A. (1997) *Living in the Landscape. Toward an Aesthetic of Environment*. University Press of Kansas.

15. See, for example, Raivo, P. (1996). Maiseman ikonografia. In Häyrynen, M. & Immonen, O. (Eds.) *Maiseman arvo(s)tus*. Kansainvälisen soveltavan estetiikan instituutin raportteja n:o 1.. Saarijärvi, pp. 47–53. Karjalainen, P. T. (1996) Kolme näkökulmaa maisemaan. In Häyrynen, M. & Immonen, O. (Eds.) *Maiseman arvo(s)tus*. Kansainvälisen soveltavan estetiikan instituutin raportteja n:o 1. Saarijärvi, pp. 8–15; Karjalainen, P. T. (1997) Aika, paikka ja muistin maantiede. In Haarni, T., Karvinen, M., Koskela, H. & Tani S. (Eds.) *Tila, paikka ja maisema. Tutkimusretkiä uuteen maantieteeseen*. Tampere: Vastapaino, pp. 227–241.

16. Karjalainen, P. T. (1999). Tunturit maan, mielen ja kielen maisemina. In Jokela,T. (Eds.) *Tunturi taiteen ja tieteen maisemissa*. Lapin yliopisto, Taiteiden tiedekunnan julkaisusarja C 12. Rovaniemi: Lapin yliopisto, pp. 18–22.

17. Tuan Y-F.(1974). Topophilia. A study of environmental perception, attitudes and values. New Jersey: Prentice Hall.

18. Relph, E. (1976). *Place and placeness*. London: Pion.

19. Muir, R. (1999). *Approaches to Landscape*. London: Macmillan Press LTD.

20. Lippard, L. R. (1997). *The Lure of the Local. Senses of Place in a Multicentered Society*. New York: The New Press.

21. Lacy, S. (1995). *op. cit.*

22. Gablik, S. (1991). *op. cit.*

23. Rogoff, I. (2000). *Terra Infirma. Geography´s visual culture*. London and New York: Routledge.

24. Sironen, E. (1996). Lauri-poika metsäss' häärii. Luonnon kokemisen paradokseja. In Kotkavirta J. (Eds.) *Luonnon luonto. Filosofisia kirjoituksia luonnon käsitteestä ja kokemisesta.* SoPhi. Yhteiskuntatieteiden, valtio-opin ja filosofian julkaisuja 2. Jyväskylä: Jyväskylän yliopistopaino, pp. 115–124.

25. Andrews M. (1999). *Landscape and Western Art.* New York: Oxford University Press. Andrews contemplates the issue with reference to the ideas of Dens Cosgrove (1998).

26. Väyrynen, K. (1996). Kant ja luonnon kunnioitus. In Kotkavirta, J. (Eds.) *Luonnon luonto. Filosofisia kirjoituksia luonnon käsitteestä ja kokemisesta.* SoPhi. Yhteiskuntatieteiden, valtio-opin ja filosofian julkaisuja 2. Jyväskylä: Jyväskylän yliopistopaino. pp. 65–87.

27. Merleau-Ponty, M. (1962). *Phenomenology of perception.* London: Routledge & Kegan Paul.

28. Varto, J. (1996). Heidegger ja fysiksen uudelleen tulkinta. In Kotkavirta, J. (Eds.) *Luonnon luonto. Filosofisia kirjoituksia luonnon käsitteestä ja kokemisesta.* SoPhi. Yhteiskuntatieteiden, valtio-opin ja filosofian julkaisuja 2. Jyväskylä: Jyväskylän yliopistopaino, pp. 125–131.

29. See Tarasti, E. (1980). Maiseman semiotiikasta. . In Kinnunen, A. & Sepänmaa, Y. (Eds.) *Ympäristöestetiikka.* Helsinki:Gaudeamus, pp. 57–72. Tarasti emphasizes that in making the subject the point of departure in landscape semiotics, we are forced to take into account the frame of reference formed by the surrounding community and culture.

30. See Andrews, M. *op. cit.*

31. Kontio, R. (1999). "Puoliväli-ilmiöitä" Pohjoiskalotin kirjallisuudessa. Kirjailija keskusta ja marginaalisen sisä- ja ulkopuolella. InTuominen, M., Tuulentie, S., Lehtola V-P., Autti, M. (Eds.) *Tunturista tupaan. Pohjoiset identiteetit ja mentaliteetit. Osa 2.* Lapin yliopiston taiteiden tiedekunnan julkaisuja C 17. Katsauksia ja puheenvuoroja. Jyväskylä: Gummerus Kirjapaino Oy. According to Kontio, there is a special northern knowledge that lives in these unique circumstances: a particular relationship to nature, people, human existence, birth and death, belief and religion.

32. Muir *op. cit.*, pp. 256–268. Muir brings out the bidirectionality of the relation between landscape and landscape painting: the way in which the depiction of a landscape guides how we see and experience it but also how we come to value it.

33. Andrews, M. *op. cit.*, pp. 22, 193. Andrews, who has done research on the history of western landscape art, emphasizes the richness of the interaction between the artist and the environment vis-à-vis that between the artist and the landscape.

34. Lacy *op. cit.*, pp. 19–20.

35. Karjalainen, P. T. (1996). Kolme näkökulmaa maisemaan. In Häyrynen, M. & Immonen, O. (Eds.) *Maiseman arvo(s)tus.* Kansainvälisen soveltavan estetiikan instituutin raportteja n:o 1. Saarijärvi, pp. 8–15. Karjalainen distinguishes three levels in a landscape: objective, subjective and representative. In his later work, he uses the terms mimetic, sensual and textual to refer to these same levels.

36. Raivo, P. (1996). Maiseman ikonografia. teoksessa Häyrynen, M. & Immonen, O. (Eds.) *Maiseman arvo(s)tus.* Kansainvälisen soveltavan estetiikan instituutin raportteja n:o 1. Saarijärvi, pp. 47–53.

37. Tani, S. (1995). *Kaupunki taikapeilissä. Helsinki-elokuvien mielenmaisemat – maantieteellisiä tulkintoja.* Helsingin kaupungin tietokeskuksen tutkimuksia. Helsinki, p. 26. The cultural geographer Sirpa Tani has written about the concept of place but here her work is wholly applicable to landscapes as well.

38. Tarasti E. op. cit., p. 69.

39. See for example Hautala-Hirvioja, T. (1999). *Lappi-kuvan muototutuminen suomalaisessa kuvataiteessa ennen toista maailmansotaa.* Jyväskylä Studies in the Arts 69. Jyväskylä: Jyväskylä University Printing House. See also Lehtola, V-P, (1997). *Rajamaa identiteetti. Lappilaisuuden rakentuminen 1920- ja 1930 luvun kirjallisuudessa.* Pieksämäki: Suomalaisen kirjallisuuden seura.

40. Häyrynen, M. (2000). Kansakunta kaleidoskoopissa: suomalaiskansallinen maisemakuvasto. In Saarinen, J. & Raivo, P. (Eds.) *Metsä, harju ja järvi: näkökulmia suomalaiseen maisematutkimukseen ja – suunnitteluun.* Metsäntutkimuslaitoksen tiedonantoja 776, 2000. Saarijävi: Gummerus Kirjapaino Oy, p. 38.

41. See Jokela, T. (1999). Heinäniitty ja erämaa – Einari Junttilan maisemat. In *Panorama Lapponica. Lapin maiseman synty.* Taiteiden tiedekunnan julkaisuja C 14. Rovaniemi:Lapin yliopisto.

42. Shusterman R. op. cit., pp. 21–55.

43. See, for example, Hautala-Hirvioja, T. op.cit., pp. 156,164.

44. Häyrynen, M. op. cit., Häyrynen sees Lapland as a new periphery which attracted attention after World War Two, also for its raw materials and energy reserves.

45. Porteous, J. D. op. cit., p. 73.

46. Eschenburg, B. (1991). Saksan maisemamaalaus 1800-luvun alkupuolella. In Reuter, B. (Ed.) *Kaipuu maisemaan. Saksalaista romantiikkaa 1800–1840.* Tampereen taidemuseon julkaisuja 41, pp. 58–75.

47. Kemppinen, K. (1960). *Lumoava Lappi. Pohjois-Suomen kauneutta.* Porvoo: WSOY.

48. Sironen, E. (1996). Lauri-poika metsäs' häärii. Luonnon kokemisen paradokseja. In Kotkavirta J. (Ed.) *Luonnon luonto. Filosofisia kirjoituksia luonnon käsitteestä ja kokemisesta.* SoPhi. Yhteiskuntatieteiden, valtio-opin ja filosofian julkaisuja 2. Jyväskylä: Jyväskylän yliopistopaino, p. 124.

49. Lehtola, V-P. op. cit., p. 119.

50. Heikkinen, M. (1993) Tie spatiaalisena metaforana. Alue ja Ympäristö 22:1, pp. 8–9.

51. Tuan, Y-F. op. cit., pp. 109–111.

52. Saarinen, J. (1999). Erämaa muutoksessa. In Saarinen, J. (Ed.) *Erämaan arvot: retkiä monimuotoisiin erämaihin.* Metsäntutkimuslaitoksen tiedonantoja 733. Saarijärvi: Gummerus kirjapaino Oy, pp. 77–93. Saarinen's works examine various wilderness discourses and their relation to the local populace.

53. Karjalainen, P. T. (1997). Aika, paikka ja muistin maantiede. In Haarni, T., Karvinen, M., Koskela, H. & Tani S. (Eds.) *Tila, paikka ja maisema. Tutkimusretkiä uuteen maantieteeseen.* Tampere: Vastapaino, p. 235.

54. Saarinen, J. (1999). Matkailu, paikallisuus ja alueen identiteetti. Näkökulmia Lapin matkailun etnisiin maisemiin. In Tuominen, M.., Tuulentie, S., Lehtola V-P., Autti, M. (Eds.) *Outamailta tunturiin. Pohjoiset identiteetit ja mentaliteetit. Osa 1.* Lapin yliopiston taiteiden tiedekunnan julkaisuja C 17. Katsauksia ja puheenvuoroja. Jyväskylä: Gummerus Kirjapaino Oy, pp. 81–92. Saarinen examines the impact of tourism on localness and regional identity in Lapland.

55. Shusterman R. *op.cit.*, pp. 9–20. Shusterman defines the role and function of pragmatic aesthetics in the Finnish and English preface to his book.

56. Hall, S. (1992). *Kulttuurin ja politiikan murroksia.* Tampere: Vastapaino, p. 320.

2

DEVELOPING AN ENVIRONMENTAL AESTHETIC: AESTHETICS AND THE OUTDOOR EXPERIENCE

Angus McWilliam

Sport Culture and the Arts is a department of the University of Strathclyde which offers degrees in Community Arts[1] and Outdoor Education. For the most part, these use separate work programmes. However, a belief shared by staff on both courses that learning in the outdoors creates experiences which stimulate the senses, awaken creativity and initiate development of an environmental ethic persuaded them to create a module which would benefit all the department's students.

This took the form of a class called *Art and the Environment*.[2] It was staffed by outdoor and art academics, delivered to both groups of students and involved them in identical experiences.

The rationale for the class was based on the argument that while activities normally associated with natural outdoor settings, for example, rock climbing or canoeing, can take place both indoors and in outdoor urban settings, there is a quality unique to activities in natural settings that attracts people as much as the activities themselves. It was also thought that if the creators or organizers of outdoor activities are sensitized to the impact of these natural environments, and are encouraged to explore the attractions or fears they engender, this will help them to think of ways of enhancing the experience for others.[3]

Outdoor education[4] creates opportunities for people to explore natural environments, to live and move in ways which are in harmony with the landscape, to get close to and feel a part of the natural world. Participants, their senses bombarded with colour, form, movement, smells

Hands at work. Photograph by Angus McWilliam

Celebration. Photograph by Glen Coutts

and sounds, commonly experience feelings of wonder or empathy. These arise sometimes from aspects of the activity itself, such as speed, effort or vertigo, sometimes from a particularly striking view or encounter with an attractive or alien life form, and sometimes simply from a greater awareness of oneself in relation to one's surroundings. These experiences, although they may be ephemeral and cannot be precisely replicated, do seem to be intrinsic to certain locations, and can often be shared. Sharing, however, requires not only a sensitivity to the qualities of such experiences and to the emotional response of others, but also a common language. This language, the language of aesthetics, was unfamiliar to our outdoor students.

The community arts students, by contrast, were comfortable in the studio and the urban settings in which they normally carried out their activities, but had limited experience of the outdoor natural world. While they were literate in an aesthetic language, few had examined their own response to the natural world or the responses of artists and how these have changed over time.

It was with these shortfalls in mind that along with a colleague, Glen Coutts, I decided to explore with both groups of students the idea of an environmental aesthetic, and to introduce them to experiences which might lead to the development of sensitivity to that aesthetic.

Aesthetics
The word *aesthetic* is derived from the Greek word *aisthanomai* which means to perceive.[5] Thus, aesthetic pleasure means literally pleasure associated with perception, and an aesthetic response is one in which perception results in the arousal of emotions or feelings. As Dewey[6] explains, beauty is neither an intrinsic quality of an object nor a chosen response of the viewer, but emerges from the relationship between the individual and the object, in what he calls 'the experience'. All experiences to a greater or lesser degree stimulate aesthetic responses, but for most of the time our familiarity with what we are experiencing, or our concerns about other matters, means that we hardly notice. An experience is aesthetic when emotional arousal commands our attention.

Not all experiences that result in an emotional response can be described as aesthetic. Aesthetic experiences have certain characteristics which set them apart from others. Stolnitz[7] describes seven key characteristics of the aesthetic experience:

- Aesthetic experiences are valued or responded to for their own sake rather than for their potential use or the satisfaction of the observer's needs.
- Aesthetic experiences are receptive experiences in which the observer lets the event or object be itself and seeks to relate to it or understand it on its own terms.
- Aesthetic experiences are centred in the present on the object as it is rather than how it came to be or what it might lead to.

- Aesthetic experiences focus attention on the uniqueness of an object or experience rather than perceiving it as an example of a class of experiences.
- Aesthetic experiences may entail a delight in the beauty, harmony or complex unity of an event, but may also involve fear, loathing or disgust.
- Aesthetic experiences can involve both emotive and intellectual responses, spontaneous feelings and a reflection on their meaning.
- Finally, aesthetic experiences can occur in the presence of any kind of object or event and involve one or all of the senses, or they may be apprehended only by the mind.

While Stolnitz's list is helpful in defining an aesthetic experience as an emotional event and distinguishing it from other emotional events which may be inwardly generated or controlled by the individual, it is still difficult to convey what an aesthetic experience actually is, although we may all insist that we know when we have had one. Why do we experience such emotions, and why are they particularly aroused by our experience of nature, wilderness and the outdoors? Two theoretical explanations have been put forward: the socio-biological and the cultural.

The socio-biological root of environmental aesthetics

The socio-biological argument simply states that in the course of evolution there have been certain survival advantages in being attracted towards some aspects of nature and being repelled by others, and that these are not learned, but genetically burnt into our psyche. What evidence is there for this? In the course of a survey of research literature in landscape aesthetics, Ulrich[8] found that irrespective of who they were or where they came from, people consistently preferred natural scenes over built views, while Kellert's[9] *Biophilia Hypothesis* claims that

> ...there is a human dependence on nature that extends far beyond the simple issues of material and physical sustenance to encompass as well a craving for the aesthetic satisfaction which results from encounters with life and lifelike processes.

The argument is that these aesthetic preferences must at some time during our evolutionary history have given us significant survival advantages. Kellert cites examples like the universal fear of snakes, which is notable even amongst people who have had no prior knowledge or experience of them. On the basis of this and other observations, he argues that the emotional arousal resulting from direct contact with nature had value and purpose, as it encouraged our ancestors to seek out and explore habitats conducive to human survival.

Iltis[10] supports this idea, claiming that there is a genetic need for natural pattern, beauty and harmony which is refined by selection over evolutionary time. Heerwagen[11] develops this by arguing that a crucial step in the lives of most organisms, including humans, is the selection of a habitat or home, and that aesthetic responses are at root emotional feelings leading to the rejection or exploration of a particular environment. Habitats with the potential to support life and growth therefore evoke strong positive responses. Psychologists and landscape architects have taken these ideas further still by trying to pinpoint the characteristics of natural landscapes that arouse an aesthetic appreciation. Appleton[12] suggests that people feel attracted to places where they feel safe and supported. This encompasses the ability to see dangers such as wild animals or enemies from a distance and to identify places of refuge for retreating to when threatened. Using these criteria, we would expect a view from an elevated position over a landscape containing open spaces and clumps of vegetation to be aesthetically pleasing.

Outdoor educators will not be surprised by this conclusion, but the fact that such panoramas are so sought after does not in itself prove a genetic "hard-wiring" of landscape types to aesthetic responses. Following a similar line of reasoning, Kaplan[13] claims that aesthetic preference is based not on irrational whim, but on a set of inclinations that direct us toward functional choices with evolutionary significance. He proposes that places which we find attractive need to be understandable and to have a simplicity based on order and pattern, with distinct recognizable features. In this kind of place you will not get lost, or even if you do, you will be able to find out where you are. At the same time, attractive places will display a degree of complexity and variety, and the potential for finding the kinds of resources needed for support. In other words, we are attracted by places with some characteristics which make them immediately understandable and others which arouse curiosity and invite deeper study. From these ideas Kaplan constructed the hypothesis that aesthetic preference is based on the following criteria:

- Coherence: the degree to which the scene hangs together through repetition of elements, textures and colours which facilitate comprehension.
- Complexity: the degree to which places display variety or diversity in space.
- Legibility: the degree to which the scene's composition can be described and it can be explored without getting lost.
- Mystery: the degree to which you can gain more information by proceeding into the scene.

The cultural root of environmental aesthetics

While Appleton's and Kaplan's theories may help predict which locations and landscapes are attractive, this still does not prove an evolutionary basis for this attraction. Indeed, historical and cultural comparisons demonstrate as many differences as similarities in what people find attractive. When we look at history and archaeology, we can find evidence of the value people have placed on the aesthetic qualities of objects they have surrounded themselves with, and of the places where they have lived. The pots they made and the buildings they lived in are not as a rule merely functional, they are also decorative, and it would appear that a desire for beauty existed even as far back as the drawings of prehistoric cave dwellers. It can be argued that these drawings and decorations were, in fact, nothing more than a signature which identified the owner; a record of events and places which needed to be remembered. It may even be that they had a mystical or ritual significance we can no longer appreciate. The care and skill devoted to them, however, and the fact that they so often feature elements of the natural landscape, suggest that even in those times people took aesthetic delight in nature.

Having said that, close inspection tends to reveal that in such early art the landscape and its animal inhabitants are seldom represented as the primary focus, but as a background for human activity. The appreciation or, at least, the celebration of outdoor natural environments as being beautiful in themselves is, according to writers such as Nash[14] and Oeschalgear,[15] a relatively recent phenomenon. They describe how classical philosophers such as Plato[16] and Aristotle drew attention to nature's abundance and the place of Humanity in nature's hierarchical system. They point to how Virgil and Horace[17] introduced the notion that nature exists as a retreat from the artificiality of the city; how during the Middle Ages, authors from Augustine to Aquinas[18] proposed a Christian view that nature was primarily significant as evidence of God's design; how Renaissance art saw nature as something to be stylized and civilized – something dangerous, unknowable and unpleasant that Man had escaped from. They describe how in the early seventeenth century, writers such as Bacon and Descartes[19] espoused a modernist world-view praising human control over natural forces.

It was, these authors argue, only with the coming of the Age of Enlightenment, the age of science and commerce, that in reaction against the squalor accompanying the industrialization and commercialization of western society the aesthetic qualities of the natural world came to be valued for themselves. Both the poetry of Robert Burns and Gilbert White's *Natural History and Antiquities of Selborne* (1789) played their part in re-establishing more sympathetic and congenial attitudes toward nature, and looked forward to the nineteenth century, when romantic literature across the western world, from Goethe to Wordsworth to Emerson, began to criticize the prevailing view of nature as mere commodity.[20] Later still, in the twentieth century, the most eloquent voices for an ecologically integrative vision of nature came from such authors as D. H. Lawrence, Aldous Huxley, John Muir and Edward Abbey.

History, then, clearly teaches us that we cannot rely on universal principles governing the way we view nature. Just as there are wide cultural variations in the kinds of building we construct and the art objects we value, so there appear to be aspects of the appreciation of nature that are culturally determined.

The learned aesthetics

The argument that our attitude towards nature may be more dependent on culture than genetics is strengthened by the observation that aesthetic appreciation can be learned. As we mature, our taste in the arts develops. We find more satisfaction in art objects as we become aware of their complexity, the skill that went into their creation and the subtlety in the meanings and stories they tell. At the same time, examining our own childhood shows clearly how much the media and fashion industries have impacted on us and moulded our tastes. Surely therefore it is reasonable to suggest that as we mature and collect aesthetic experiences in the outdoor world, our appreciation of nature may grow and become more discerning.

So the appreciation of nature can be learned, but is it something that can be taught, and is there a point in teaching it? When we read authors such as Thoreau[21] and Abbey,[22] it becomes increasingly evident how their delight in nature and places increases with each encounter. What can be surprising to the modern reader is that these were not global tourists who searched the world for novelty and sensation, but people who spent most of their lives exploring the places they lived in. Dillard[23] describes how she learned to perceive Tinkers Creek in all its myriad variations through the changing seasons, and how this perception was a revealing of the coherence and complexity of what she was seeing. Her aesthetic satisfaction was enhanced by the developing ability to read that complexity, and to be aware of the mysterious depths that were being uncovered.

This suggests that if aesthetic experience is as I proposed at the beginning of this chapter a matter of pleasure derived from perception involving both senses and intellect, then it is more than just a question of seeing – it takes time. Time to allow sensations to impinge on our senses, revealing the form and diversity of the places we visit, time for the interplay of the senses with our accumulation of experience, time for reflection on the meaning and impact of what we have experienced. This is essentially no different from any other area of education – as teachers are constantly reminded, experience without reflection is unlikely to lead to learning, and reflection itself is an art that needs to be learned.

So, to develop a natural aesthetic, we need to be exposed to nature and natural environments, and we need to reflect on our experience of them. We need to become aware of how our emotions are aroused, and explore why we feel the way we do. And in order to reflect, we need to develop an appropriate language for reflection. This may call on words, music or images, and may be analytical and argumentative or intuitive and creative, but only in this way will we deepen our understanding of ourselves, our relationships with the places we inhabit, and the objects and creatures we share it with.

There is a degree of urgency about this. Kohak[24] asks how can we expect people to defend nature if they do not see it as 'good'. Leopold[25] suggests that without a love of the land, an environmental ethic is a *dry concept which touches no-one*. Aesthetics is about delight in beauty, and anger at ugliness. Outdoor experiences need to foster delight in places and engender anger at their removal.

Developing the learning experience

If one accepts the argument that an environmental aesthetic is a meaningful concept, that it can be learned, and that learning it can bring personal and social benefits, then one can argue that learning experiences designed to develop an environmental aesthetic should include opportunities to explore the work and responses of artists, to explore natural locations, to play with natural materials and, finally, to engage in a creative act in a location which has become known to the students and represents their desire to communicate something about it.

These were the considerations that informed *Art and the Environment*. In planning it, it was important to ensure enough time for reflection, time to listen to artists, time to read and talk, time for the development of a language which would allow aesthetic ideas to be considered and shared.

Art and the Environment took place over five days, followed by a further period of fourteen days for research and writing, and included:

- Researching the history of the relationship between art and the natural world.
- Examining the work and the writings of environmental artists, for example, Chris Dury, Andy Goldsworthy, Richard Long, and Timo Jokela.
- Visiting locations in which artists had placed works of art in natural settings and sharing feelings and responses to these intrusions – The Gallery of Modern Art in Edinburgh and the Sculpture Park in Perth.
- Working with natural materials.
- Exploring a location in a natural setting to discover what makes it unique.
- Creating a work of art in that setting.
- Discussion in groups.
- Personal research.
- Journals and reflective writing.

Findings

The initial findings of this experiment in learning, which is still evolving, are presented below. They are not in the form of a rigorous analysis using strategies of triangulation, inter-rater reliability and methods of reducing sampling bias, but are based purely on the writings that the students submitted for assessment. The eight texts that were used can be seen and explored further on the ACE website.[26] Each of these electronic documents was incorporated into a NVivo[27] Project, where it was coded against themes representing learning experiences and learning outcomes. The texts were then combined to re-create for the reader the experiences and thoughts of the students as they progressed through the course. This was done by stitching together extracts from their writings, using, wherever possible, the students' exact words. The resulting vignette is not 'true', insofar as it does not represent the experience of any one individual on the course, nor is it a carefully balanced evaluation distilled from the experiences of all the students. Rather, it represents the range of messages that the most articulate students wished to communicate. We felt that this was the best way to present the essence of the experience and its impact on its participants.

Art in the environment

This was a course I was looking forward to. I really like being in a natural environment and as a child spent a lot of time outdoors. For me the experiences would encourage emotions and memories which connected with my childhood. 'Art in the Environment' was a five day module which included classroom work and excursions designed to give an insight into the impact of environmental art. The excellent part of the module was its intense nature, allowing us to bond and to surround ourselves in the environment. This resulted in everyone developing unique ideas and perceptions of the location and the work of art they wished to develop.

Concentration. Photograph by Angus McWilliam

The Sculpture Trail

Day One involved an exploration of a sculpture trail. This was located on the bank of a river. The gardens and ponds were filled with natural beauty and the energy of spring. As we walked along the trail I heard many of my colleagues saying that the environment made more of a statement than did the art. Many of the pieces were large, constructed with artificial materials making them intrusive, reminding us of the domination of industry and technology.

I found myself thinking that the real intention of the art was revealed in the impact on, and the drained reaction of the viewers. I tried to capture this feeling in a picture and thought about incorporating it into my final work. Walking around the sculpture trail allowed me to think about and appreciate environmental art for the first time. One of the pieces which was really liked by the others I didn't have any feelings about but I did think about it. Perhaps the artist's aim was to make people stop and think. I was unsure about the mixture of materials used in the piece. The stone base blended in with the natural environment but the marble top looked modernised and made it stand out.

Doug Cocker, River Arch. (Perth, Scotland). Photograph by Glen Coutts

Another piece which inspired me was a bench. I especially liked the fact that the material was all natural being made from wood. The artist left the curves and wavy edges. I feel that the use of natural curves and shapes helped the artwork blend into the environment and thought how nature has no straight lines. One piece was very clever. It made you look beyond it and appreciate the outdoor environment. Depending where you stood you got a different view through the frame. It let you decide what part of the landscape is the most beautiful. Amazing!

The visit

Ardmore point was the perfect site because there were so many contrasting types of land in a small, condensed area. The beauty of the site was represented in the natural cycle of the tidal effect, the abundance of wildlife and the rolling Scottish hills in the background. The ugliness of the site came from the way the land has been mistreated. Unfortunately those who use this spot do not seem to appreciate the beauty and leave much of what they bring with them behind. This has had a devastating affect on the aesthetic value of the area, and the plants and animals which live there.

The rubbish looks unsightly but it does tell a story of the surrounding areas and ways of life. The rubbish highlights the impact that modern society has on the environment. The old pieces of plastic nets and other bits represent how much Scotland used to rely on fishing for income and how the Clyde was once a busy passage with ship building and importing and exporting goods by ship.

Looking across the water in complete contrast is the built up area of Greenock, with several high rise buildings and houses. I have connections with the surrounding areas. I learned to sail in Helensburgh as a child. I have a friend who stays near Rosneath where we go trail cycling and I stayed in Dunoon for the whole of last summer where I worked. When looking out from Ardmore point I have many happy memories and feelings.

The area would provide a wealth of opportunities and materials to create artwork. There was a lot of beautiful, natural driftwood on the beaches, thousands of different coloured pebbles, litter and man-made objects which had been left there by other visitors. I thought about what I would create. The artwork would have no lasting effect or cause any damage to the area. I was inspired to construct a landscape picture of the coastline.

The planning

During the intervening days I considered what I would do. Thoughts about the balance between natural and the manufactured, between life and death had all been running through my mind. I had two ideas – the first was to develop a piece of art that would be pleasing

Observation. Photograph by Angus McWilliam

Exploration. Photograph by Angus McWilliam

Construction. Photograph by Angus McWilliam

Elation. Photograph by Angus McWilliam

to the eye, whilst capturing the atmosphere of the area and not damaging it in any way. An artwork that succeeded in 'fitting' with its surroundings which had something mystical and majestic about it, which amplified the ordered beauty within nature itself. It would be obvious to the eye that someone or something had been at work; something had left its mark and the onlooker would question why make such a figure and what is its purpose for being there.

The second was to depict the frustration and anger of the place towards those who had no concern for its beauty. I would violently interact with my art. I would suspend a blatantly artificial object from a completely natural frame and smash the sphere into the River Clyde. It would be a dark, powerful and shocking statement representing change, consequence and destruction.

Creating the piece

Since I knew that our artwork was going to be temporary, I decided to place it very close to the tide line so that by the end of the day, most of it would be gone. At this location, the viewer can enjoy views of the surrounding landscape and the water, allowing a definite feeling of calmness and piece. I collected mussel shells to imitate the sea. The insides of the mussel shells resemble the pattern of coastlines with the blue sea around it. I also liked the shapes as they resemble the swirling tides and currents. The stones were chosen by their colour, size and shape.

The structure was a labour to construct but the physical exertion in the collection of the branches and the piling of rocks was all part of the personal interaction with the piece. Physical work in one's environment becomes a type of meditation in which the body opens pathways to sensations, to the environment. The feelings that are experienced are calmness, you feel at one with nature, you can get caught up in the environment around you, relaxed and fulfilled.

Reflecting on the piece

The constructed work of art remains as much a part of the landscape as the living nature that surrounds it. Made with the materials afforded to them by the surroundings, environmental artworks are able to blend into their locales. However, they are interesting and unique enough to the place that they merit investigation. Art that entices one's curiosity to investigate and meditate on 'why' such an object is where it is, 'who' could have done this and 'what' is it here for, has accomplished a wonderful thing. It has drawn a person from within their own 'small story' to engage with the 'place' in which they are walking. It has caused one to stop and identify with the space in which it is standing. To place an art piece that stands against nature rather than within it would invoke an entirely different reaction. It would seem, for want of a better phrase, 'out of place'.

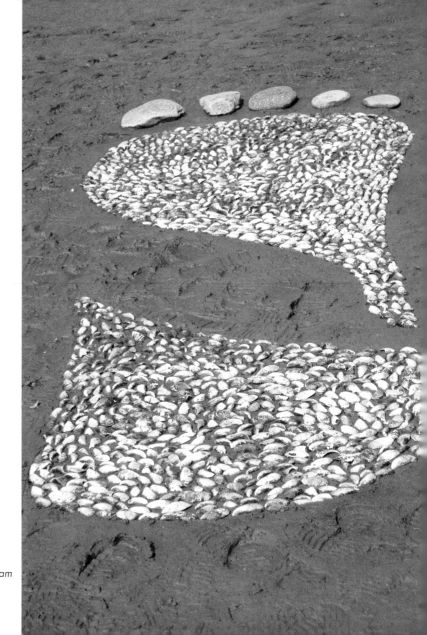

Impact. Photograph by Angus McWilliam

Completion. Photograph by Glen Coutts

Reflecting on the learning

What did I learn from this experience? It has ignited a desire to pursue further knowledge and experiences. I have realised the way in which I view my surroundings has changed. The pieces of wood were no longer simply pieces of wood, they became objects with meaning and thought behind them, they became a sculpture that was pleasing to the eye, explored the relationship between nature and industry and, although it may have been swept away by the end of the day, the photographs and memories will last forever. It has made the environment more colourful in many ways because I can now connect this awareness of 'natural' art with my career.

I believe that it is very important to educate young people about the value of environmental art and how much fun art in the outdoors can be. Making a simple collage out of twigs and leaves is a fun and practical method of teaching art and appreciation of the environment. Some of the children I work with are from the inner city. I believe work in the natural environment could in some ways provide a therapy for them. It may also encourage them to think about beauty and what it really stands for.

Discussion

In reading what the students had written, what was striking was the apparent passion aroused by the experience. The entire spectrum of emotions, from sadness, to anger, to love, was expressed in both the works of art they made and their reporting of how the class had impacted on them. In a comparatively brief space of time a relationship had developed between these students and a specific location – Ardmore Point had become a place of worth.

Martin Heidegger[28] describes how growing up in an age of technology has impacted on the relationship between individuals and their environment. We tend to see nature as a 'standing reserve', having worth only because of its usefulness to us. Ardmore Point was already familiar to many of the students, who had used it for ecological studies and for outdoor activities. They had acknowledged its usefulness for these purposes and recognized both the contribution it had made to their learning and to their enjoyment, and the problems and hurt the place had experienced. But they had never really looked at it, encountered it as itself and or felt hurt on its behalf. In engaging them in the creative act of art, we challenged them to reveal the essence of the place and of the material and objects which existed in that place, to value it for itself and, in doing so, to awaken in themselves a sense of belonging and a sense of responsibility.

Notes and references

1. The BA Community Arts and the BA Outdoor Education Degrees prepare students to engage members of the public in the arts and in outdoor activities, e.g. drama, visual arts, canoeing, climbing.
2. This class was an elective chosen by students. It occupied one week of full-time lectures and workshops followed by two weeks of private study.
3. The University of Strathclyde Calendar Elective modules SC409. More detail can be found at URL: http://soolin.mis.strath.ac.uk/classcatalogue/control/classpage?startentry=1, (accessed 14th June 2007).

4. Outdoor Education is defined as 'a means of approaching educational objectives through direct experiences in the environment' Hunt, J. (Ed.) (1989). *In search of Adventure.* Guildford: Talbot Adair Press.

5. Heerwagen, J. H., Orian, G. H. (1993). Human Habitats and Aesthetics. In S. R. Kellert and E. O. Wilson (Eds.), *The Biophilia Hypothesis* (pp. 138–172). Washington: Island Press.

6. Dewey, J. (1934). *Art as Experience*, London: Putnam.

7. Stolnitz, J. (1960). *Aesthetics and Philosophy of Art Criticism*, Boston: Houghton Mifflin, p. 35.

8. Ulrich, R. S. (1993). Biophilia, Biophobia and Natural Landscapes. In Kellert, S. R. & Wilson, E. O. (Eds.) *The Biophilia Hypothesis.* Washington: Island Press.

9. Kellert, S. R. (1993). The Biological Basis for Human Values of Nature. In Kellert, S. R. & Wilson, E. O. (Eds.) *The Biophilia Hypothesis.* Washington: Island Press.

10. Iltis, H. (1967). To the Taxonomist and the Ecologist, Whose Fight is the Preservation of Nature. *Bio-Science*, December 1967, p.887.

11. Heerwagen, J. H. & Orians, G. H. (1993), *op cit.*

12. Appleton, J. (1975). *The Experience of Landscape.* London: John Wiley and Sons.

13. Kaplan, S. (1987). Aesthetics, affect, and cognition: environmental preference from an evolutionary perspective. *Environment and Behaviour*, 19: pp. 3–32.

14. Nash, R. (1882). *Wilderness and the American Mind.* Newhaven: Yale University Press, pp. 8–23.

15. Oeschlaegear, M. (1991). *The idea of wilderness*, Newhaven: Yale University Press, pp. 31–68.

16. *Ibid.*, pp. 53–59.

17. *Ibid.*, p. 104.

18. *Ibid.*, pp. 66–67.

19. *Ibid.*, pp. 85–88.

20. *Ibid.*, pp. 113–119.

21. Thoreau, H. D. (1862). *Walking*, New York: Harper Collins.

22. Abbey, E. (1968). *Desert Solitaire.* New York: Ballantine Publishing.

23. Dillard, A. (1974). *Pilgrim at Tinker Creek*, New York: Harper's Magazine Press.

24. Kohak, E. (1992). Perceiving the good. In Oelschlaeger, M. (Ed.) *The Wilderness Condition* Washington: Island Press.

25. Leopold, A. (1949). *A Sand County Almanac.* Oxford: Oxford University Press.

26. These can be seen at the ACE website at URL: http://ace.ulapland.fi/ (accessed 15th February 2008).

27. *NVivo* is a qualitative software package created by QSR, which allows electronic texts to be coded, indexed and collated into themes.

28. Heidegger, M. (1997). The Question Concerning Technology. In *The Question Concerning Technology and Other Essays*, Lovitt, W. (Ed.) New York: Harper & Row, 1977, pp. 3–35.

3

STRATEGIES FOR THE CONVIVIAL CITY: A NEW AGENDA FOR EDUCATION FOR THE BUILT ENVIRONMENT

Malcolm Miles

Introduction

Work in several disciplines over the next decade is likely to be characterized by responses to the problem of urban sustainability. One aspect of this will be an urgent reappraisal of notions of 'the city' in face of urban crises; another, a search for alternative models of what urban settlement might be. A possible third aspect may be a multi-disciplinary approach underpinned by critical attitudes to the professional ideologies of those, such as planners, architects, designers and artists, who contribute to the built environment.

Because urban forms are produced historically, for example, through processes of planning and design, rather than being 'accidents of history', a number of possible futures are open. Whilst the dominant conceptualization of 'the city', to which a city's material form more or less corresponds, reflects the dominant values and structures of power in a society, these values and structures, like the model of a city, are never the only ones imaginable. When a society re-writes its (urban) histories, it begins to foresee its (urban) futures. The question, in a democracy, is: who determines the concept of 'the city' which informs these histories? Or, as sociologist Sharon Zukin writes:

> To ask 'Whose city?' suggests more than a politics of occupation; it also asks who has a right to inhabit the dominant image of the city.[1]

At one level, this is a political question. But at another, it concerns the implicit rather than explicit ideologies of the professions which shape the built environment, ideologies affirmed as much through education as practice, and embedded in the methodology of design. This paper asks how education might, referencing alternative models of practice, construct design as a critical practice, how imagination might reconfigure notions of 'the city'.

A riverside walk

A walk along the South Bank of the River Thames takes the stroller through a set of seemingly convivial urban spaces. Between the Festival Hall and Tower Bridge, then on towards Docklands, several recently re-developed pedestrian spaces link to form a riverside axis, creating what urbanist Kevin Lynch might have called 'good city form'.[2] The walk offers many views, each an image of the city framed by the (spatial) viewpoint from which it is observed and the (social) point of view of the observer. Seen across the river, disparate buildings form a skyline; Victorian-style street lights suggest an imperial past while seats offer repose in the shade of mature trees. This riverside boulevard exhibits a sense of place – a place of ease, of liberal civitas – embellished with nature and art; it is also a space for disciplined publics, rather than the flaneur or provocateur.[3]

For things are seldom (only) what they seem. The boulevard – a term first used in the sixteenth century to describe the walkway on a city rampart, later a promenade laid out on a demolished rampart, then a street planted with trees – offers detachment from the press of everyday urban toil; another kind of detachment is experienced in the view of a street from a tall building.[4] The view of a person in a crowd, amidst busy streets, or in social terms from the 'grass roots', may be different. And if the notion of a liberal society is expressed through the leisure of its citizens, this ease may not, in certain kinds of social and economic organization, be open to all. Such is the subject matter of Seurat's *Bathers* (National Gallery, London), which, despite the calmness of its atmosphere, conveys a revolutionary programme; the citizens who laze by this river have been freed from the economic problem of scarcity by a socially just distribution of the benefits of industrialization (represented by the factory chimneys on the far bank). Seurat derived this idea of society from the writings of Peter Kropotkin. Kropotkin's ideas are set out in his key work, *Mutual Aid*, parts of which were first published in the 1890s. The leisure of those who stroll by the Thames today has been produced by a different response to the problem of scarcity.

Hays Galleria, London, with security guard in foreground.

The elements of urban form encountered during the walk each construct a kind of city around them. William Pye's stainless steel sculpture outside the Queen Elizabeth Hall suggests Utopian purity in its material, and affluence in its status as blue-chip art. Nearby, a homeless person sits on the pavement and skateboarders appropriate space for their own society.

The phoney facades of Gabriel's Wharf represent the city as a space for the tourist gaze[5] and mini shopping mall, both setting up relations of consumption rather than sociation. Further on, near Tower Bridge, Hays Galleria is an ersatz space designed as instant heritage, replete with kinetic sculpture, its purpose consumption and its ambience controlled by CCTV and a security presence. Coin Street, in contrast, is a development where the tenants of social housing, thanks to one of the last acts of the Greater London Council before its abolition by a Conservative government, control the development process. Canary Wharf can be glimpsed from a pier nearby, part of a global city of corporate enclaves; in the water of what was once a dock is another shiny sculpture: Wendy Taylor's *Spirit of Enterprise*, acting as a kind of logo for the development.

Each element is read within a code brought to it by the observer, but also encodes the space around it. Sometimes the codes collide.

Context: An urban nightmare?

Around half the human inhabitants of the planet now live in cities. Although the most rapid rates of growth are in the cities of Asia, Africa and Latin America, the dominant concept of 'the city' remains that derived from the industrialized west. In this story, the city, often represented (for example, in postcards) as a skyline, stands for security against the wild, a citadel in which life is ordered, its manner of unfolding predicted; and when the heath, coded by the city's light as darkness, has been turned into the countryside, another kind of wildness, first attributed to the vagrant and insane, then to other categories of non-productive deviance, is confined in institutions within the city.[6] By the nineteenth century, civic order is expressed in a geography of categorization. Foucault cites an ironic view of this regulation in an anonymous contribution to La Phalange (1836):

...here is the improved plan in which all like things are gathered together. At the centre, and within a first enclosure, hospitals for all diseases, almshouses for all types of poverty, mad-

Spirit of Enterprise by Wendy Taylor, London Docklands Development.

houses, prisons, convict-prisons for men, women and children. Around the first enclosure, barracks, courtrooms, scaffolds, houses for the executioner and his assistants...[7]

Categorization, however, is only one approach to order. The cities it has produced, its mechanism today extended into a geography of enclaves and margins, business parks and areas of deprivation, is full of contradictions.

The rupture of the liberal image of the city is both threatening and exciting. Richard Sennett writes of New York as 'a city of differences par excellence, a city collecting its population from all over the world',[8] but in which difference is contained rather than celebrated, in which edges become disengaged. Yet, it is in the cracks that the possibility for alternatives appears, and where Sennett, who writes like a novelist, begins to imagine himself as flaneur.

But the rupture is actuality, seen in the uneven impact of urban development on diverse publics. Rosalyn Deutsche writes: 'the visibility of masses of homeless people obstructs belief in positive images of New York, constituting a crisis in the city's official representation' and 'Today's homeless...are refugees from evictions, secondary and exclusionary development – the conversion of neighbourhoods into areas they can no longer afford'.[9]

The rupture is also seen in the representations of cities in mass culture, as in Kathryn Bigelow's film *Strange Days*, set in Los Angeles in 1999. Architect Lebbeus Woods uses the trope 'architecture as war', stating 'Building is by its very nature an aggressive, even warlike act'.[10] Perhaps such representations appeal to a masculine taste, like war stories, but, again, the representations are supported by evidence: Mike Davis describes 'the carefully manicured lawns of Los Angeles' Westside [which] sprout forests of ominous little signs warning: "Armed Response!"'.[11]

One, rather obvious, explanation of urban dis-ease is that (western industrial) cities are a product of capitalism. Aram Eisenschitz writes:

The history of capitalism demonstrates its scant regard for human life. The truth of this statement may be seen in contemporary Britain where being poor means increasing constraints in access to the basics of life and in the ability to participate in ordinary society.[12]

Cities are a product of planning and design, and whilst these professions serve a dominant ideology, their methodologies also embody attitudes to society, are also ideological. Yet the workings of these professions may seem opaque to many citizens, shielded by notions of nature, culture and expertise. It is necessary to de-construct these mystiques before turning attention to the methodologies of the professions which shape the built environment.

Naturalizing explanations of urban dysfunction, as in the terms 'planning blight' with its image of the city as a crop of potatoes, or 'urban sprawl', conceal, like the term 'accident of history', decisions which determine urban form. The advantage of naturalizing explanations to the interests of capital is precisely that they conceal the consequence of social divisions on some development decisions, or make certain kinds of change (rather than others) appear inevitable. Deutsche writes of the late capitalist city:

> ...growth, far from a uniform process, is driven by the hierarchical differentiation of social groups and territories. Residential components of prosperity – gentrification and luxury housing – are not distinct from, but in fact depend upon, residential facets of poverty – disinvestment, eviction, displacement, homelessness.[13]

A means of legitimizing enclaves like Broadgate, Docklands and Cardiff Bay, or Battery Park City in New York, is embellished with 'public art'.

Statues and memorials constructed national myths in the nineteenth century, and subsumed personal loss into national exaltation in war memorials. Neoclassical forms were also used to lend value to new industries, for example, in the design of station facades embellished with neoclassical figures. Public art, today, lends cultural value to urban development; by commissioning work from artists of international status, developers legitimize the global city of trans-national corporations and financial services, and cities which regard themselves as marginal seek to be located on an international culture-map – an Oldenburg in Middlesbrough and a Gormley in Gateshead. Heritage culture is used in a similar way. But the importation of art or heritage to 'humanize' developments such as Docklands contradicts the erasure of the real histories of work and dwelling of such sites.

The design of an environment contributes to civic order and is a work, conventionally, of expertise. Just as the museum is a place where citizens behave in a suitably improving way, so built environments organize the publics who use them. Amos Rapoport writes:

> Such sets of rules apply...to the use of urban space, so that we find two clear traditions, one where urban space is used for many activities and another where such activities are prohibited. In other words, different groups will decide...which behaviour is appropriate in what setting, thus relating environments and behaviour[14]

and Michel Foucault has argued that the disciplining mechanism of the panopticon design of a prison applies also to the organization of cities.[15] Public participation in urban planning and design is often inhibited not only by the lack of formal procedures through which to exercise influence but also by the specialist languages within which planning and design operate. These act as mono-disciplinary 'keep out' notices. What remains difficult to explain, and goes beyond notions of expertise, is how decisions are made by people who subscribe to the values of liberal society, which yet cause obvious misery for other members of society. Robert Moses, for example, who oversaw the construction of expressways through New York in the 1950s and 60s, is quoted as saying, 'When you operate in an over-built metropolis, you have to hack your way with a meat ax'.[16] What kind of detachment allows such a de-valuing of other people's habitation, and what kind of methodology enables such detachment from everyday life?

The method of design

Design and planning depend on representation, and representation is a kind of abstraction or reduction of reality to a graphic system. This is more than just a technical matter, or one intended to put off unwary interlopers. The conventional city plan is a view from above, the site of god's powerful and masculine eye. This began with Alberti's formulation of a method of mapping cities from their surrounding walls. Detachment enables objectivity, but also objec-tification, and the inscription of new plans on an extant urban fabric as if it had no value (like white paper). This was the basis for Baron Haussmann's re-planning of Paris for Napoleon III, and Le Corbusier's desire that 'the centres of our great cities must be pulled down and rebuilt'.[17] Le Corbusier was never empowered to effect this, but perhaps all planning, in as much as it is inscription (as if) on a blank ground, is a kind of fantasizing, and, perhaps, this applies to the design of buildings too. Henri Lefebvre writes:

> the architect ensconces himself in his own space. He has a representation of this space... -bound to graphic elements – to sheets of paper, plans, elevations, sections, perspective views of facades...This conceived space is thought by those who make use of it to be true, despite the fact – or perhaps because of the fact – that it is geometrical.[18]

The site of ensconcement is the study, a discrete, masculine domain in European domestic architecture from the fifteenth century – 'a small locked room off his bedroom which no one else ever enters, an intellectual space beyond that of sexuality'[19] – developed into, amongst other things, the studio.

Lefebvre writes of a society's spatial practice as 'representations of space' -- conceived space -- and 'representational spaces' -- the spaces of lived experience. He argues that both are necessary and complementary, whilst modern society privileges conceived space over lived or felt space. Redressing this balance might, then, be part of a re-visioning of design education; this could, possibly, involve new technologies of representation which take as a point of departure the view, not from above, but in the street. But it will also entail, in a re-integration of design and everyday life, a new approach to professional expertise, in which the expertise of urban dwellers on their lives is given equal value to the knowledges of professionals. And a new approach to aesthetics, in which beauty is related to need. Imagination is not the preserve only of artists and designers, it is the potential of every citizen to foresee a future.

Strategies in education

Design education generally affirms the exclusivity of professional expertise through the divisive specialism of courses. Its site is usually the white-walled studio, denoting a value-free space. This continues despite frequent claims for 'relevance' (to what?). Planning and architecture are overwhelmingly male preserves, whilst education in art, architecture, design and planning replicates a common professional ideology still based in Modernism. Where artists and architects work together, they tend to produce conceptual schemes which reproduce the value-free space of Modernist art; this reflects that they share a belief in innovation, individuality and abstraction. Innovation privileges stylistic or technical development for its own sake over its impact on recipients, yet it tends to figure implicitly in the criteria for success in art, design and architectural education. Individuality, expressed in 'signature buildings' and the signature on a painting, constructs the fiction of an isolated person, apart from society, exactly the kind of fantasy made possible in a white-walled studio. And the methodology of design, depending on representation, locates the designer, or planner or architect, in a position of power, whilst professional mystique, expressed in specialist languages, constructs a barrier to the involvement of ordinary people in determining their cities. Towards all this, art and design education needs to take a critical approach, re-visioning design as a critical practice.

How does education foster critical practice? At one level it interrogates the baggage of received ideas, questioning ideological and institutional frameworks and picturing possible alternatives. The university thus becomes a site for a continuing work of social criticism. Part of this is to seek a transparency, or construct strategies by which artists and designers might create transparency, in urban processes of development; this may involve learning social skills as much as art or design skills, participating in the discourses of sociology, geography and critical theory as much as of design or art. It may also employ new media to overcome the inaccessibility of architectural language, and construct courses thematically rather than according to categories of material practice or discipline.

At another level, critical practice requires models which constitute alternatives to the products of the dominant culture, just as students require a diversity of role models in staff. These alternatives are available in both art and urban planning, in some cases addressing specific issues, in others envisaging a whole new process.

Kevin Atherton's *Platforms Piece* at Brixton Station, a set of three bronze life-casts on the platforms, seeks to democratize the monument by taking as models three commuters: two female, one male; two black, one white. Even an aggressive response to the work, as in daubing with white paint the face of the white commuter, makes visible the tensions of the neighbourhood. Colin Wilbourne's *Red House* is part of a series of works made during his long-term residency in the redevelopment zone of Sunderland. It embodies the memories of place and family homes of many people now living in the housing district which has replaced the shipyards; the reception of the sculptures by residents is very positive, and there has been no serious vandalism despite the high incidence of deprivation in the city. These projects remain fairly conventional as art practice. Others reject the notion of the art object entirely in favour of social process. The work of artists in this field has been termed 'new genre public art'.[20] Examples include Culture in Action,[21] a series of projects in Chicago in the summer of 1993. HaHa, an artists' collective, initiated Flood, a volunteer network which used a vacant shop for a hydroponic garden, supplying the uncontaminated vegetables produced there to AIDS hospices. The site was used as an information, resource and meeting centre for education about living with HIV. Another group, Street Level Video, used video production as a way to work with members of street gangs.

New genre public art references the 'happenings' of the 1960s, though with a more defined social, and sometimes ecological, purpose. Other, often ephemeral, acts interrogate readings of urban form whilst denying any incorporation into the art market such as the covering of a house in Vauxhall, London, with newspaper. Similarly, new developments such as 'action planning' and the use of 'urban design action teams', in which professionals participate in workshop sessions with members of defined communities to understand the needs of a neighbourhood before beginning detailed processes of planning, and John Forester's proposals for 'equity planning' in situations of conflict between developers and communities,[22] reference Davidoffs 'advocacy planning' of the 1960s.[23] In these practices, urban dwellers are empowered to use their expertise on the everyday life of a neighbourhood in partnership with professionals.

Two radical alternative models are the Open City at Ritoque, Chile, and the village of New Qurna, Egypt. Both re-figure architecture in ways which, whilst appropriate to what the west calls 'developing' countries, are equally relevant to the west itself. The Open City was founded in 1970 by architect Alberto Cruz Covarrubias and surrealist poet Godofredo Lommi. The city interrogates notions of site, has no master plan or zoning, is built on and to coexist with sand dunes, and develops according to the needs and desires of its inhabitants. The founding of a site for a building is a collective poetic act.

Decisions are made by open meeting of those living in the Open City, and buildings use recycled material and are constructed without the use of either heavy machinery or inappropriate technologies.[24] The role of the architect is thus mediated into a contributor to a process in which building is artisan work carried out collectively. This in no way excludes an aesthetics of built form, but relocates it within a sustainable pattern of settlement.

Nearly fifty years ago, the Egyptian architect Hassan Fathy worked with masons using traditional skills and mud brick to design and build the village of New Qurna, on the left bank of the Nile opposite Luxor. Fathy researched patterns of sociation amongst the extended families of the existing village and designed a series of interlocking units offering a mix of private space and communal street. The houses remain cool in the sun, and the brick radiates warmth during the cooler nights. The mosque references a type found near Aswan, and a theatre doubles as a cinema and meeting place. Although the villagers, who had made a living for generations from the tombs on top of which their old village sat, refused to move into the new village, it has since been occupied and become a stable community. A few modifications have been made, but mostly in mud brick, and the small acts of appropriation which have taken place may account for a sense of ownership. New Qurna remains a model for sustainable development, a kind of 'no-cost' architecture which functions in its construction in a way equivalent for the villagers to that of the Open City for its mainly academic community. It, similarly, re-positions the architect as enabler, the dweller as co-designer.

The implications of the Open City and New Qurna for design education are wide. They are similar in some ways to the aspirations of Ivan Illich for a 'de-schooling' of society. Fathy writes:

> We need a new way of knowledge. The enforced academic knowledge of schools has alienated us from nature just as industrialisation by force has taken away the possibilities of our participating in satisfying our needs.[25]

If, then, there is a benefit in bringing together artists, architects, planners and designers, or courses in these fields, it is that professionals and students might be able to set aside their baggage and work with non-professionals to identify what needs of urban living, rather than manufactured wants or consumer wishes, are to be satisfied, and to develop strategies and languages for doing so. In effect, this means that design professionals will relinquish the exclusivity of current definitions of professional expertise, definitions which separate those whose knowledges are, in pursuit of a convivial city, complementary. For it is not only experts who have imagination; those who experience a city through the attachment of meanings and values to spaces (rather than through schematic representations) have much to offer and are the city's rightful owners.

Imaginative work and the principle of hope

By changing its stories, or frameworks, a society imagines its futures. In face of urban violence it is possible to imagine a city of conviviality, in which the built environment is determined by patterns of sociation which accommodate difference, rather than one in which the environment determines the sociation it contains. In the latter case, of course, it is the structures of power and value through which the built environment takes its particular form which are the determining factors, mediated by decisions of planning and so forth. Imagining a convivial, or sustainable, city entails a reformulation of the aesthetic, or beauty, as something integrated in and expressing the possible fulfilment of everyday life, not something outside it acting like an opiate. Ernst Bloch writes, in *The Principle of Hope*,

Interior of the mosque in New Qurna designed by Hassan Fathy.

We say of the beautiful that it gives pleasure, that it is even enjoyed. But its reward does not end there...it remains even after it has been enjoyed...hangs over into a land which is 'pictured ahead'. The wishful dream goes out here into what is indisputably better, in doing so...it has already become work-like, a shaped beauty. Only: is there anything more in what has been shaped in this way than a game of appearance?[26]

Bloch suggests that 'the beautiful' articulates the imagining of what is potential in a socially produced human consciousness. It is a picturing, which enables sharing, of a process of becoming. His work, completed during the 1950s in the German Democratic Republic, puts forward the principle of Hope, related to work in the arts, as a counter to society's degradation through the alienation of repressive political and economic systems. Just as the beautiful imagines a life which is better, so Hope is the bringing into realization of what is pre-con-scious. This realm of ideas not yet formed is differentiated from the Freudian unconscious as a realm of repressed material. Hope begins the process of ending alienation by opening a space for an alternative; creative work is a means to articulate this.

If artists and designers seek to share a critical view of social forms from a position within society, then art and design become means to give form to pre-conscious desires for fulfilment:

More than anything else, Bloch placed great faith in art and literature to raise the not yet conscious to a point where it could grasp the direction humankind would have to take to bring about the fulfilment of those needs, wants and wishes that he saw scattered in dreams and daydreams.[27]

which is a re-thinking of the idea of the avant-garde which informed the work of Courbet and Millet in the nineteenth century. The aim, then, of art and design education is to set up spaces of engagement in which people are enabled to imagine possible futures, possible joys.

This chapter was originally published in *The Journal of Art and Design Education*, vol. 17, no. 1, pp. 17–25.

References
1. Zukin, S. (1996). Space and Symbols in an Age of Decline. In King, A. (Ed.) *Re-Presenting the City: Ethnicity, Capital and Culture in the Twenty-First Century Metropolis*. London: Palgrave Macmillan, p. 43.
2. Lynch, K. (1981). *Good City Form*. Cambridge, MA: MIT Press.
3. Benjamin, W. (1973). *Charles Baudelaire*. New Left Books.
4. de Certeau, M. (1988). *The Practice of Everyday Life*. University of California Press, pp. 91–110.
5. Urry, J. (1990). *The Tourist Gaze*. Sage.

6. Foucault, M. (1967). *Madness and Civilisation*. Tavistock.

7. Foucault, M. [(1975) 1991]. *Discipline and Punish: The Birth of the Prison*. Penguin, p. 307.

8. Sennett, R. (1990). *The Conscience of the Eye: The Design and Social Life of Cities*. Norton, p. 128.

9. Deutsche, R. (1991). Uneven Development – public art in New York City. In Ghirardo, D. (Ed.) *Out of Site*. Bay Press, pp. 157–219.

10. Woods, L. (1995). Everyday War. In Lang, P. (Ed.) *Mortal City*. Princeton Architectural Press, pp. 47–53.

11. Davis, M. (1990). *City of Quartz*. London: Verso, p. 223.

12. Eisenschitz, A. (1997). The View from the Grassroots. In Pacione, M. (Ed.) *Britain's Cities*. Routledge, pp. 150–76.

13. Deutsche, R. *op. cit.*, p. 158.

14. Rapoport, A. (1980) Cultural Determinants of Form. In King, A. (Ed.) *Buildings and Society*. Routledge Kegan Paul, pp. 283–305.

15. Foucault, M. [(1975) 1991]. *op. cit.*

16. Cited in Berman, M. (1983). *All That Is Solid Melts Into Air*. Verso, pp. 293–4.

17. Le Corbusier, [(1929) 1987]. *The City of Tomorrow and its Planning*. Dover, p. 96.

18. Lefebvre, H. (1991). *The Production of Space*. Blackwell, p. 371.

19. Wigley, M. (1992). Untitled – the housing of gender. In Colomina, B. (Ed.) *Sexuality & Space*. Princeton Architectural Press, p. 347.

20. Lacy, S. (1995). *Mapping the Terrain: New Genre Public Art*. Bay Press.

21. Jacob, M. J. *et al.* (1995). *Culture in Action*. Bay Press.

22. Forester, J. Planning in the Face of Conflict. In LeGates, R. and Stout, F. (1996) *The City Reader*. Routledge, pp. 433–46.

23. Davidoff, P. *Advocacy and Pluralism in Planning*. In LeGates, R. and Stout, F. *op. cit.*, pp. 421–32.

24. Pendleton-Jullian, A. (1996). *The Road That Is Not a Road*. MIT.

25. Fathy, H. (1984). Palaces of Mud, Resurgence #103 March/April, pp. 16–7.

26. Bloch, E. [(1959) 1986]. *The Principle of Hope*. Blackwell, p. 210.

27. Zipes, J. [1988]. The Utopian Function of Art and Literature, Cambridge, MIT, cited in Leach, N. [1997] *Rethinking Architecture*. Routledge, p. 42.

Part Two
Communities

4

BEYOND PROCESS: ART, EMPOWERMENT AND SUSTAINABILITY

Mark Dawes

Among many sections of the population there is a perception that creativity and the arts are associated with childhood and school, and the examples of work with and by children that follow do demonstrate a tendency for inclusive and innovative collaborative work in the arts to happen first and foremost with children and young people. It is widely acknowledged, however, that the arts can play a more wide-ranging role in both personal and community development,[1] and the purpose of this chapter is to look at meaningful ways of maximizing that potential.

A process-based model can be a highly successful approach to working with people in the arts, but the short-term nature of most projects of this kind limits more profound possibilities for growth within communities. The model recommended by the Cultural Commission Report is *Cultural Planning*, which has been successfully employed in North America, Australia and other parts of Europe over the past two decades. This model is also mentioned on numerous occasions throughout the Scottish Executive Draft Culture Bill.[2]

Contexts and approaches: Empowerment in the arts

Artistic processes have evolved dramatically in Scotland in the last few decades. The meaningful inclusion of communities[3] in the creative process has enabled a real dialogue to emerge between artists and local people. Integrated approaches to the commissioning and creation of public artworks have resulted in a sense of community ownership which was often missing from work produced in earlier decades. Neil Livingstone's 1977 sculpture *Concept of Kentigern* is a good example.

Concept of Kentigern, bronze, by Neil Livingstone 1977 as sited in Glasgow, 1998. *Photograph by Brian Lochrin*

Aspiring to represent the spiritual qualities of Kentigern, mother of St Mungo, Glasgow's patron saint, the sculpture, monolithic and abstract in execution, for many years occupied an entirely inappropriate site in a busy pedestrian precinct in the shopping area of the city's Buchanan Street. It was removed during renovations in 2003. As a symbol representing Glasgow and its people, it occupied a questionable place in the city's cultural history, and it may seem obvious now that failing to involve local people in the creative process might engender resentment within communities who are 'gifted' cultural artefacts, especially in the context of regeneration projects which may be contested and unpopular in their own right. It may also seem obvious that in trying to answer the question 'what do *they* want?', the best thing to do is to ask them.

But does this go far enough? Rather than asking '*them*', shouldn't we be trying to dissolve boundaries and distinctions between *them* and *everyone else*? While it may be a sign of progress that cultural professionals are now paying attention to '*their*' aspirations – what 'the people' want – shouldn't we now be reaching beyond that to what *we* want as communities?

We and *they* are the terms of distinction which put professionals and bureaucracies at the centre of creative processes and keep real people and real communities on the periphery. If empowerment is an important function of the arts, then the direction of travel should be towards complete and permanent integration of the arts within public construction partnerships, and away from the 'visitations' of short-term projects which appear to value the creativity, ideas and energy of communities for only a finite period. If people are to be truly empowered, why limit their involvement to when a sculpture or other artwork is in the planning, commissioning and creation stages? Or, at best, to a token follow-up consultation to say how worthwhile the experience was?

By definition, a 'project' has an endpoint, and while this has advantages, it can also be a failing. How can we decide on an endpoint to empowerment? How can we declare an endpoint to growth, when growth has only just begun? Although the Cultural Commission strongly supports the Scottish Executive's acknowledgement of the value of cultural activity,[4] and the central role it can play in policy areas such as education, justice, health and employment, the benefits of inclusive arts projects are being only partially realized because the inclusion is neither sustained nor expanded. The way forward is to look at new bureaucratic structures aimed at developing a coherent cultural planning approach for local communities.

Examples of empowerment in the arts with young people
Mosaic Bollard Project, Woodlands, Glasgow
In 1997 the artist Karina Young initiated a project to enhance existing street furniture in the Woodlands area of central Glasgow. The population of Woodlands is drawn from a wide range of social and ethnic backgrounds. It is close to Glasgow University and other West End amenities and has been subjected to stringent measures to limit the impact of traffic on its distinctive sandstone tenement flats. Economy

Mosaic Bollard Project, Woodlands, Glasgow, Scotland, 1997. Project led by Karina Young with pupils from Willowbank Primary School. *Photograph by Brian Lochrin*

was the guiding principle – plain grey concrete bollards were use to close off most of the area's peripheral streets. This solved the traffic problem, but looked horrendous.

Karina Young worked in partnership with Willowbank Primary School, located at the heart of Woodlands, to find a way of addressing this problem. A total of 150 children created designs which were then scaled up and applied to the bollards as mosaics using small, coloured tiles. In an interview in 1998, Young had this to say:[5]

> I basically feel that the idea of some people being professional artistically and other people being amateur is divisive, and that a lot of so-called amateurs have a great deal to offer, and that any artistic process that people are involved in has a lot to offer them in terms of accomplishment, raising self-esteem, the actual enjoyment of working with materials towards an end product.
>
> I think it's really important that the children growing up in this area are going to have a direct link to their environment on a daily basis, and that they've made a stamp on it, that there's a sense of pride and ownership over what they've done.
>
> I feel that the project was quite organic in the sense that it was springing from the community and then flowing out, and then beneficially affecting the community. It has become an integral feature now of the local environment.

The sense of ownership fostered by this project amongst the local children is a key factor in its success. Each artwork carries a brass plaque with the artist's name engraved on it. The bright, vibrant designs speak eloquently of the diversity of the local population, and the children involved could hardly have been more visibly implanted in the area. Not only does their art outline the shape of their community, it demonstrates a humane underlying value base which is there for all to see.

Future In Hand **sculpture, Port Glasgow, Inverclyde**
Port Glasgow is a former shipbuilding town on the banks of the River Clyde to the west of Glasgow. There is a recent history of unemployment, poor housing and other social difficulties, but parts of the town are currently being regenerated. This initiative, however, is not without cost. Areas like the former council housing estate of Woodhall are changing dramatically, and while this can be seen as a positive step away from poor housing stock and problems with drugs and anti-social behaviour, many law-abiding residents who are active within the community are concerned that new housing developments will leave them marginalized and disenfranchised.

A nearby regeneration initiative in the Robert Street area has seen extensive landscaping and street furniture projects. This formerly run-down area is now the site of a new public sculpture developed by the artist Nina Saunders and students from the local high schools, Port Glasgow

Future in Hand, bronze, by Nina Saunders and students from Port Glasgow High School and St Stephen's High School, Port Glasgow, Inverclyde Scotland, 2006. *Photograph by Darrell Wilson.*

High School and St Stephen's High School. Roy Fitzsimmons, Principal Teacher of Art and Design in Port Glasgow High School, had no doubts about the value of what had been achieved:

> Two sections of S3 Standard Grade pupils (were) involved. Nina arranged visits of historical interest to Newark Castle, and a 'Story Teller' was invited to give talks on local folklore to the pupils. From here Nina along with department staff organised sculpture workshops with the pupils, with ideas being stimulated by the various stories and the construction of small table pieces of sculpture being produced by individuals. Thus all the pupils were involved in promoting ideas. Finally, from the various ideas a piece was selected by the putting together three selected elements from the work of three pupils.

> The initial brief was related (to) their environment....visits were arranged to the Powder Hall bronze casting foundry for all the pupils in S3 showing the processes involved in scaling up and the production of the final sculpture.

> Finally the work was erected within a renovated landscaped area and all the pupils took part in the opening. Many of the pupils, not just the ones whose work was selected regard the work as their own as they belong to the immediate area where the work is sited. Another positive off-shoot of the project was the production of a small bronze maquette of the sculpture purchased by the school which will be awarded yearly as a trophy for 'citizenship' within the school community.

> I feel this was an immensely positive experience for the pupils....(It) proves that it is possible to break into a tight curriculum to give the pupils that little bit extra experience and involvement in a 'real world' project.

The young people involved in this high-profile project are some of the young people who will actually live around this sculpture. They and their peers are often stereotyped as belonging to the 'ASBO generation',[6] indulging in anti-social behaviour and vandalism in their own communities. This project valued the involvement of young people in public realm projects and attempted to cut across negative perceptions of young people by fostering a sense of pride in the area. Clearly public artworks play only a part in modifying the behaviour of young disenfranchised people in our communities. But projects such as this attempt to reverse the sense of disenfranchisement at source within young people themselves. Methods of social and legislative control cannot change young people's behaviour alone. Arguably, the logical way to change young people's anti-social behaviour is to literally change their behaviour; rather than having no involvement in communities and social processes, young people stand to become agents of change themselves when they are allowed to participate in meaningful public projects in their own locale.[7]

The *Room 13* network

Room 13 defies brief description. It serves as an example of empowerment which moves beyond facilitating participation in the creative process, towards the democratization and self-determination of a group of artists – who happen to be children – within an educational context. Much has been written by Room 13 participants themselves which eloquently describes their experiences, and this material should be seen as the 'primary text' on this remarkable phenomenon.

Since the students of Caol Primary took the first initiative in 1994, Room 13 has evolved into a network of similar studios worldwide and is host to a growing international movement of young artists.

Each Room 13 studio is organized and run completely by the students. Every year it elects a management team, who are responsible for arranging projects, raising funds to meet day-to-day running costs and employing an artist in residence to work with them. They also make sure the studio is stocked with materials, keep the working environment and office in order, oversee the cleaning and maintenance of equipment, deal with correspondence and administration, and keep track of finances in the studio's own bank account. In Room 13, no adult is allowed to sign the cheques! As the children themselves put it:

> Each Room 13 is a democratic, autonomous organisation. The only things we depend on our schools for are light, heating and the use of the room itself. Together, these autonomous studios form the Room 13 Studio Network.

> Room 13 strives to provide even the youngest artists with access to professional equipment and the best possible materials. Works on canvas using oil or acrylic paint, collage, drawings, sculpture, photography, digital prints, film, performance art, sound art, text, installations, original compositions and mixed media are among the works produced by artists from Room 13.

> Every artist's work is original and unique. In Room 13 artists are encouraged to think for themselves, and every artist must think very seriously about what they are doing and why. Each piece of work is a product of an individual's exploration of his or her own ideas. Open discussion of ideas, philosophy and thinking about anything and everything is a constant in any Room 13.[8]

Cultural planning and the community development perspective

Cultural planning is a cross-sector approach to sustainable community development, through a series of socially engaging creative projects that puts people and culture at the centre, and like any other endeavour in this field it needs appropriate policies and resources to flourish.[9] It is expensive to develop and maintain truly inclusive, truly integrated arts projects, whatever the economic, social and personal benefits that may be claimed on their behalf. So if children can be empowered through involvement in public artworks, should we also consider looking to other sectors of society for a cost-effective way of representing hidden interests and unheard voices? The elderly, ethnic minorities, prisoners and asylum seekers are just some examples of groups whose perceptions could bring considerable enrichment to the social mix.

Deciding on the depth and scope of the cultural empowerment agenda should not be solely a matter for cultural professionals or politicians. The model of cultural planning suggested in the Cultural Commission Final Report has the potential to move the arts bureaucracy in Scotland in a meaningful direction, encouraging a citizen-centred, creative atmosphere and promoting the empowerment of both individuals and communities. To paraphrase the economist E. F. Schumacher, 'creativity as if people mattered!'

While specific cultural polices may have a sectoral focus, e.g., the arts, the overall process of cultural planning has a broader remit which includes territorial and developmental aspects[10] and requires a sensitive understanding of urban planning and policy.

A run-down inner-city housing scheme, for example, may be seen as uncared for, dangerous and deprived, and its inhabitants as underprivileged, under-employed and disengaged from society. Any regeneration agenda that eventually targets such a place will almost inevitably lead to a reduction in social housing, and the expansion of private sector housing driven by commercial developers and the desire for local authorities to make short-term gains from the sale of land.

As is evidenced by the likes of the Woodlands project, however, the things that really contribute to the desirability of a neighbourhood are attractive artworks, thoughtful landscaping and a sense of ownership by the local community. Without them, economic viability and the development of a positive community spirit will not happen. Yet, these factors are seen as non-essential; the 'project' involves building a certain number of houses, renovating a number of others and creating or improving some basic amenities such as small businesses and a community centre. Everything else is secondary. The more creatively inclusive aspects of the development are not central to the process and may not even feature in the budget.

But let us imagine a scenario in which creative and committed individuals *have* been put in place and are fully committed to inclusion and participation. Funding has been secured, the planning authorities are supportive of the proposed artefacts, and local people are keen to be involved. The designs are relevant, representative and expressive of local aims, and take note of the history and character of the area. The project is successful. The artworks that have been produced give a real buzz to the area, attracting media coverage and creating a real sense of partnership amongst the stakeholders of the community. A celebratory launch day helps foster a sense of pride and excitement. In the months that follow, evaluations show that the project has been popular with the majority of people in the area, and there is debate about what other improvements could be made. Local people are seen by themselves and others as creative and engaged, whereas only a few years before they had never considered the arts as an outlet for their aspirations or a conduit to greater social involvement.

The patina begins to deepen and mature on the bronzes. Planted areas spring up with greenery, and footpaths begin to wear with the caresses of a multitude of footprints. And the presence of the artists, the architects and the funding officers slowly dwindles. One day people notice that the creative people who facilitated involvement in the development process are no longer there. They exist only in memory and in the objects they helped the local community to create. Dreams fade, ideas gradually weaken, discussions and meetings about the development of the area become less frequent and less passionate in their intensity. A sense of normality returns, a normality with no creative process at its heart, with little engagement or sense of community. The evaluations are complete. The project is complete.

Once a community is empowered to the extent of regaining its cultural identity, what can be done with that empowerment to cement its inhabitants' role as co-designers of their space, to ensure that they occupy the place where its form is determined?[11]

The time and money spent on such a project is not wasted and can mobilize commitment and produce ideas and energy to spare. The community, to a certain extent, has been 'healed'. But this 'medical model' of the regeneration process is neither holistic nor sustainable. It sees a problem, offers a diagnosis, finds a cure and tries to include the patient in the process of treatment. But in the afterglow of being healed, the patient is susceptible to relapsing into the same condition as before. There is nothing to prevent this relapse except a short-term sense of well-being. No preventative solutions are in place. There are no programmes of development to continue the improvement of health beyond mere wellness into positive growth. The future is postponed; for now, the sickness has gone and the patient is cured. That was what the medical process set out to do. There was no question of addressing any future needs or anticipating future problems.

So, is there an alternative, an approach that is both holistic and sustainable and does not view a community as a problem to be solved, but rather as the key resource to be employed in its own development? If we adopt such an approach, then what would otherwise have been seen as the endpoint of 'the project' becomes the beginning of 'the process' – of independent, self-directed and inclusive growth, of practical self-help enabled by the initiation of involvement in development agendas once the professionals have departed. The learning experience would encompass not only the practical skills required to complete the 'project', but 'soft outcomes', like confidence building, social and communication skills and capacity-building. It might include training in community development, committee management, financial management and educational skills, as well as specific creative and technical skills, and would involve not only consulting a broad group of people from within the community on what they want and how much involvement they would like to have in 'making the piece', but encouraging them to develop transferable skills which will come into play at the point where 'the project' ends and 'the process' begins.

Under this scenario, the community becomes the kind of informal 'free university' espoused by Joseph Beuys. The model has a lot in common with gardening, or vocational training – the aim is not just to perform in the short term, but to learn how to perform, to begin performing and then to create opportunities for others to learn to perform. Cultural practice in Scotland has certainly taken steps down this road, but there is still some way to go. As well as looking beyond merely 'making things', empowerment in the arts should perhaps also look beyond 'participating in processes'. We need a future-focused, holistic approach whose key outcome is the growth of people within a culture, rather than an item of culture constructed by people.

Future directions in Scotland

Some of the recommendations made by the Cultural Commission Final Report include the following:

- That community planning be adopted as the operational cornerstone for delivery of culture locally and nationally and best practice be shared.
- That local authorities should take the lead in establishing and servicing Cultural Planning Partnerships which include the voluntary, private and public sectors.
- Three-year funding for established voluntary cultural sector groups.
- Funding for the voluntary cultural sector to participate fully in cultural community planning.[12]

These recommendations, amongst others proposed in the report, clearly state the belief that integrated approaches to engaging communities in creative partnerships can put citizens at the centre of cultural activity. Since the publication of this report, the Scottish Executive has published a Draft Culture Bill (in December 2006) which refers not only to cultural planning, but also to cultural entitlements. It proposes a duty on local authorities to engage in the planning and publication of such entitlements in consultation with local people. Anything less than full compliance with this requirement would stop short of the goals outlined in the Cultural Commission Final Report.

I will conclude with some findings quoted in the report which clearly demonstrate the potential of regeneration projects to foster positive outcomes for local people. Describing examples in Glasgow (the Castlemilk Arts and Cultural Development Office), Edinburgh (the Fireworks project in Wester Hailes), Dundee (Partnership for Arts) and South Uist (the Ceolas project), these findings show that cultural initiatives played a key role in personal and community development as well as improvements in the local economy. Specific outcomes included:[13]

- In the Castlemilk scheme in Glasgow, five out of the seven participants interviewed in 2001 believed that being involved in the arts project had helped them get a job or move into training.
- The participants in the Fireworks project in Edinburgh felt they had become more confident, more interested in learning, had a chance to do new things, made a positive contribution and made new friends.
- In Dundee, 29 out of 32 stakeholders questioned believed that the arts projects had had a positive impact on the quality of life for individuals in Dundee and had improved the image of the area.

- In South Uist, 80 per cent of the local volunteers on the Ceolas project thought that the image of the area had been improved as a result, and reported a positive impact on their own lives and skill development.

These outcomes suggest that by engaging in fully-integrated, citizen-focused approaches which truly embed the arts within a range of social processes, we can ensure that empowerment becomes not just an indicator of short-term success, but the foundation on which future success is built and extended.

Notes and references

1. Cultural Commission (2005). *Cultural Commission Final Report.* Edinburgh: Scottish Arts Council/Scottish Executive p. 74.
2. Scottish Executive (2006). See http://www.scotland.gov.uk/Publications/2006/12/14095224/0 (accessed 12th February 2008).
3. 'Communities' here refers to any community – schoolchildren, local populations, communities of interest etc.
4. Cultural Commission, *op. cit.,* p. 5.
5. Artist interview in Dougall, P., Coutts, G. & Dawes, M. (1999). *Scanning the City: A Virtual Journey around Public Art and Urban Design in the City of Glasgow,* Glasgow: University of Strathclyde, DEG@S [CD-ROM].
6. 'Anti-Social Behaviour Orders' or 'ASBOs' were introduced by the UK Government in Section 1 of the Crime and Disorder Act 1998 and first used in 1999. An ASBO sets conditions on the liberty of individuals who indulge in nuisance behaviours such as graffiti, litter, noise etc. Although breaching the terms of an ASBO can lead to imprisonment, 'the ASBO generation' is often seen to be dismissive of such orders. This is seen as particularly true amongst some young people in Britain who consider punishments such as ASBOs as a 'badge of honour'.
7. Port Glasgow Online (2005). *Robert Street Sculpture Unveiled.* Available from URL http://www.portglasgowonline.com/news/itemDetails.php?id=560 (accessed 8th May 2007).
8. Room 13, 2007. Available from URL http://www.room13scotland.com/ (accessed 8th May 2007).
9. Cultural Commission, *op. cit.,* p.170.
10. Ghilardi, L. (2006). *Culture at The Centre.* Glasgow: National Cultural Planning Steering Group, p. 8.
11. Miles, M. (1997). *Art, Space & the City.* London: Routledge, p. 178.
12. Cultural Commission, *op. cit.,* p. 208.
13. *Ibid.,* p. 25.

5

COMMUNITY ARTS PROJECTS AND VIRTUAL LEARNING ENVIRONMENTS

The need for Web-based communication in Lapland and in the Barents region

Maria Huhmarniemi

In terms of land mass, Finland is a large country, the seventh largest in Europe. The distance from North to South is over 1000 kilometres, and 33 per cent of the population of 5.2 million live in rural areas, in some cases as much as 100 kilometres from the closest village. Finland is also, however, a modern country, with advanced technology and educational policies, and considerable investment has been made in ensuring that everyone has equal access to information channels.

The University of Lapland, located in the region's capital city, Rovaniemi, on the Arctic Circle, is committed to an active role in regional development. Its objectives include the promotion of knowledge of the Northern regions, their social and cultural development, and ensuring the welfare of their inhabitants. The main focus is on the Barents region, which includes the northernmost parts of Sweden, Norway, Finland and northwest Russia, and is Europe's largest area to benefit from international cooperation.

The *Art, Community and Environment* programme, run by the Department of Art Education, encourages participation in the cultural life of the North and supports local people in the further development of their own neighbourhoods. Art education and school students, villagers, museum visitors, local unions and entrepreneurs can all cooperate in bringing art to communities and in using art to meet local needs.

Local teachers, tourist industries and high school students in northern Norway participated in a seminar, a distance education course, and a workshop in snow and ice sculpting. *Photograph by Timo Jokela*

In this kind of project, art is understood as promoting place-specific processes and localized strategies. There have been a number of other examples in various parts of the world. According to Kester,[1] contemporary environmental artists have developed collaborative projects ranging from portable bio-gas generators designed for rural African villages, to proposals to uncover long-hidden rivers in the heart of London, to recycling centres on Chicago's South Side. In Lapland, the tourism and experience industries are among the fastest growing areas of commercial enterprise and a welcome antidote to the high rate of unemployment in rural areas. Community art and environmental art projects have been used to get artists, students, local communities, tourist industries and other groups working together[2] and to generate new practices for developing provincial areas and celebrating regional identity. Communication technology, new media and distance-learning pedagogy are a vital part of these processes.

Communication and dialogue can play a central role in contemporary art and art theory. Kester uses the concept of 'dialogical art' to describe practices whereby an artist invites groups of people to meet to discuss topical issues and problems.[3] Virtual communication should not be intended to replace these meetings. Collaborative physical activities play a vital part in awakening interaction and understanding between participants in community or environmental art projects, and this cannot be approximated by interaction through the Internet. However, there is evidence that virtual communication can result in other levels of dialogue not achieved in pedagogy based on face-to-face meetings.[4] For example, shy people can benefit from virtual interaction.

Although information and communication technology is a powerful tool in combating social problems in provincial areas, and can have a positive impact on personal well-being, economic growth and regional equality, it concerns researchers that global communication may weaken local identity in provincial areas. The special characteristics of small cultures are under potential threat from globalization, multinational production and the spread of information through the Internet.[5] It is not simply a question of encouraging communities to present a homogeneous local identity and public face. Individuals and minorities should also have the opportunity to produce information about their own culture.

Structuring Web-aided learning in Art, Community and Environment Studies

The *Art, Community and Environment* programme consists of a theoretical introduction to the field (via video lectures and literature published on the Internet) and an independent, practical, project. This chapter explains how the studies are structured in terms of project management.[6] A community art project starts with an analysis of the community and the environment, and proceeds first to defining problems and future visions, then to planning the activity and creating it in cooperation with local partners. Each project includes the reporting and evaluation of all its fields of action. In every phase of the process, students use the web-environment to describe their progress, in verbal as well as illustrated form, to both the tutor and their peer group. Ideas and comments are shared in discussion lists and, throughout the proceedings, students have the opportunity to work collaboratively, to cooperate with each other and to form project teams.

Light installation. *Photograph by Maria Huhmarniemi*

Master's degree students who live a long way from the university benefit particularly from this mode of study. They often have access to networks of people in their home provinces, an essential element of community-based art studies, and generally collaborate with at least one local partner to realize a community art project in the area where they live. This allows them both to empower their home communities and to strengthen their personal networks, while at the same time the students' knowledge of their everyday environment feeds back into the course contents of the *Art, Community and Environment* unit. The motivation engendered by personal responsibility for the projects brings an authenticity to the learning process.

The initial project survey has five dimensions: exploration of place as an objective, subjective and textual entity, and the community's social and cultural circumstances.[7] Students are encouraged to observe their everyday environments through art practices, taking photographs and sketching. They are also advised to interview members of the community and to collect information from literary sources. In the course of the survey of sociocultural context, students make a map of associations and societies in the area.[8] This helps them to find partners for their project and to identify topical issues in the community.

The project design explains why the project is needed, its potential significance, its goals and objectives and possible modes of action. The project plan briefly states who is responsible for the creation of the project, what will take place and where, and with whom the students will collaborate. It also includes a summary of both the fundamental approach to art education and the specific theories that inform the project. The third element of this part of the process is a draft document outlining strategies for environmental and community analysis, communication, documentation, financing and reporting.

During the project's initial stages, participants take a collaborative approach in a virtual learning environment. Each student presents a draft for a project plan and studies drafts produced by other members of the peer group. They then comment on each other's work and give feedback. Students are encouraged to use theoretical underpinning for their plans, and to use the collaborative process to refine and proceed to an independent realization of them. The forum's design ensures an appropriate level of contribution from each student, and there is a flexible time limit.

As the students themselves are responsible for documentation of the project, its success is very much dependent on their documentational skills. The aspects covered are:

- Environmental and community analysis;
- The creation of artworks and events from sketches, thematic development to various stages in the work, working methods, the learning process and how it was perceived;

Fire sculpture event in Easter 2006. Photograph by Maria Huhmarniemi

- Events or artworks in the environment, observed from near and far, during different seasons and at different times of day;
- Achievement of project goals, level of cooperation/active participation/interaction between learners.

The documentation is in digital format, which makes it possible to use photographs and video clips as well as text. As Coutts[9] argues, multimedia is an ideal vehicle for the presentation of public art. It offers tools for creating a rich visualization of social and cultural contexts from the perspective of both the artist and the community.

In due course a report of the completed project is submitted to the virtual learning environment. Its first section is a formal, detailed account of the project's aims, actions that were taken and the resulting evaluations. Potential problem situations and development needs are identified, with a view to avoiding pitfalls in similar future projects. This part of the report also includes a critical analysis of the processes and methods used in the project, and of how they might be adapted to other environments and communities. The second section is a digital slide show, representing the entire project from the initial stages to the completed artwork or event and conveying a flavour of its emotional impact on those involved. The third and final section summarizes the project in English for publication in the ACE archive on the Internet.

The study programme ends with a discussion in which students comment on the project report of the peer group. They are encouraged to reflect on how they experienced the project and, thus, deepen their understanding of community art.

Assessing the virtual learning environment

Several guidelines have been developed to audit the quality of virtual learning materials and online courses. For example, Herrington et al.[10] present a checklist based on the determination of critical elements within three main areas: pedagogies, resources and delivery strategies. The pedagogies of a high-quality virtual learning environment should feature:

- Authentic tasks and real-life settings;
- Opportunities for collaboration;
- A learner-centred environment, where the focus is on learning rather than teaching;
- Engagement (learning environments and tasks that challenge and motivate learners);
- Meaningful assessments (students are assessed on unit activities rather than separate assignments and have the opportunity to present polished products, rather than simple drafts).

Resources should be accessible, well organized and current, reflect a rich variety of perspectives, and demonstrate social, cultural, and gender inclusivity. Students should be able to navigate to and download error-free materials within a reasonable period of time, and should have communication channels for dialogue. The user interface, graphics and overall design should also be of high quality.[11]

The *Art, Community and Environment* unit is formally assessed to ensure that it complies with these criteria, but this needs to be supplemented by feedback on how successful actual groups of students are in using the learning environment to achieve the goals of their studies. The *Art, Community and Environment* programme has been run twice as a distance course, with approximately forty students on both occasions. Most of the students were artists or teachers in rural areas of southern Finland. The course was part of their master's degree studies in art education, which leads to a qualification for teaching art. Most students opted for school or public art projects in their home town or village, ranging from winter art in schoolyards, to murals, outdoor installations, playground designs and environmental artworks in forests and parks. Such a wide variety was to be expected, as there were significant differences between the places and communities involved, and the students were taking on a number of different roles, acting as artists or teachers in primary, secondary or upper-secondary schools, in art schools for children and young people, or in polytechnics. Some projects involved entire school and village communities.

Thirty-two students were asked what they had found helpful in the planning of the project. In total 79 per cent found the introductory video lectures very helpful or helpful, and 22 per cent said that the lectures had offered some help. Surveys of the location and its sociocultural context were considered very helpful by 13 per cent, helpful by 41 per cent and somewhat helpful by 44 per cent. The opportunity to study the project designs of the other students was widely appreciated: 69 per cent said they had learned 'much' or 'very much' from this. The list of discussions classified by theme was less successful. Of those that responded, 28 per cent found it very helpful or helpful, 47 per cent found it to be of some help, and 25 per cent said it did not give any support at all. For too much of the time, discussions consisted not of coordinated threads but of a series of unlinked comments. More active participation from course tutors was needed to encourage better interaction. On the other hand, the discussion lists did motivate students to study the project designs of their peer group and, thus, to a certain extent fulfilled their purpose.

Feedback was gathered again at the end of the same course, via an assessment form in the distance-learning environment containing multiple-choice questions and text fields for verbal feedback. The outcome was that 82 per cent of the students reported that they had learned 'very much' during the course. During the same exercise, 86 per cent believed that the programme would have a meaningful impact in their future profession. Some of the students had encountered problems in the course of their projects, but most were satisfied with their own results and impressed by the work of the other students.

A virtual environment requires the ability to self-direct learning. This is an important aspect of academic studies, especially in teacher education where trainees are being prepared to meet the demands of future employment and perform a responsible social role.[12] Students enrolled in

Our Friend in Vasa. 2005. Photograph by Evelina Lindahl

Art, Community and Art Environment programmes generally show interest and ability in self-directed learning, but when studies are entirely Web-based, they tend to seek a more direct relationship with their tutors. According to the course feedback, some students felt that their tutors left them to face the challenges of creating a project with little or no support. Some also reported that shared comments in discussion lists often lacked individuality. Better guidance in these areas and more interactive systems need to be developed. On the other hand, students need to learn how to seek support and accept help from colleagues when this is appropriate.

Photography and project galleries

Documentary photographs, reports and presentations have been published in a range of media. Projects have been disseminated to a wide audience through seminars, exhibitions, exhibition catalogues and photographic galleries on the Internet. The University of Lapland maintains two photographic galleries. Its Site Specific Art Gallery (http://olos.ulapland.fi/mm/katoavapublic) contains documentation of land art, environmental art, performances and community art projects, while the Winter Art Gallery (http://olos.ulapland.fi/mm/talvipublic) documents snow and ice sculpting projects in villages, schools and tourist environments. There are about 2,000 easily accessible and downloadable photographs in these archives, which date back to the early 1990s. Each photograph is presented with some background information, such as the name of an artist, the title and description of an artwork, and the aims, methods and results of the projects they were part of.

These galleries function as a learning environment for students who are planning new projects. They are also a source of inspiration and information for art educators and other workers involved in local communities in Northern areas. Producing and publishing new content to these galleries is simple and cheap, an important issue when addressing relatively low audience numbers in small communities. Some of the materials and strategies on show, such as snow sculpting, have been developed specifically for northern environments, but many could equally well be put to use by other communities whose circumstances are quite different; for example, in urban surroundings as well as in rural and provincial areas.

Within the University of Lapland, the Web-galleries are used when evaluating community and environmental projects, but this resource has also attracted new collaborative partners. Disseminating the project in this way has clarified fundamental principles of environmental, socially active art and raised the profile of art education in the Barents region.

The Universities of Lapland and Strathclyde in Scotland have opened an *Art, Community and Environment* project archive (http://ace.ulapland.fi), containing summaries of students' project reports. The web pages have been developed in collaboration between staff and students in both universities. A key aim of the ACE archive is to keep students up to date with projects in both countries, but it is also both an educational resource that can be used to stimulate debate about the current practices of the *Art, Community and Environment* unit, and a valuable research tool, allowing visitors to the site to read about a vast array of projects and compare methodologies.

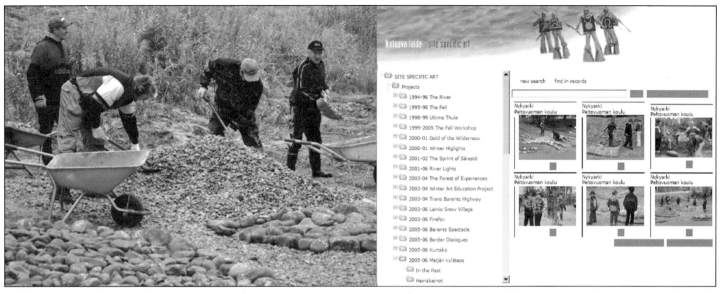

Photos from Peltovuoma village. *Photograph by Saara Sarparanta*

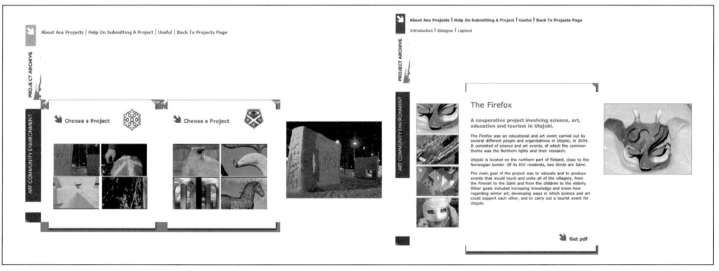

Projects presented in four photographs. *Screenshots by Maria Huhmarniemi*

Elderly people create snow sculptures in the schoolyard. *Photograph by Maria Huhmarniemi*

Project descriptions in the ACE archive are published in PDF format as collages of text and photographic documentation. This means that downloading them is not too time-consuming. However, there are plans to make future reports more inspiring and evocative by adding a sound background and video screens to the PDF files, and there are other development needs if the effectiveness of the archive is to be maximized. At the moment it is not possible to make online comments on reports, and there is no virtual channel to allow interaction between students, cooperation partners in projects, colleagues in other universities and the general public.

Future uses of virtual learning environs in community art projects

New media, particularly digital media, have always had an essential role in community art. Artists and project leaders commonly use new communications technology to widen both participation and audiences.[13] Many classic large-scale projects have activated recruits through the Internet. For example, the Empty Bowls project uses its Web space to invite new participants to create ceramic bowls. Since the project began in 1990, Empty Bowls events have been held throughout the world, and millions of US dollars have been raised to combat hunger.[14]

The virtual learning environments of the *Art, Community and Environment* studies have been used effectively by both students and tutors, but there is still a lot of untapped potential for increasing interaction and participation. While members of the community should obviously be at the physical heart of community art projects, the experience can still be enhanced by Web-based communication.

Virtual learning environments for community projects should be developed as open environments, where all participants have easy access. They should be used as a publication channel, but also as a medium for interaction, for example, as a data-sharing tool for project management, evaluation and documentation. Community art education projects aim to 'give a voice' to local communities. The imaginative development of virtual learning environments could provide a really effective channel for these voices.

Notes and references

1. Kester, G. (2006). Collaborative Practices in Environmental Art (online). Available from URL: http://greenmuseum.org/generic_content.php?ct_id=208. (Accessed 19th December 2006).
2. See, e.g., Hiltunen, M. (2007). Embodied Experiences. Constructing a Collaborative Art Event in the Northern Environment, in Kylänen, M. & Häkkinen A. (Eds.) *Articles on Experiences 5 – Arts & Experiences*. Rovaniemi: Lapland Centre of Expertise for the Experience Industry, pp. 62–89; Huhmarniemi, M., Jokela, T. & Vuorjoki, S. (Eds.) (2004). *Talven tuntemus: Puheenvuoroja talvesta ja talvitaiteesta*. (Sense of Winter. Statements on Winter and Winter Art) (trans. V. Välimaa-Hill). Rovaniemi: University of Lapland.
3. Kester, G. (2004). *Conversation Pieces. Community + Communication in Modern Art*. London: University of California Press, p. 10.
4. Graham, C. R. (2006). Blended Learning System. Definition, Current Trends, and Future Directions, in Bonk, C. J. & Graham, C. R. (Eds.) *Handbook of blended learning: Global perspectives, local designs*. San Francisco, CA: Pfeiffer Publishing, pp. 3–21; Korhonen, V. & Pantzar, E. (2004) Verkko-

opetuksen ja vuorovaikutuksen erityispiirteitä tunnistamassa. In Korhonen, V. [ed.] *Verkko-opetus ja yliopistopedagogiikka*. Tampere: Tampere University Press, pp. 17–48.

5. Sinko, M. & Lehtinen, E. (1999). The Challenges of ICT in Finnish Education (online). Jyväskylä: The Finnish National Fund for Research and Development. Available from URL: http://www.sitra.fi/Julkaisut/sitra227.pdf (accessed 19th December 2006), pp. 242–243.

6. See also Jokela, T. & Hiltunen, M. (2003). Art pedagogical projects in northern wilderness and villages, *Lifelong learning in Europe*, vol. 8, no. 2, pp. 26–31.

7. Jokela, T. & Huhmarniemi, M. (2007). Environmental Art and Community Art Learning in Northern Places, in Mason, R. & Eça, T. (Eds.) *Intercultural Dialogues in Art Education*. London: Intellect Books; Jokela, T., Hiltunen, M., Huhmarniemi, M. & Valkonen, V. (2006) Art, Community & Environment (online). Available from URL: http://ace.ulapland.fi/yty/english.html (accessed 19th April 2007).

8. Kurki, L. (2000). *Sosiokulttuurinen innostaminen. Muutoksen pedagogiikka*. Tampere: Vastapaino.

9. Coutts, G. (2004). Multimedia, curriculum, public art, *Art Education*, vol. 42, no. 4, pp. 33–39.

10. Herrington, A., Herrington, J., Oliver, R., Stoney, S. & Willis, J. (2001). Quality guidelines for online courses: The development of an instrument to audit online units. In Kennedy, G., et al. (Eds.) *Meeting at the crossroads: Proceedings of ASCILITE 2001*, Melbourne: The University of Melbourne. Available also from URL http://elrond.scam.ecu.edu.au/oliver/2001/qowg.pdf. (Accessed 19th December 2006), pp. 263–270.

11. *Ibid.*

12. Virta, K. (2005). Sloyd teacher trainees´ self-directed learning and metacognitive regulation and the web-based support. Kullas, S. & Pelkonen, M-L. (Eds.) *The relationship of Nordic handicraft studies to product development and technology*. Turku: Turun yliopisto, pp. 50–73.

13. Lacy, S. (1995). Departed territory. Toward a critical language for public art. In Lacy S. (Ed.) *Mapping the terrain: New genre public art*. Seattle, WA: Bay Press, pp. 171–185.

14. Empty Bowls. Available from URL: (http://www.emptybowls.net) (accessed 19th April 2007); see also Gablik, S. (2004) (1984) *Has Modernism Failed?* London: Thames & Hudson, pp. 150–151.

6

COMMUNITY-BASED ART EDUCATION IN THE NORTH: A SPACE FOR AGENCY?

Mirja Hiltunen

I have adopted the term 'agency' to define the process whereby one individual or group of people acts as a conduit, facilitator or enabler on behalf of others or themselves. In the context of community art, this means the empowerment or emancipation of a community through the agency of the community itself together with art education professionals. In talking about a 'space for agency', I am referring to the physical, social or metaphorical space in which this process takes place; the moving forces in the process I describe as 'actors', which derives from the same Latin root as 'agency'.

My aim in this chapter is to illustrate agency as a characteristic aspect of community-based art education in the North by analysing two projects that took place in Finnish Lapland,[1] an area whose intimate relationship with the environment and traditional livelihoods co-exists with a lively tourist industry. I will first look at Pelkosenniemi, a tiny village in eastern Lapland, the site of the *Tunturin taidepaja* (Fells Art Workshop) project. From there my journey continues to Utsjoki, Finland's northernmost municipality, host to the *Tulikettu* (Fire Fox) project. I will argue that in Utsjoki, art education itself can be seen as an actor and a space for agency for the entire village community.[2]

Community-based art education takes place between several sectors of society and can be approached from different perspectives. Like community art itself, it is concerned with the empowerment and emancipation of individuals and communities through art. Community art has been hitherto studied mainly from within art institutions, or explored from the perspectives of social policy and health care. Its educational dimension has not normally been the wider focus of study. The working methods which play a central role in community art have also been to a large extent ignored, and their strengths – analytical, social and organizational skills, knowledge of social structures and organizations and the ability to cooperate – downplayed.[3]

The concept of agency is multidisciplinary. According to the social psychologist Suvi Ronkainen, although the concept is used to refer to an individual's capacity to make decisions and to implement and reflect on them, agency is not the characteristic of an individual. Agency relates both to individuals and their resources and to the environment and its possibilities and restrictions. It presupposes the possibility of doing things differently and can be perceived as a space, because it always needs a situation, a context. The process of creating a space for agency comes down to the question of perceiving and naming someone or something as an actor.[4] In the projects I have studied, art education can be perceived as both the actor and the space for constructing agencies.

Towards agency

The starting point of the *Tunturin Taidepaja* workshop was to offer a learning and working environment in the field of art education to unemployed young people at risk of social alienation. It is a labour market, political youth education project which simultaneously aims at developing cultural travel to the area and at improving the employment situation.[5] Students from the University of Lapland's Department of Art Education have worked as environment and community art educators on the project in the course of completing their teaching practice, and the quotations used in this chapter are taken from their reports. The purpose of these reports is to discuss the students' own role and pedagogy in the teaching practice or 'project environment' and to present their own development visions and reflective and critical evaluations.

In 2002, two students acted as instructors for a fire art workshop which was a part of the *Turjan taika* winter theatre performance in *Tunturin Taidepaja*. It took place on a stage made of snow and ice in a forest near a local ski resort. The target audience was mainly tourists, but the performance was also seen by a number of local people. *Turjan Taika* was realized in its entirety by the young unemployed people studying in *Tunturin Taidepaja*, under the instruction of the art education students and other art professionals.

The students' report concluded that the project-based nature of the *Tunturin Taidepaja* activities required cooperation from instructors specializing in a number of different kinds of task. At the same time, everyone had an opportunity to learn from each other and participate actively in the work. Communality, the sharing of experiences and peer-learning, emerged as the most significant field practice outcomes for the students.[6]

It became clear that in a small, working community it is of primary importance to be able to interact with different kinds of people and to give everyone the chance to express their opinions:

Cooperation between the instructors and the workshop participants was smooth. Due to the lack of time, both the instructors and the workshop participants had to give a large work contribution. The artworks had to be made during that one week, and there was no time for any fine tuning. Despite long workdays the work climate was positive.

On the other hand, it was felt that the project was not without its difficulties:

The problem of the workshop is that information does not move where it is needed, and the personnel and visiting teachers have conflicting objectives.

The struggle to meet the production deadline was a new challenge:

Sometimes you have to balance between your own art educational views and commercial demands, which can be difficult for an inexperienced person to do successfully.

The reports suggest that agency involves walking a fine line between possibilities and restrictions. Conditions imposed by the tourist industry and production schedules cannot be perceived as mere restrictions, because tourism is itself one of the factors concerned in the construction of the local space for agency. The question to be addressed is the extent to which some of the conflicting and partly contradictory intentions of art education and the tourist industry can be resolved.[7]

In a winter art workshop held in *Tunturin Taidepaja* in 2003, the roles of teacher and pupil were successfully reversed: the art education student leading the workshop moved 'into the background', and the workshop participants acted as instructors to a group of upper-secondary school pupils in making snow sculptures. The student reported the outcome as follows:

The communication was interactive; the workshop participants instructed [the pupils] in using the tools, and the upper secondary school pupils gave advice in building shapes.

The workshop participants also organized a snow sculpture workshop for tourists at the *Hotel Pyhätunturi*. They all seemed to find a space for their agency and seemed comfortable with the possibilities and restrictions of the environment, but challenges related to the division of tasks, the organization of the workshop and communication continued to exercise minds. The workshop leader stated in the evaluation section of his final report that a winter theatre performance in which the workshop participants had been simultaneously involved had taken up a lot of time that might otherwise have been available to the project. He had been forced to considerably condense many of his original ideas.

Turjan Taika (the Magic of Turja). A winter theatre performance in a snowy forest. Left: Photograph by Mirja Hiltunen. Right: Photograph by Elina Rissanen

It is important to pay attention to how activities are organized and realized in the often diverse and piecemeal environments characteristic of community-based art education. The various goals and objectives of the different parties involved should be turned into strengths that can serve as starting points for a new approach. However, before this can happen it is of primary importance to establish a culture of dialogue within which differences are embraced, and activities are targeted towards a shared goal. I see art as having the potential to serve as a common language in this process, a space for dialogue as well as its 'product'.

Dialogue is one of the most central characteristics of community art. Community art is communication between those involved in the creation of a work of art and a participating audience. It is not mere representation: it is primarily based on interaction and participation and consists of situations which people enter in order to collaborate with the artist[8] in creating meanings, and a medium and space where they can share them and give them form and voice. According to Kester, dialogical projects develop, unlike object-based artworks, through 'performative interaction'.[9] In other words, it is a question of agency.

All community art activities are underpinned by the idea of learning and change through art. They involve intent, but their outcomes are often open-ended and unpredictable. This is also true of community-based art education projects that are realized in cooperation with different partners; for example, the tourist industry, but in this case the process of trial and error and the open-ended ideal may be subject to practical limitations, like the meeting of production schedules.

Learning by doing is central to art education.[10] The starting point for all learning is the learner's phenomenal, physical and sensory relationship with the environment, and the multisensory physical work done in *Tunturin Taidepaja* is closely tied in to the surrounding environment and culture.[11] The fire art and winter art workshops are good examples of how *Tunturin Taidepaja* embodies tensions between art, art education and tourism, but is at the same time a space that renders new forms of activity possible in the everyday lives of local people.

A multicultural village as a space for agency

My journey now continues towards Utsjoki which is situated about 450 kilometres to the north of the Arctic Circle in Finnish Lapland. The first *Tulikettu* week, an event that sought to promote art and science education and to empower the entire population of the village, was organized by several cooperating partners in 2004, mainly with the help of volunteers, and the theme of the week, the Northern Lights, emerged from an initial discussion of local interests, the Northern environment and folk tales.[12] A group of the University of Lapland's art education students took on a number of different roles, and snow and ice sculpting and lantern and mask making workshops were organized in several locations in the village. In the course of the week, visiting professors gave lectures about both the science of the Northern Lights and the mythology surrounding them.[13]

Funding from The European Social Fund (ESF) in 2005 ensured *Tulikettu's* continuing role in the cultural and educational agenda of the municipality. An action week in Utsjoki beginning on the 28th of February 2005 took as its theme the Northern Lights and the ending of the *kaamos*, the winter darkness.[14] The starting point of the project was familiarization with the theme and the environment, and an extract from an email sent by one art education student about three months before the action week was to take place describes very well the confusion that participation in a large project can bring about:

What are the tasks of us participants? Developing the theme/deciding about it? Inviting different schools and other partners to participate in the project? Responsibility for choosing and obtaining the materials? Drafting tasks for the workshops etc, and "curricula" for those doing their field practice and for the pupils for the whole week (or even for a longer time)? Working in the workshops and teaching? Everything...?

Due to the nature of community art projects in general, it is not possible to plan every aspect in advance, and this open-endedness can trigger feelings of insecurity. Communication was one of the areas that had been criticised the previous year, and one of the goals of the students was to improve it. Increasing and improving the possibilities of 'coming together with others', a quintessential part of community art education, was chosen as a prime objective:

One of our goals was to make different kinds of people meeting each other equal or better than the previous year. For this reason we chose a separate building in the schoolyard as our headquarters.

This separate space served as a meeting point and a common ground for the pupils from both the Sami-speaking and the Finnish-speaking classes. Before the activities began the art education students collected learning material from varied points of view with a view to encouraging

Fire sculptures in the opening of the exhibition with the Fox in the foreground. *Photograph by Mirja Hiltunen*

the active participation of local partners, schools, children's day care centres, the village authorities, and the elderly. This involved designing artworks in advance, making models, drafting posters and taking part in a snow sculpture contest.

A participating international exchange student at the University of Lapland was particularly impressed by one of the activities:

> At first pupils were supposed to work in groups of 3 or 4 people to create a common sculpture. They did so, but some of them liked the experience so much, that they created a second and even a third sculpture, in some cases.

She also discussed the aesthetic qualities of the sculptures, and said that making some of them had required a high level of both group work and technical skills. She observed that the participation of different groups from the community seemed to increase cooperation:

> It is also interesting to note that the common creation of a snow sculpture increased the level of cooperation in the community. The big snow fox could be a reason for the enthusiasm, too, since the citizens were witnessing the creation of a huge sculpture and understood that with cooperation the range of possibilities widens.

The massive fox sculpture created by the international snow sculpture workshop and upper secondary school pupils is a memory that still lingers in the minds of the villagers, although the sculpture itself melted a long time ago.

In the *Tulikettu* project, art acts as an open space that invites action. The public sculptures are an indication of the many skills the villagers possess, and they also speak of a desire to cooperate. When people work together as a group, and observe the work of others, unique opportunities for learning open up, as in the case of the fire art workshop that was part of the same event:

> Actually, the fire sculpture happening influenced some of the adults participating since they included some fire in their ice sculpture. It is nice to see that what the young people are doing can have repercussions in adults' lives.

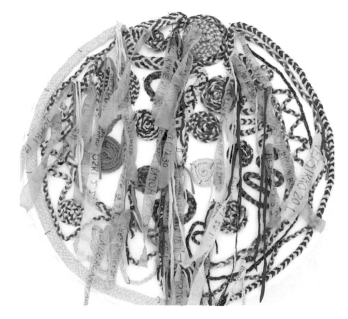

Traditional Sami plaiting.
Above: Photograph by Heidi Koljonen
Right: Photograph by Mirja Hiltunen

Age does not matter when making snow sculptures. *Left: Photograph by Mirja Hiltunen. Right: Photograph by Minna Saastamoinen*

The possibility of doing things differently

The participation and agency of villagers from different age groups and cultural backgrounds can be seen to have increased during the *Tulikettu II* project in 2005, and this development has also been noticed in the context of the other projects that were active in the village at the same time. The final report on *Ikäihmiset yhteisönsä voimavarana* (The Elderly as a Valuable Resource of Their Community) states that the elderly were active participants in *Tulikettu*, passing on oral tradition in the form of stories about the Northern Lights and the significance of the first sunrise after the polar night. The elderly also taught traditional Sami plaiting, passing on different techniques, knowledge and skills to pupils of the local school and to other villagers.[15]

Art can make things visible, as was the case with the Fox sculpture, or it can give a voice to a group of people, such as children or the elderly, who might not otherwise have had a chance to be heard. The voices of different groups of people can be heard through their participation in community art projects and in the works they produce. While openness to the possibility of doing things differently is always a prerequisite, in the northernmost municipality of Finland, the only municipality where the Sami people are in the majority, this is of particular importance. One art education student, who herself has basic skills in the Sami language, had this to say in her teaching practice report:

> The majority of the elderly Sami people have experienced forced 'Finnishisation', discrimination and disregard in their childhood. Due to this, some workshop participants felt at times that the workshop was oppressive, because it had been brought from the outside.

The same student went on to say that the situation was resolved by warm-hearted discussions with the local project worker, who has a good command of the Sami language, followed by the singing together of a familiar and well-liked song about the Northern Lights. The episode however does point up the dangers inherent in this kind of activity. Even if community artists do not emphasize their role as activists, let alone their educational intentions, and even if their main aim is to give new expression through art to phenomena already present in the environment and the community, or to simply act as a reporter, they will inevitably exert some influence over the community involved.[16] The artist and the art educator must always be aware of the responsibility that this entails. The art sessions for the elderly in the *Tulikettu* project have been voluntary, and the starting points for all activities have been joint planning and listening.

If we have to label any one part of a community art project as 'the artwork', it could be the social bond that is generated between the participants.[17] In most cases, the community artist seeks to create situations that render it possible for people and communities to make themselves visible and heard, but often the artist also aims to empower individuals and communities to manage their own lives or, for example, to increase awareness of environmental issues. Listening to the participants, recognizing their wishes to do things differently and, even if necessary, recognizing their refusal to act all require a special sensitivity.[18]

Expanding networks, opening spaces

As community art is active by nature, and aims at change, it can be perceived as activist art, which, according to Felshin,[19] raises questions about the appropriateness of using public space as socio-political and cultural space, and encouraging communities or audiences to participate in art activities that aim at social change. In 2006, the *Tulikettu* project continued to expand, as new groups of actors joined *Tulikettu III* as instructors and as course participants. The following extract is from the report of one art education student:

> When the chairperson of the local Committee of Education and Culture, wearing a red fox hat, gave a speech in the opening ceremony of Tulikettu, he said that the event was so significant to Utsjoki, that it felt as though the Olympic Games were being held there, and suddenly I realised the significance of the event to the municipality.

The opening ceremony set the tone for a remarkable week in which contemporary art was one of the main themes. An exhibition portraying the works of the Finnish artist Osmo Rauhala[20] was opened, and throughout the event there were lectures on contemporary Sami art. With the expansion of the project, joint planning had become increasingly challenging. Art education students from the University of Lapland were given the freedom and responsibility to initiate and develop activities, together with the locals, from starting points planned in consultation with all the cooperating partners. I also invited a group of student teachers who were minoring in music to join the project, along with their instructor from the University of Oulu. Without extensive cooperation it would not have been possible to carry out such a large operation.

The main theme for art and science in 2006 was water in its different modes. Lectures, exhibitions and other events were organized for and by local people, and the theme brought together people working in local schools and day nurseries. A major feature of the event was the *Deatnu*, a river of snow and ice that flowed through separate sections each containing a startling variety of mythological water creatures and other phenomena, as well as snow sculptures representing a group of real buildings near the *Teno* River (*Deatnu* in Sami). The school's history teacher had designed the models for the buildings with the pupils, and supervised the sculpting in snow, an integration of normally separate disciplines that resulted in a tangible monument in the schoolyard.

Over the weekend, the local people created their own snow sculptures in the yard of the village hall. Elderly villagers took part in music sessions and painted their 'water memories' with acrylic colours on sheets, which were then frozen in the form of ice lanterns and placed in the yards of the service centre and school. They also created a salmon net installation and took part in the building of a snow sculpture entitled *Vesihiisi*, after a mythological creature that dwells in lakes, rivers and ponds. People attending mental rehabilitation facilities also participated in the activities.

In community-based art education, artistic learning can be achieved through different forms of collaborative and cooperative learning. *Left: Photograph by Heidi Koljonen. Right: Photograph by Mirja Hiltunen*

In their report summary, the art education students who had been involved concluded that the project team had functioned well, and everyone had been flexible and ready to offer help to others. A number of development tasks, however, still remained: inviting villagers to events, encouraging entrepreneurs to participate, taking weather conditions into consideration, discussing working schedules at the local school and addressing the fact that the scale of the project, in line with the pattern of previous years, had generated more work than the art education students could handle.

Tulikettu shows that project art can be seen as a space where people from different age groups and cultural backgrounds can meet. The goal set in the ESF project plan for *Tulikettu*, to give the inhabitants of Utsjoki the opportunity of increased participation in learning in the fields of education and culture, seems to have been achieved. The concept of equal learning opportunities is closely interwoven with accessibility. In order to create a true community project, communality has to be present at the planning stage. This is a challenge in northern Finland, where the population is sparse and distances between communities can be considerable. There have been various attempts to find ways round this difficulty. E-mail has been found to be problematic and cumbersome, and although video conferences have turned out to be reasonably successful, interaction tends to remain superficial if several sites participate at the same time. Having said that, without these technical advances, however imperfect, it would not have been possible at all to realize community-based art education projects based on cross-sector collaboration.

Seeing and naming

Modernization has been seen as a threat to traditional ways of life and to both local and national identities. It has been claimed that in the modern world small communities with homogeneous values no longer exist, and people make connections through multicultural and multidimensional networks instead. This, however, can also be seen as an opportunity to explore new forms of communality. A community can be a unit with geographical boundaries, but it can also be a symbolic entity bound together by something less tangible, like feelings of togetherness.[21]

It could be argued that community art, in responding to changes in communal understanding, also makes new forms of communality, and *Tulikettu* is a typical case. Public awareness of the project and its potential for empowerment has been a central goal from the outset. The skills of the community have been celebrated annually during festivities at the end of the action week, the winter artworks have been showcased in an outdoor art gallery, and there have been numerous other art exhibitions in the village hall, library and school. A section of the website of the municipality of Utsjoki is dedicated to *Tulikettu*, and the project is described and documented in the University of Lapland's Web-galleries.[22] It has also featured on television and in north Finland's most read newspaper, *News in Northern Finland*, as well as in Finnish- and Sami-language local newspapers. This indicates that it has been embraced as a joint event among both Sami- and Finnish-speaking people,

The mythical boat was part of the Deatnu – snow sculpture river streaming through the yards. *Photograph by Mirja Hiltunen*

one of the project's major successes. It has made visible and celebrated the strengths of a unique multicultural community and outstanding natural environment.

Changes in agency, tensions and empowerment

My perspective in this exploration of the characteristic elements of community-based art education has much in common with the socially active movements of contemporary art and postmodern multicultural and socially reconstructive art education, both of which feed into critical pedagogy and sociocultural animation.[23] In the course of the chapter, the voices of art education students have been heard in reports which highlight their dual role in projects like *Tulikettu* – on the one hand a reflective learner, and on the other a teacher who acts as designer, organizer and art educator. These reports build a picture of a polyphonic choir consisting of the students themselves, teachers, school pupils, elderly people and numerous other participants. They also help to clarify the role of the various interest groups and cooperative partners involved in the process. Part of my purpose has been to define my own place[24] among these voices, all of which are welcome and necessary, the critical as well as the enthusiastic.

Implicit issues of power underlie everything I have written about here. When working in a region like northern Lapland, it is essential to bear in mind that the larger cultural context has an impact on the activities of the project. The issue of Sami cultural autonomy and land rights is a good example. I do not intend to discuss this in detail here and will confine myself to the observation that in the course of the *Tulikettu* project, tensions have emerged which have clearly originated from collisions of political interests both within and between certain groups of people. These tensions have been visible in the workshops, where there has been concern that all participants should be offered equal opportunities to participate, and about whose physical space can be used to work in.
That said, art has served as a space that is freer and more neutral than many arenas of everyday life, a space where people have been able to meet each other and express different points of view. The tensions that emerged during the *Tulikettu* project have been tempered by growing trust, listening and mutual understanding, and feedback from participants in the action weeks has been mainly positive. In particular, the opportunity to spend time with others and to do things together was often mentioned.[25]

So what kind of changes in terms of 'space for agency', 'naming of agency' and opportunities for choice have arisen from *Tulikettu*? One general development has certainly been a shift in focus to the local level. Opportunities for participation have expanded annually, and a number of new groups have come on board. The potential for choice has also become greater, as is indicated by development plans made by the local agents for the project.[26] These plans also suggest that people's own resources have increased, that something has been learned, become visible, been publicly acknowledged.

One venue at the first Tulikettu 2004 was the historical church cottage area in Utsjoki. *Left: Photograph by Mirja Hiltunen. Right: Photograph by Anna Pakkanen*

Every year an improvement in winter art skills has been manifest in the work of pupils, teachers and other villagers, while participation in a range of art workshops, exhibitions and presentations has developed knowledge in the domains of art and science. Changes in attitudes and action models are more difficult to assess, but at the very least, participation in multidisciplinary and multicultural activities has enabled people from different backgrounds to meet in the course of everyday life, made the importance of cooperation visible and offered models for further development of related activities. The project has had a positive impact not only on local people, but on the agency of the participating art education students – their role as 'actors'. Their readiness to take responsibility for the different activities in cooperation with the local population has shown a marked increase during the course of the project, and the value of the experience of participation is clearly manifest in their evaluation of their own role as art educators. This is in tune with one of the central objectives of project studies, which is to support the development of art students in the role of teacher across a range of environments and communities, while expanding the domain of art education into different sectors of society.

Community-based art education, like the pedagogy of liberation, is never perfect and does not seek to offer final answers. It is, rather, a process which is constantly being reshaped, as McLaren and Giroux put it, as part of the struggle for critical understanding, emancipatory forms of solidarity and the rebuilding of democratic public life.[27] Community-based art education can be seen as a collage or a social sculpture built cross the domains of art and science, in which private and public intertwine. The process may be slow, however, in the art education projects I have studied there are signs of the first green shoots of animation and empowerment.

Notes and references

1. The projects are based on an environment- and community-based learning model which has been developed at the University of Lapland in the context of art teacher education. See Jokela, T. (2006). Nurkasta ulos – kuvataiteen opettajankoulutuksen uusia suuntia, in Kettunen, K. *et al.* [eds.] *Kuvien keskellä. Kuvataideopettajaliitto 100 v.* Keuruu: Like, pp. 71–85; Jokela, T. & Hiltunen, M. (2003) Art Pedagogical Projects in Northern Wilderness and Villages, *Lifelong Learning in Europe*, vol. VIII, issue 8:2, pp. 26–31; Jokela, T., Hiltunen, M., Huhmarniemi, M. & Valkonen, V. (2006) *Taide, yhteisö & ympäristö. Art, Community & Environment*, Rovaniemi, Lapin yliopisto. Available from URL: http://ace.ulapland.fi/yty/english.html (accessed 15th April 2007).
2. I use the concept of agency to refer to the capacity of individual human beings to act independently and to make their own free choices. There are different factors, such as social class, religion, gender, ethnicity and customs which seem to limit or influence the opportunities open to individuals. I use the concept of actor to mean one who exerts power, or has the power to act, who develops a unique voice and gains control over his or her own being.
3. In art criticism, projects of community artists have often been treated as documentations and have been discussed from the perspective of their technical realization: see Haapala, L. (1999). Taiteilijan muuttuva rooli – yhteisötaidetta 90-luvun Suomessa, in Erkkilä, H. *et al.* [eds.] *Katoava taide – Förgänglig konst – Ephemeral Art*, Ateneum 1999. Helsinki: Valtion taidemuseon museo, pp. 81–82. Education and learning are the focus, for example, in Williams,

J. (2003) Where the Arts, Education and Society Intersect, *Lifelong Learning in Europe*, 8:2, pp. 32–38; see also Matarasso, F. (1997) *Use or Ornament? The Social Impact of Participation in the Arts*. Comedia. London; Delft, M. Van (1998) *Community Art – Implications for Social Policy*. Themes from Finland. 6/1998. Sosiaali-ja terveysalan tutkimus-ja kehittämiskeskus.

4. Ronkainen, S. (1999). *Ajan ja paikan merkitsemät. Subjektiviteetti, tieto ja toimijuus*, Helsinki: Gaudeamus, pp. 84–89; Ronkainen, S. 2006. *Toimijuus*, a lecture. Tutkijakoulu, Lay. 23.5.2006.

5. The *Tunturin Taidepaja* art workshop started as an experimental project in 1997. The project has subsequently received support from The European Social Fund (ESF) as well as national and local funding. The project ended in 2005, but some activities are still continuing.

6. Communality in the context of art education refers to a socio-constructivist concept of learning and knowledge, which emphasizes the significance of interaction. It requires joint construction of meaning in addition to reciprocity.

7. Hiltunen, M. (2007). Embodied Experiences. Constructing a Collaborative Art Event in the Northern Environment, in Kylänen, M. & Häkkinen, A. [eds.] *Articles on Experiences 5 – Arts & Experience*. Lapland Centre of Expertise for the Experience Industry. Rovaniemi: University of Lapland Printing Centre, pp. 62–90. Available from URL: http://www.leofinland.fi/includes/loader.aspx?id=7fca337f-63ab-4f24-8600-26d8e18ae522 (accessed 16th February 2008); Hiltunen, M. (2004) Erämaa opettaa. Kehollisesti ympäristön, taiteen ja yhteisön maisemissa. *Aikuiskasvatus*. 1/ 2004, pp. 54–59.

8. Sederholm, H. (2000). *Tämäkö taidetta?* Porvoo:WSOY, pp. 113–116, 192.

9. Kester, G. H. (2004). *Conversation Pieces: Community and Communication in Modern Art*. Berkeley and Los Angeles: University of California Press, p 10.

10. Dewey, J. (1980). *Art as experience*. New York: Putnam; Kolb, D. (1984) *Experiential learning. Experiences as the source of learning and development*. Englewood Cliffs, NJ: Prentice Hall; Räsänen, M. (1997) *Building Bridges. Experiential Art Understanding: A work of art as a means of understanding and constructing self*. Doctoral dissertation. Helsinki: Publications Series of the University of Art of Design. UIAH A18.

11. Hiltunen, M. (2007). *op. cit.*, pp. 62–90.

12. The name *Tulikettu* is derived from the Finnish word for the Northern Lights, *revontulet*, the 'fox's fire'. There is an old belief that the Northern Lights are born when a fire fox runs across the night sky.

13. The main coordinator at the local level, and the originator of the entire idea, is the mathematics and physics teacher Juhani Harjunharja; the art director is local artist Minna Saastamoinen. The Meteorological Institute of Lapland (Sodankylä), the Department of Astronomy at the University of Oulu and *Ursa* Astronomical Association have all been involved in *Tulikettu* from the beginning, see Hiltunen, M. (2005) The Fire Fox. Multisensory approach to Art Education in Lapland, *International Journal of Education through Art*. 1:2, pp. 161–177.

14. Snow and ice were the main artistic media, but a shadow theatre and fire art workshop were also organized, and there were lectures on astronomy as well as other science programmes. The Department of Art Education instigated a winter art workshop for a group of ten international art students, and a group of local upper secondary school pupils joined the group.

15. The Elderly as a Valuable Resource of Their Community. Final report. 2005, p. 23. Written by the project worker Anna-Maija Hilliaho. The Archives of Utsjoki municipality and the archives of author.

16. Lacy, S. (1995). Debated Territory: Towards a Critical Language for Public Art, in Lacy, S. [ed.] *Mapping the Terrain. New genre public art.* Seattle: Bay Press, pp. 174–177.

17. Haapala, L. (1999). *op. cit.*, p. 81.

18. Kester, G. H. (2004). *op. cit.*, pp. 116–118, 151.

19. Felshin, N. (1995). Introduction, in Felshin, N. [ed.] *But it is Art? The Spirit of Art as Activism.* Seattle: Bay Press, pp. 9–12.

20. The exhibition in Utsjoki consisted of two video installations, *Against the Wind* (2003) and *System Complexity* (2004), and three showings of Arto Koskinen's documentary film *Joki taivaalla* (*River in the Sky*) on Osmo Rauhala's works and their underlying ideology. Rauhala is currently one of Finland's best-known artists in the international arena. He combines science and art in his works, and rivers are one of his main themes, see also http://www.osmorauhala.net/ (accessed 15th January 2007).

21. Hautamäki, A. 2005. Johdanto, in Hautamäki, A., Lehtonen, T., Sihvola, J., Tuomi, I., Vaaranen, H. & Veijola, S., *Yhteisöllisyyden paluu*, Helsinki: Gaudeamus, pp. 7–13.

22. Utsjoen Tulikettu, municipality's web pages: http://www.plappi.fi/kunnat/utsjoki/projektit/tulikettu__talvitaiteen_ja_tieteen_koulutustapahtuma/; University of Lapland, Department of Art Education: *Katoava taide – site specific art-gallery*, http://olos.ulapland.fi/mm/katoavajulkinen; ACE – art, community, environment project archive, which is maintained by the University of Lapland's Department of Art Education and the University of Strathclyde in Glasgow, Scotland, http://ace.ulapland.fi/ (accessed 15th January 2007).

23. See Danvers, J. (2003). Towards a Radical Pedagogy: Provisional Notes on Learning and Teaching in Art and Design, *Journal of Art & Design Education*, vol. 22, no. 1, pp. 47–57; Davenport, M. (2000) Culture and Education: Polishing the Lenses, *Studies in Art Education*, vol. 41, no. 4, pp. 361–375; Garber, E. (2004) Social Justice and Art Education. *Visual Arts Research*, vol. 30, no. 2 (issue 59), pp. 4–22; Mason, R. 2004. Cultural Projection and Racial Politics in Arts Education, *Visual Arts Research*, vol. 30, no. 2 (issue 59), pp. 38–54; Efland, A. D., Freedman, K. & Stuhr, P. (1996) *Postmodern Art Education: An Approach to Curriculum.* Reston, VA: National Art Education Association; Freire, P. (2005) *Sorrettujen pedagogiikka*, in Kuortti, J. [trans.] Tomperi, T. [ed.] Tampere: Vastapaino, 2005; Kurki, L. (2000) *Sosiokulttuurinen innostaminen. Muutoksen pedagogiikka*, Tampere: Vastapaino.

24. I have worked as an educational coordinator, a member of project steering groups, a supervisor of students' project studies and theses, and an art educator and action researcher participating in the practical realization of various projects. From the perspective of the art institution, my role could also be seen as community artist or curator.

25. Hiltunen, M. (2005). *op. cit.*, pp. 169–172; Hiltunen, M. (2006) Elettyä taidetta – yhteistä toimimista, in Kettunen, K. *et al.* [eds.] *Kuvien keskellä. Kuvataideopettajaliitto 100 vuotta.* Keuruu: Like, pp. 28–32.

26. The local school continued the *Tulikettu* tradition with a winter art event in the winter of 2007 and organized a summer school in 2007 that combined art and science in the spirit of the *Tulikettu* project. The social welfare sector has also been active in developing art-based activities. The winter art equipment remains in the possession of the local Department of Cultural Affairs and is at the disposal of the inhabitants of the municipality.

27. McLaren, P. & Giroux, H. (2001). Radikaali pedagogiikka kulttuuripolitiikkana. Kritiikin ja antiutopianismin tuolle puolen, in Vainonen, J. [trans.] Aittola, T. & Suoranta, J. [eds.] *Henry A. Giroux & Peter McLaren. Kriittinen pedagogiikka.* Tampere: Vastapaino, p. 68.

7

CROSSING THE LINE

Sarah Bennett

The title of this essay refers not to the reactionary act of crossing the picket line, but to the act of crossing from one place to another – crossing thresholds or boundaries, sites of differentiation. I am writing this piece as a practitioner,[1] crossing into new professional territory by writing about a collaborative art project called *Window Sills*, initiated in 1998 by staff from the Exeter School of Arts and Design[2] at the University of Plymouth. *Window Sills* investigates the space of the window, as the interface between our personal experiences and memories, and the broader cultural and historical realm in which we live. The project examines changing cultural divisions between public and private space, and the barriers between public artwork and its publics.

The act of crossing a boundary may be political, or transformative, or an act of transgression, but boundaries are integral to the process of crossing, in that each defines the possibility of the other. Conventional thinking sees this as a binary problem, but Edward Soja[3] has added another dimension with the idea of '*thirdspace*', which opens new ways of thinking about spatial practices, and activates a space of the 'between'. It is this transitional space, the fluid and overlapping space between shifting margins, that is the focus for this project, not the polarized positions of 'either side' that propose a set of oppositions which are no longer clearly delineated or desirable. Estella Conwill Majozo,[4] when preparing her contribution for *Mapping the Terrain* (which takes its subtitle from Majozo's own text '*to search for the good and make it matter...*'), in the course of meditating on this theme, '*found myself thinking about territories, both public and private, about political turf and definitive lines, those that exclude and those that include. I began to reflect on the earth and all the redrawn borders that we who are involved in public art must bring to the map if there are to be positive new directions for the world's cultures.*'.[5] But have the redrawn borders provided new spaces, interstices between the old definitions?

Window sills

The *Window Sills* project aims to develop collaborations between contemporary artists, local residents, fine art students and professionals and organizations in the public and cultural sectors. It takes its lead from the model of *'new genre public art'*[6] in the USA and from strategies developed by groups such as *Common Ground*, *The Art of Change* and *Platform* in the UK. Individuals, such as Alison Marchant, whose project *East Londoners* was commissioned by the London Borough of Newham in 2000, have also developed process-based ways of working. These are frequently ephemeral and often related to local rather than global narratives. *Window Sills*'s intention is to foster understanding and identify common ground between all the different groups involved in order to encourage inclusive and sustainable social change through art, and to increase opportunities for people to participate in the representation and recording of their own culture.

The opportunity for dialogue and exchange between the artists on the project and the residents of St Thomas and Exwick in Exeter arose from the initial idea of the window space as a boundary between public and private realms. What currency, if any, do the terms *public* and *private* hold in a new century? Categories and definitions previously taken as given are now seen as mutable, and there has been seepage in the social ordering of space. While the term *public* once related to all that was fair and democratic, and *private* to the capitalist project, the private sphere, notably the domestic space of the home, has now been politicized through feminist discourse,[7] and much of the public sphere has been literally privatized through government policy. No longer can one be privileged over the other. What takes place in public settings can be of a private nature; we tolerate the most public of spaces in our private homes in the form of television, and advertising via the Internet turns the entire world into a consumer market. Our relationship to the spaces of the city has become the subject of much academic interest from fields such as architecture, geography, linguistics, sociology and cultural studies. As Jos Boys states:

> This has led to a very fruitful unravelling of older, enlightenment 'ways of seeing' based on the flawed logic of binary oppositions; to valuable critiques of the limitations of modernist identity politics (including those earlier feminist studies of the built environment) which remain in binary ordering in both their analyses and plans for change; and to a series of reconceptualisations concerned with framing a 'thirdspace', beyond the simple dualisms and oppositions found in so many western socio-spatial concepts.[8]

The concept of *thirdspace* was applied to the case of Barcelona by Malcolm Miles in a recent unpublished paper.[9] Miles developed the idea of the in-between space in which the semi-public sphere is customized by the private individual. Such a space could be represented, for example, by the balcony, particularly in Mediterranean countries where it commonly extends the interior space of the home into the social space of the street. Steve Pile[10] writes: '*The home is not simply an expression of an individual's identity, it is also constitutive of that identity*', and perhaps what is meant by 'home' includes such transitional spaces, including the space of the window sill, which was the starting point of the project[11] under discussion in this essay.

The identity of the residents of St Thomas and Exwick depends on difference. This difference is not of the kind found in a metropolitan city, but there are still issues of diversity, even in a place where the label of 'community' might seem easy to affix. The truth is that this kind of labelling is no more appropriate here than anywhere else. As Lucy Lippard points out, 'like the places they inhabit, communities are bumpily layered and mixed, exposing hybrid stories that cannot be seen in a linear fashion'.[12] The 'communities' of St Thomas and Exwick are set apart from the rest of Exeter by geographical demarcation, being historically outside the city walls and on the other side of the River Exe. 'Down in St Thomas' refers to the elevated viewpoint enjoyed by much of the rest of the city, which was once a Roman fortress and is set on a hillside with an outlook to the river and sea beyond.

The area contains a mixture of housing: some Victorian, some suburban, large housing estates, several shopping precincts and numerous parks and playing fields which reflect its history as a market garden centre exploiting the alluvial soil of the valley. Its geographical boundary, represented by the river, is intertwined with the social and hierarchical boundaries of power. Such boundaries are culturally constructed in order to set one thing apart from another, for example, the University from the city. The School of Art and Design is a case in point, having moved 1½ miles from its original site in the city centre to south of the city (down river) in 1974.

How, then, can we dip our institutional toe into the waters of the city, be they river, pond, fountain or flood, or retrace our steps back across the lines that differentiate us from our locale? There are some precedents for working across cultural boundaries. For example, *River Crossings*, organized by *Camerawork* and *Darkroom* in East London in 1992, engaged a broad public in the debate about the changes being made in the Docklands during the late 1980s, the River Thames itself becoming a metaphor for communication and exchange.[13] The mainly photographic works occupied sites on either side of and underneath the River Thames and were accompanied by Richard Layzell's 'performance in transit', which took place on a river cruiser. In *Creative Camera*, Helen Sloan, co-organizer of *River Crossings*, stated that

> The works in the exhibition approach issues of the effects of urban development on local communities; historical methods of transport and communication; and look at the more generic implications of communication networks in the global/local context.[14]

Window Sills creates an interface between the University of Plymouth and the residents of St Thomas and Exwick. Students from both the undergraduate Fine Art: Contextual Practice Pathway and the Integrated Masters Programme in Fine Art collaborated on the project. Some of them lived in the areas of St Thomas and Exwick where it took place. The Contextual Practice Pathway undergraduates have since 1986 worked off campus in numerous locations in the city and surrounding area, addressing issues of audience, site and context. As Sally J. Morgan observes,[15] 'these off-campus projects...put developing artists in touch with a palpable audience'. Her paper makes the case that such activities have become almost mainstream within fine art courses. Students are encouraged to question the boundary walls of the

...my father was one of the wardens during the floods. They went over the bridge and down Okehampton Road, past Beech Brothers and along to Emmanuel Church. The water was very deep , especially down Cowick Street. Many women were going around helping out and making cups of tea....

'Memories of the Exeter Floods'. Text and water print made in a collaboration between Edwina Fitzpatrick and residents of Lucerne House, Alpington, November 1999.

institution as well as the ideological restraints of modernist, studio-based art practice and to seek a more accountable range of practices. It is equally the role of the staff, through their own practices as well as broader research, to (in Exeter's case) 'navigate upstream' to the city and contribute to sustainable regeneration through creativity, dialogue and partnership. This process also provides opportunities for students to collaborate on 'live' projects with professional artists and the public, thereby preparing them for their future roles as professional artists.

Because some of these students are already from the area, after graduation they will return with specialist and transferable key graduate skills. As residents, in one sense, they never actually leave the place they come from, but as artists they do cross institutional and cultural boundaries.

What is seldom asked is what happens when they re-cross them on their way back.

Hybrid places

Doreen Massey[16] speaks of places as 'hybrid'. Whatever the historical boundaries defining them, she asserts that places are never 'pure'. If we accept this, then we can *think of places as essentially open, porous, and the products of links with other places, rather than as exclusive enclosures bound off from the outside world*. The act of returning, 'transformed' through learning, is perhaps one of the keys to re-thinking pedagogic methods and processes with a view to reopening links between St Thomas and the University.

The space of the river is constantly in flux. It is a place of fluidity and transformation. The river transgresses its borders, floods the land, seeps and creates new watery places. The memory of floods (a frequent occurrence in St Thomas until a flood prevention scheme was carried out in the 1970s) was central to the dialogue that Edwina Fitzpatrick, one of the *Window Sills* project artists, established with residents of the St Thomas area during the early stages of the project. Mapping memories through traces left by the floodwaters, Fitzpatrick facilitated a space for reminiscence about the floods.

As part of the process of representing and recording their own culture Fitzpatrick's co-artists from Lucerne House, some of whom are very elderly and suffer from short-term memory loss, made collaborative artworks that reflected their personal memories through image and text. The residents who participated saw this exercise as having great significance to them, which suggests that not only were they interested in their personal histories, but they had also enjoyed the process of exchange between themselves and younger people. One participant said during the interim evaluation period that *'it is important for memories to be heard so that other people can learn from them about the area and older peoples thoughts'*.[17] Lucy Lippard elucidates this point when she suggests that *'one reason to know our histories is so that we are not defined by others, so that we can resist other people's images of our pasts, and consequently our futures'*.[18]

Both the history and the future of the city of Exeter and the area of St Thomas, with its quayside location, are inextricably linked through time and space to the river. It laps up against the walls of the empty warehouses on the quay, whose downfall was precipitated by the short-sightedness of the City Council in past generations, notably during the nineteenth century. Until it was too late, the council refused to offer financial support to the building of a rail link from St Davids Station to the quay to facilitate the transport of imported goods. This led to the decline of the import and export trade, and the present council's plans for the West Quay seem to be restricted to looking at new commercial and leisure uses for the maritime buildings, with inevitable consequences for the present occupants.

On the east side of the quay is a piece of public sculpture by Roger Dean entitled *Armillary Sphere*. Privately commissioned as a personal memorial, only a small amount of its cost, along with its site next to the Customs House, was donated by the City Council. A celebration of Exeter's maritime history, it is one of very few pieces of public art in the city. The others are a fountain by the same artist commissioned by the City Council in commemoration of the Exeter blitz during the Baedeker raids, an insipid figurative sculpture of a family group by Carole Vincent commissioned by Devon County Council as a contribution to the Year of the Pedestrian in 1989 and 1990, a piece by Ray Smith commissioned by Sainsbury's for one of their 'out of town' sites, mosaics by local artist Elaine Goodwin and a smattering of poorly executed murals.

This is as far as it goes in Exeter, arguably not because members of the council have recognized the folly of the widespread wholesale visual pollution of public spaces prevalent in the 1980s, but for the rather less principled reason that they have never intrinsically valued the contemporary visual arts in 'their' city. Be that as it may, in contrast to the experiences of other cities whose public spaces have been colonized by impositional artworks, Exeter is perhaps more in tune with the traditions of 'community arts'. A proliferation of leisure activities under this banner has flourished in the city. It is now vital to build on this by recognizing that cities are hybrid places of diverse publics, and that the contemporary arts have developed processes like new genre public art which can contribute positively to the cultural development of a city. One of the aims of the *Window Sills* project is to show how the inclusive strategies developed by the artists with the project team can contribute to sustainable urban futures. These futures will not be enhanced by pieces of public art parachuted into the city, or wholesale commissions which may mean nothing to many residents.

The local
The 'local' is key to the project. In its early stages in 1998, when the research team wanted to initiate a collaboration with the residents of a street in the city, we went looking for a location that evidenced the way in which people represent themselves within the threshold of the window space, through the display of objects, images, curtains etc. We spent some time looking at our own neighbourhoods, on the grounds that as individuals our identities as artists/educators coexist with other multiple identities, including association with places in which we and our families are stakeholders. When artists, through their own practice, reflect on their own sense of place, wherever that may be, this may

become a useful starting point for inclusive strategies towards a truly public art, informed by the preoccupations and concerns of local residents and seeing their experiences as central to the process.

David Harding[19] argues that a 'transformative experience' is available to both professional and non-professional artists, i.e. the public, through collaboration. This is at the core of the *Window Sills* project, which seeks to create a sustainable forum for creativity, decision-making and activity within various city localities. Whether one is 'local' or not emerged as a theme with clients of Hatherleigh Road Day Centre in St Thomas in their discussions with project artist Brendan Byrne, and this led to a suggestion that a signpost should be erected outside the centre pointing to the towns where they were born, bearing legends like '72 years, Eva, 52 miles west'; and '79 years, Gerty, 1.5 miles north east'.

The project includes a number of other memorable strands. *Mapping Home*, the outcome of a collaboration between artist Neil Musson and groups of both the young and the elderly in the area, involves the production of sound recordings triggered by sensors placed at points on the boundaries of an individual's home 'territory'. Rebecca Eriksson, with student Kathy Woolner and 21 residents of St Thomas and Exwick, has collected 21 photographic 'moments' based on the window spaces of their homes, for presentation in public spaces such as the local newspaper, buses and bus shelters and community notice boards.

The market gardens that used to be a feature of the area became the focus of research by Edwina Fitzpatrick and a team of co-artists, and gave rise to plans to locate scent dispensers and window boxes in the streets to re-create the smells of the flowers that once were grown locally.[20]

All these activities have sown the seeds of a positive dialogue in Exeter about the role the arts can play in encouraging meaningful reflection on people's lives and personal histories. This has the potential to lead to a climate of renewal. Ownership of the project by the residents of St Thomas and Exwick was central to its underlying strategy. As Miles suggests, in relation to the role of the citizen in urban planning:

> Perhaps dwellers are also experts on their city and if so, their expertise begins in their awareness of the spaces around their bodies and the lattices of memory and appropriation they assemble as a personal reading of the city.[21]

Several government reports have pointed to the 'arts' as strategic players in the processes of urban renewal, local and regional development[22] and social inclusion.[23] These reports reiterate what those of us who have been involved in art and design education have always known, that 'the Nation benefits artistically, socially and economically from having a healthy and vigorous cultural life involving as many of its people as possible.'.[24] The importance of partnerships as a key strategy for the future is emphasized by Ken Robinson[25] in *All Our Futures*, the DfEE/DCMS-commissioned report on creativity, culture and education:

'Dunsford Hill Tulip Fields' Sclater's Nurser, early 20th Century. *Courtesy of Gerald Sclater, St Thomas Exeter.*

New working partnerships are now needed involving schools, higher and further education, local education authorities, local authorities more widely, cultural organisations and local commerce.[26] ...Each partner could contribute funding and other resources, and the total activity would contribute to the vitality of education and cultural life in the locality.

With a view to contributing to a creative future for the city, The School of Arts and Design at Exeter[27] has developed partnerships with other agencies, both arts and non-arts organizations, notably the Family Education Development Trust, the Royal Albert Memorial Museum and Spacex Gallery (with which it already had strong links). This future needs to involve all Exeter's citizens, not only those who currently take part in cultural activities. We, therefore, need to investigate those transitional or hybrid spaces which are the sites of important activities in everyday life. It is with these in-between places, seldom figuring on a city map, that the *Window Sills* project is concerned.

A version of this chapter was published in *The International Journal of Art and Design Education*. Vol. 19. No. 3.

Notes and references

1. Author's note. I originally wrote this essay in 1999, during the development of the 'Window Sills' Project (see below). When the editors invited me to include it in this edited publication, I considered revising it to bring it up to date with the current debates concerning arts within public contexts. This would allow me to reflect on the findings of the many texts that have been published in the interceding years, notably Miwon Kwon's excellent 'One Place after Another' (2002) which provides a critical overview of the approaches of artists/arts organizations working in relation to locational identity (that we attempted to interrogate within our research project and explored further in Bennett and Melling 2000). However, I realized that to revise my text would remove it from the specific context in which it was written. I have, therefore, decided to submit it for publication in its original, present-tense form, and hope that it will perform some usefulness in relation to the newer texts included in this publication.
2. Window Sills project was developed by the author with John Butler and Gill Melling. It was funded through the University of Plymouth QR funding, the Regional Arts Lottery Programme and Exeter Arts Council (local authority funding). A Symposium 'Divers[c]ities' took place in Exeter in September 2000. Consultants to the project were: Sally Morgan, UWE; Alison Marchant, artist; Louise Short, artist; Nigel Hillier, Consultant to Family Education Development Trust; Catherine Bailes, Exeter City Arts Officer; and Maggie Bolt, Director Public Art, South West.
3. Soja, E., *Thirdspace: Journeys to Los Angeles and Other real-and-imagined Places*, Cambridge, Massachusetts: Blackwell 1996.
4. Majozo, E. C., To Search for the Good and Make It Matter. In S. Lacy (Ed.) *Mapping the Terrain*, (Washington: Bay Press, 1995 pp. 88–83).
5. *Ibid.*, p. 88.
6. Lacy, S. (1995). *Mapping the Terrain: New Genre Public Art*, Washington: Bay Press.
7. Massey, D. (1994). *Space, Place and Gender*, Cambridge: Polity Press.
8. Boys, J., Beyond maps and metaphors? Re-thinking the relationships between architecture and gender In R. Ainley. (Ed.) (1998) *New Frontiers of Space, Bodies and Gender*, London and New York: Routledge, pp. 203–217.

9. The paper was presented at the Public Observatory which was an ELIA-funded project coordinated by Dr Toni Remesar, University of Barcelona. The paper was further developed in 'After the Public Realm...' in the *Journal of Art and Design Education* 19.3, 2000.
10. Pile, S. (1996). *The Body and the City: Psychoanalysis, Space and Subjectivity*, London and New York: Routledge, p. 55.
11. The particularity of window sills was brought to my attention by an exchange student from Barcelona. A lesser known usage of the verb 'to window sill' is to support oneself on the way home from the pub by leaning on the window sills of the houses in the street.
12. Lippard, L. (1997). *The Lure of the Local: Senses of Place in a Multicentered Society*, New York: The New Press, p. 24.
13. Sloan, H. (1993). *River Crossings: Light and Sound along the Thames. Creative Camera* (Feb/March), pp. 14–15.
14. Morgan, S. J. (1999). The Border-guards have lost interest: The 'problem' of Public Art and the Rise of Contextual Practice, *Drawing Fire, 4,* vol. 2 pp. 26–31.
15. *Ibid.,* pp. 26–31.
16. Massey, D. (1995). The Conceptualization of Place. In D. Massey and P. Jess (Eds.) *A Place in the World?* Oxford: Oxford University Press, pp. 45–77.
17. Bennett, S., Butler, J. and Melling, G. (1999). *Window Sills Evaluation Report*, unpublished paper.
18. Lippard, L. op. cit., p. 85.
19. Harding, D. (1997). Public Art: Contentious Term and Contested Practice. In D. Harding and P. Buchler (Eds.) *Decadent*, Glasgow: Foulis Press, pp. 9–19.
20. 'Window Sills' event/exhibition of collaborative artworks which took place within the locality of St Thomas and Exwick during the Exeter Fringe Festival in July 2000.
21. Miles, M. (1997). *Art Space and the City: Public Art and Urban Futures*, London and New York: Routledge, p. 200.
22. Fleming, T. (Ed.) (1999). *The Role of the Creative Industries in Local and Regional Development*, Government Office for Yorkshire and Humber and The Forum on Creative Industries.
23. Policy Action Team 10 (1999). Research Report: Arts and Neighbourhood Renewal Department for Culture, Media and Sport 1999.
24. Arts Council of England (1997). *Leading Through Learning*. London: ACE.
25. Robinson, K. et al. (1999). *All Our Futures: Creativity, Culture and Education*, NACCCE Report, London: Department for Education and Employment and Department for Culture, Media and Sport.
26. *Ibid.,* p. 129.
27. The School of Arts and Design relocated to Plymouth from September 2007, where the author continues with research into the arts' role within urban re-developments.

Bibliography
Bennett, S. and Melling, J. (2000). 'Window Sills: Art of Locality' in Bennett, S. and Butler, J. Location, Regeneration and Divers[c]ities: Advances in Art & Urban Futures, volume 1. Portland, Oregon and Bristol: Intellect Books.

Part Three
Education

8

ART AND DESIGN EDUCATION AND THE BUILT ENVIRONMENT

Eileen Adams

Education that focuses on the built environment and public art can contribute to young people's intellectual, emotional and social development as well as their moral and cultural well-being. Education through art enables young people to experience the world, to understand it, to think about it, to feel, to value and to take action in certain ways that are not possible through other disciplines. Educational projects that create links between art, design and the environment establish new relationships between learners and their surroundings. They offer young people opportunities to explore, investigate and discover. They nurture different ways of thinking and feeling; provide opportunities for active learning and problem solving; develop skills of perception, communication and invention; and encourage the exploration of different social roles and relationships. Sometimes they enable young people to take action, to put their ideas into effect. Most importantly, involving young people in public art and environmental design projects develops their capability to deal with the process of change positively and creatively.

Raising standards

In the relentless quest to raise standards, schools, children and teachers are monitored, inspected and judged more than ever before, with *target-setting*, *indicators*, *assessment*, *inputs* and *outcomes* the current watchwords. Anything that can be measured *is* measured. Other considerations do not seem to matter. Teachers play safe. The norms of organizing learning in schools – routine, timetable, length of lessons, rules relating to behaviour, relationships between teachers and pupils, the requirements and perceived constraints of the National Curriculum, pressures brought about by target-setting, assessment and inspection – all create a climate and habits of learning and teaching that do not necessarily support art and design education or built environment education. The imperative of gaining qualifications for employment has skewed the purposes of general education and is prompting debate in the press:

Gordon Brown's [then Chancellor of the Exchequer] pre-budget statement last week focused grimly on the need for all of us to work harder, learn more and compete more effectively in the international marketplace. Education is his priority – not for what it brings to our lives, but because it will turn us into better-qualified, richer and more productive workers...Our education system is increasingly geared towards examinations and results. For a substantial minority of children, these benchmarks are absolutely meaningless, and yet they are offered nothing worthwhile to take their place...The exam-driven, results-focused system is failing too many children.[1]

A heavy emphasis on (verbal) literacy and numeracy and a stress on teacher-directed whole-class teaching have meant that arts education has been severely damaged in primary schools and is in retreat in many secondary schools. Teachers are not able to invest the time and attention in art and design activities that they once did. Educators who should know better even talk about *packages* and *service delivery*, using models based on consumerist principles. There is a danger that children and young people are becoming more passive as learners. Parents and teachers are doing more of their thinking for them, organizing their time and their activities, controlling their access to educational, environmental and social experience. Young people are becoming more dependent on the use of the computer and access to the Internet to shape their understanding of the world. Children should be learning to be thinkers, makers, carers and doers, and we must place greater emphasis on nurturing young people's capability as independent learners, paying attention to the ways they are helped *how* to learn and the ways they are encouraged to love learning.

In its publication *Excellence and Enjoyment* (2003), the Government explains its strategy for primary schools. Moving on to a broader focus and encouraging teachers to take more professional responsibility, it sets out its vision for '*a rich, varied and exciting curriculum, which develops children in a range of ways*':

High standards and a broad and rich curriculum go hand in hand. Literacy and numeracy are vital building blocks, and it is right to focus attention on them. But it is important that children have a rich and exciting experience at primary school, learning a wide range of things in a wide range of different ways. The new Primary Strategy will support teachers and schools across the whole curriculum, building on the lessons of the Literacy and Numeracy Strategies, but moving on to offer teachers more control and flexibility.
    Excellence and Enjoyment[2]

There is a tension between a narrow focus currently evident in schools on specific skills development and the broader view of child development in the Government's stated policy that *Every Child Matters*. The Children's Act (2004) defines five broad outcomes seen as important for the well-being of young people: *Be healthy; Stay safe; Enjoy and achieve; Make a positive contribution;* and *Achieve economic well-being.* These give ample scope for art/design and built environment education. The design and management of the environment impacts directly on our health and well-being; our perceptions of the environment and our relationship to it determine how safe we feel; an understanding and love

Students from Eccles Sixth Form College, Manchester, worked with sand, water and other materials found on the beach to create a large-scale temporary artwork. *Photograph by Eileen Adams*

of art, architecture and the built environment enhance young people's relationship with place. Engaging young people in consultation and decision-making processes, both within school projects and at community level, helps them develop capabilities for life as well as self-confidence and skills of reasoning, argument and communication. And, of course, environmental art/design education offers many different career opportunities to ensure economic well-being.[3]

This move towards broadening the curriculum is reflected in recent changes to the Qualifications and Curriculum Authority's (QCA) programmes of study related to the National Curriculum for pupils aged 12–15 in schools in England, which emphasize the breadth of art and design education. At the time of writing, these changes have not yet been put into effect, but teachers will probably be advised to include work from a range of contexts, including different cultures and contemporary art and design practice. They will also be urged to make links with other areas of the curriculum. Hopefully, this will be interpreted to mean that the built environment and public art are accommodated more comfortably within art and design education. Making such links can contribute to:

- Language development (verbal, visual, spatial, kinaesthetic);
- Cultural development (learning about people and place, shared values and ways of viewing the world);
- Emotional intelligence (feeling response, education of the emotions, empathy);
- Social and moral development (skills of cooperation, judgement-making, shared decision making).

Creativity

The notion of *creativity* has surfaced again in Government rhetoric in the last few years, much influenced by the efforts and publications of Ken Robinson, who has described creativity as '*imaginative activity fashioned so as to produce outcomes that are both original and of value.*' He identifies four characteristics of creative processes:

- They always involve thinking or behaving imaginatively.
- This imaginative activity is purposeful, directed to achieving an objective.
- These processes must generate something original.
- *The outcome must be of value in relation to the objective.*[4]

These ideas inform inter-professional collaboration in education, which is used to lever change in attitudes and practices in schools. This has been important in the development of built environment education in the UK since the 1970s and, since the 1990s, has been a significant influence in arts education. It has been given a powerful boost through *Creative Partnerships*, a generously funded programme developed jointly by the Department for Culture, Media and Sport (DCMS) and the Department of Education and Skills (DfES). Launched in 2002 and

Pupils from Colmore Primary School in Birmingham created temporary installations of cutout figures in an allotment, then made a permanent record of their installations through photography. *Photograph by Eileen Adams*

managed by the Arts Council, this has brought schools into working partnerships with *'creative and cultural organisations, businesses and individuals'*...and was established...*'to develop schoolchildren's potential, ambition, creativity and imagination.'*

In effect, it has meant that thousands of opportunities have been created for artists to work with teachers and pupils. How should artists act as educators and facilitators? How might they bring out other people's creativity? Through demonstration, explanation and example, artists are expected to illuminate the ways they think and work. The assumption is that they can share their expertise with others and, through working with artists, children and teachers, will think and act more creatively. However, making this happen requires the experience, specialist knowledge and professional skills of an educator. It requires artists not only to know about their subject, but also to be able to share that knowledge effectively and to support other people's learning. Artists are not always able to do this. Their efforts are sometimes well intentioned but uninformed, and in most cases they are untrained to work with children and young people. They learn a lot about this by observing how teachers interact with their pupils.

There are modes of thinking and ways of working in artists' practice that can be usefully adapted to enable children to learn effectively, but adopting a model of professional artistic practice and applying it directly to work in schools does not necessarily foster creativity in either the children or their teachers. Some projects provide interesting study activities and a fascinating environmental experience for children, and everyone has a wonderful time, but there might be very little creative endeavour on the part of the pupils. In many cases, artists have been content to use other people as a creative medium, believing that this has educational value.

In response to concerns about the place of the arts in the curriculum, a number of initiatives, campaigns and awards have sprung up to influence what is taught in schools, such as *Big Arts Week*, *Art in Action*, the *Artworks Young Artist of the Year Award* and the *Young People's Art Award*. *Artsmark* was initiated by the Arts Council to raise the profile of arts education in primary schools. All these schemes are valuable in providing validation of young people's work, but the benefits are limited, as there are not necessarily any strategies in place to disseminate the results effectively. Although there may be attempts to recognize, promote and spread good practice, the emphasis tends to be on finished products rather than on educational processes.

Learning outside the classroom

Children are learning all the time, in any environment where they find themselves – in the supermarket, in the car, or at home in front of the computer or television screen. Learning does not take place only in the classroom, nor are teachers the only people who have responsibility for educating the young. In November 2006, the British Government launched its *Learning Outside the Classroom Manifesto*, which states:

Every young person should experience the world beyond the classroom as an essential part of learning and personal development, whatever their age, ability or circumstances.

These, often the most memorable learning experiences, help us to make sense of the world around us by making links between feelings and learning. They stay with us into adulthood and affect our behaviour, lifestyle and work. They influence our values and the decisions we make. They allow us to transfer learning experienced outside to the classroom and vice versa.

Learning outside the classroom is about raising achievement through an organised, powerful approach to learning in which direct experience is of prime importance. This is not only about what we learn but importantly how and where we learn.

We believe that every young person should experience the world beyond the classroom as an essential part of learning and personal development, whatever their age, ability or circumstances.[5]

Those who have championed *experiential, investigative and authentic* learning for many years are delighted that the Government has woken up to the value of this approach and is giving it such strong endorsement. The emphasis needs to be on helping young people learn how to learn: how to get to grips with new experiences, new ideas and new ways of thinking. This sits at odds with a system that places greater emphasis on didactic, programmed learning, with control and containment of pupils within the classroom seen as the safer option, and with teachers weighed down by the need for risk-assessment, fears over health and safety and the demands of continual monitoring and assessment.

Public art provides experience of art outside the classroom – in the street, the park and other community settings. The point of the artwork may be to change people's perceptions of place, or the way they think about an idea or an issue or simply the place itself. Contemporary practice obliges educators to place art and design in a broader cultural context, related to a more *'democratic conception of creativity'*[6] – a significant force that young people can use to shape their environment and their lives. The need is to acknowledge a wider range of purposes in links between art, design and education, and to recognize new forms of cultural expression, production and activity.[7]

The experience of public art and environmental change offers a useful focus for exploring notions of creativity and collaboration in community settings. Art is not about objects, it is about ideas. Art education should be pushing at the boundaries of how people understand what art is and what artists do. Art can frame how we are able to understand experience and ideas and permits certain ways of perceiving, knowing, responding to and interacting with the world. Art values a personal, emotional response. It is about making sense of experience. It is about making things to crystallize and symbolize thought. It is about making things happen. Engagement in environmental art stimulates and

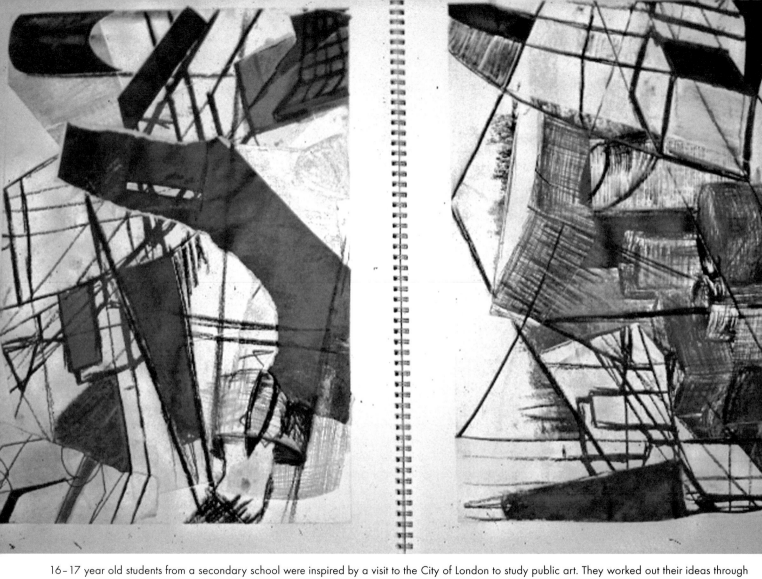

16–17 year old students from a secondary school were inspired by a visit to the City of London to study public art. They worked out their ideas through drawing (above) and maquettes then made use of scrap metal (right) to create large-scale artworks for the school grounds. *Photograph by Eileen Adams*

Each year, 70 students aged 14–17 from Glasgow schools spend 10 days at the Castle Toward summer school. They use the beach, woods, farm and gardens as inspiration for making art, connecting with the work of contemporary artists. This twig construction (this page) can be seen as a hanging sculpture or a three-dimensional drawing. *Photograph by Eileen Adams*

Everywhere at Coombes Infant School, near Reading, offers opportunities for play and learning. Children's early experience of environmental design and public art i of a place that is constantly changing, with all kinds of artworks, including those made of natural form, to explore and investigate. *Photograph by Eileen Adams*

challenges young people to interact with others, to shape their environment, to create feelings of pleasure and satisfaction, to construct meaning in their lives.

One strategy to take learning out of the classroom and into the environment well established in British schools has been the field course for subjects such as geography and the summer school for art/design. These provide an often intense immersion experience, with a depth of study not possible in school. This ensures that learning is relevant and related to young people's direct experience. The use of time is very different from the drip-feed approach evident in the normal school timetable. The relationship between pupils and teachers is also likely to be very different, with each aware of being part of a shared endeavour.

For the last twenty years, learning outdoors has been promoted by *Learning through Landscapes* in England and *Grounds for Learning* in Scotland. These organizations have encouraged a view of landscape as something that is shaped and formed by human activity, reflecting interactions between people and nature. Teachers and pupils can see how they can be involved in shaping and caring for the school environment. They have participated in the development of school grounds, contributing ideas for ephemeral works, seating, play structures, playground layouts and sculptures, as well as making major changes to the school landscape through planting schemes and building projects. Often the intention is to create an artwork, but more importantly, the experience should aim to nurture creativity. This includes the ability to wonder, to question, to experiment, to treat failure positively, to take risks, to value difference, to collaborate with others and to explore different points of view. Schools must respond to children's urge to make things, to do things, to change things – to create. Transformation and invention are at the heart of this – transforming what we have learned from our experience into knowledge, inventing new understandings and new meanings. That is what environmental art/design education is about.

Commission for Architecture and the Built Environment

The Commission for Architecture and the Built Environment (CABE) seeks to promote high standards in architecture and urban design. It is *'dedicated to helping young people improve their understanding of the built environments they inhabit and opening their eyes to the way good and bad design affects the quality of their lives.'*[8] Its publications for schools have promoted the ideas embodied in the Government's *Learning Outside the Classroom Manifesto*. A series of books published by CABE, *Getting out there ...local safari guides*, has been targeted at art, design and geography teachers in secondary schools, and others such as *Neighbourhood Walks* at primary schools. Most of these suggest study methods for analysing and interpreting the built environment, for developing critical skills and for thinking about design and environmental change.

A joint initiative by the Arts Council England, CABE and the South East Development Agency (SEEDA) has given young people the opportunity to develop these skills through *Shaping Places*, a programme developed by the Kent and Solent Architecture Centres in 2003 to 2005. This brought artists, designers, architects and landscape architects together with teachers from a number of disciplines and their pupils in primary and secondary schools, with the aim of engaging young people in the urban design process. Their efforts resulted in the publication of a

Pupils involved in the *Shaping Places* programme made use of drawing, including manual and computer-aided technique and other 2D media, 3D constructions, photography and words to develop appropriate study methods to think about possibilities for environmental design and change in their local areas.

Young children involved in the *My Square Mile* programme explored their local area.
Their field notes identify key characteristics that contribute to a sense of place.

book of case studies and study methods, which was distributed to every school in the south-east of England to encourage teachers to develop similar projects. The Solent Centre for Architecture and Design has developed this further, 2005 to 2008, through its Partnership Programme, embedding built environment education in schools through collaboration between teachers and architects. This has resulted in a wealth of Web-based learning and teaching resources and a professional development programme (http://library.solentcentre.org.uk).

Architecture Centre Network

Although architecture centres have existed in the UK since 1977, the recent emergence of the Architecture Centre Network (ACN), in close working partnership with CABE, means that there is now an *'agency that drives the movement forward, co-ordinates activity, provides a national voice'*, a mechanism for growth and development. Architecture Centres seek *'to secure greater knowledge, access, participation and influence, at all levels, in the creation of an excellent built environment for all'* (www.architecturecentre.net). The Architecture Centre Network offers support for individual centres, as well as training and dissemination and, very importantly, continuing professional development for its members. This means that there is more chance of ensuring coherence and continuity where development of the field has been inhibited by lack of long-term funding and the fragmentation of effort.

Design Commission for Wales

Although a much smaller organisation than CABE, the Design Commission for Wales (DCfW) has a similar mission, engaging in design review, providing advice on design quality and influencing public understanding of design. It commissioned a book and CD, *My Square Mile*, and distributed the pack to every primary school in Wales. Intended to develop children's design awareness, this initiative is based on the results of a two-year pilot programme in 2005 and 2006, to promote studies celebrating local distinctiveness and identity and to nurture emotional attachment and a sense of belonging. In discovering their local area, children recognize that they are part of the place, and the place is part of them. Pupils and teachers in Swansea and Ceredigion primary schools worked with artists to explore the aesthetic and design qualities of the local neighbourhood. They identified environmental issues and considered ideas for change and improvement in the design and management of the environment. The results of their work are now being used to inspire other schools to develop similar programmes of study.

Access and inclusion

Opportunities for learning outside the classroom are always available in museums and galleries. In recent years, these institutions have received considerable extra funding from the Government to build up education and public programmes in an attempt to bring in new audiences. Museums, galleries and heritage sites have all taken up the challenge to widen their appeal to a greater range of visitors, and have had to review ways of managing the 'visitor experience' and to pay attention to how people learn in these settings. Through its various programmes, *The Campaign for Drawing* has done a lot to promote access and inclusion through developing appropriate drawing strategies for engaging the public, interpreting traditional collections and contemporary exhibitions, and helping visitors connect with heritage buildings and sites.

The Campaign for Drawing has shown how drawing can be not only a private passion, but shared, public and collaborative. At *Big Draw* events at Bishopswood, an environmental study centre in Worcester, children and their families work with artists to explore ideas familiar in public art. They create temporary and ephemeral works, such as these mud prints on banners, which are hung in the trees. *Photograph by Eileen Adams*

The *Big Draw* is a national celebration of drawing. Having grown from one day in October to a month-long festival of drawing around the UK, it is supported by an intensive media campaign to make drawing visible, accessible and enjoyable. Many events held during the autumn half-term holiday are aimed at families, with the emphasis on fun and active involvement. The *Big Draw* has spread from museums and galleries to include heritage sites, science centres, libraries and archives as well as community groups and schools. A key message is that everyone can draw if they have the opportunity. The challenge is to move from regarding the practice of drawing as personal, solitary and individual, concerned with personal expression, development and taste, to viewing it also as a public activity, encompassing dialogue, shared judgement and action.

Through its education programme, *Power Drawing*, the campaign has demonstrated the effectiveness of drawing as a medium for engagement and interpretation. It has created a focused and serious regard for drawing as a medium for learning and thinking in schools and informal education, and presents new knowledge about drawing's role in perception, communication, invention and action. Crucially, it has developed a model of research and development that can be used to lever changes in attitudes and practices in environmental art/design education. Knowledge gained from the first five years is now being reinvested through a professional development programme to embed the use of drawing in educators' practice in a variety of settings, including schools, museums, galleries and heritage sites, as well as community organizations. Over the next three years, *Power Drawing* publications will be distributed more widely, a programme of workshops and courses will be provided across the UK, and reports on new developments disseminated through the campaign's website.

Teacher education

The Training and Development Agency was set up by the Education Act of 2005, its stated aim being to 'secure an effective school workforce that improves children's life chances'. The notion of life chances does not necessarily mean a broad and balanced education, but is more likely to be interpreted as securing qualifications needed to compete in the job market. This raises the issue of what schools are for and has implications for teacher education, both pre-service and in-service. Very few of the 31,000 new entrants to initial teacher-training in 2006, for example, will have received any formal training in relation to environmental art/design education. Their exposure to public art and built environment topics will have been dependent on individual tutors, resulting in piecemeal and erratic provision. Changes in local government's responsibilities for education and the demise of local authority advisers – some of whom have been replaced by inspectors and school improvement officers – have meant that most of the responsibility for in-service training has fallen on individual schools. And as schools inevitably have other priorities, again the result is piecemeal provision.

In summary

The bad news is that public art and the built environment must fight for attention in an overcrowded and increasingly fragmented curriculum. Pressures on schools to raise standards of literacy and numeracy have resulted in neglect of other areas of the curriculum, particularly the arts. A subject-based curriculum means that areas of study that cross subject boundaries – such as environmental art/design – are likely to be given lower priority than areas that improve test results and inspection scores.

The good news is that there are signs the picture is improving. Support is available from sources outside schools; resources are becoming more readily available and government policy is moving to broaden the scope of the school curriculum, promoting learning both in and out of school. The potential exists. The need is for teachers to see the educational value of studies linking contemporary practice in art with built environment education, and for curriculum managers to build this strand of work into art and design education programmes.

Notes and references

1. Russell J. (2006). *The Guardian* newspaper, 12 December.
2. DfES (2003). Excellence and Enjoyment.
3. CABE (2006). 360 degrees, issue 11, December.
4. National Advisory Committee on Creative and Cultural Education (NACCE), (1999). All Our Futures: Creativity, Culture and Education, London: Department for Education and Employment.
5. DfES (2006). Learning Outside the Classroom Manifesto.
6. NACCCE, (1999). *op. cit.*, pp. 29–30.
7. MacDonald S. (1999). Art and the Built Environment: Strategies for Sustainable Creativity. In *Built Environment Education in Art Education*. Guilfoil J. and Sandler A. (Eds.), Virginia, USA: National Art Education Association.
8. Information about CABE is available from URL: www.cabe.org.uk. (Accessed 27 May 2007).

Information about *The Campaign for Drawing* from URL: www.campaignfordrawing.org (accessed 6 February 2008).

Bibliography

Adams E. (1999). Education for Participation: Art and the Built Environment. In *Richer Futures, fashioning a new politics*, Worpole K. (Ed.), London: Earthscan.

Adams E. and Ingham S. (1998). *Changing Places: young people's participation in environmental planning*, London: The Children's Society.

Adams E. (2004). Space and Place, *The Campaign for Drawing*.

Adams E. (2006). *Getting Out There ... Art and design local safari guide: A teacher's guide to using the local environment*, CABE.

Adams E. (2006). *Shaping Places*, Kent Architecture Centre.

Adams E. (2007). *My Square Mile*, Design Commission for Wales.

DfES (2006). Annual Report of Her Majesty's Chief Inspector of Schools.

Connections between Public Art and Art and Design Education in Schools

Eileen Adams

Introduction

As we approach the millennium, the mood is inevitably one of reflection on what has gone before, while looking forward to an uncertain and exciting future. As a researcher interested in strategic planning and the practice of art and design education in schools, I must ask what can we learn from our previous work which can be invested in future practice? I base this paper on experience of certain research projects for which I have been responsible and which span a twenty-year period. In it, I make connections between art and design education in schools and public art.

Research

For the ideas concerning education, I draw specifically on experience gained from two curriculum development projects which linked art and design education with the environment. These are the *Front Door* Project [1974–1976], part of the Royal College of Art's study into *Design in General Education*, and the Schools Council's *Art and the Built Environment Project* [1976–1982]. The aims of the research were to find ways of influencing art teachers' practice, of extending the boundaries of design education and linking both of these with a study of the environment. The objectives were to create strategies and techniques to develop students' awareness of aesthetic and design qualities and encourage a critical stance to environmental experience. As the work progressed, it was evident that these aims were unnecessarily limited. If young people were able to make informed judgements about environmental quality, the question arose as to how they might engage in thinking about changing and improving their environment. The research was developed first in trial schools in the UK, then more broadly through interprofessional working parties of teachers, architects and planners [Thistlewood 1990], in-service courses and teacher education in the UK and abroad.

The origins of my research into public art was the preparation of a report for The London Arts Board to inform a review of their policies and practices, *Public Art Review* [1994], followed by a commission for a case study, *A Study into the Interface between the Practice, Process and Reception of Public Art* [1995–1997]. Concurrent with this, I undertook an investigation of *Public Art: People, Projects, Process,* [1996–1997], commissioned by the Southern Band, a consortium of four regional arts boards in the south of England and the Arts Council for England. The results, including accounts of 32 public art projects, have just been published.

Theory

When the work in curriculum development began in this field which links art, design, environment and education, there was little theoretical background to draw upon. The theory has developed through reflection on teachers' practices. Over the years, a number of theorists have helped to interpret and illuminate the nature of learning and teaching processes in art and design education linked with environmental study and to explain the strategies for curriculum development which have been attempted. I identify the work of Colin Ward in environmental education, Ken Baynes in design education, the work of Malcolm Ross and Brian Allison in art education, and that of Elliot Eisner in critical study, as being particularly influential in the 1970s and 1980s. In the 1980s and 1990s, the work of environmental psychologists such as David Uzzell helped us understand children's perceptions of the environment, while Roger Hart enabled us to appreciate more fully the issues involved in children's participation in environmental change. Geographers such as John Huckle and Ian Robottom have contributed to our understanding of how young people might engage critically with the environment through environmental education in schools. John Elliot's work on action research illustrates the effectiveness of teachers taking control of managing change in their own practice and contributing to curriculum development.

The theory concerning public art is derived in the main from experience in the USA. There are fewer theorists in the UK. Here, writers on the subject tend to be advocates such as the Public Art Development Trust or critics such as Peter Dormer. Writers discuss general issues, such as the benefits of public art [Selwood 1995] or focus on certain aspects such as art in health-care settings [Miles 1989]. They provide frameworks, such as guidelines on commissioning [Greene 1996] or funding strategies [Shaw 1991]. There is more documentation now appearing in reports [Boyden Southwood 1996], but still much work to be done on evaluation of case studies. We might make connections between these disparate fields to influence both professional art practice and the art and design curriculum in schools concerned with general education.

Outcomes

The various publications and teacher education programmes which have resulted from many of the research projects in which I have been involved are aimed at supporting practitioners, to inform their praxis, to clarify the ideas behind their work, the rationale for it and the strategies and methods they can adopt to make it more effective. From the research on public art, a framework for evaluation has emerged intended to support the process of project development. For this, I have been much influenced by my work in curriculum development, using action research as a way of initiating change and sustaining development. Thus, lessons learnt from the experience of curriculum development in art and design education have been applied to public art. The question for me now is what connections can be made between public art and art and design education in schools to inform the process of curriculum development?

Public art and art education

In this paper, I identify issues which have emerged from both the study of public art and my experience of work in schools. The text should be seen in conjunction with the images which show evidence of the kinds of work done by students and artists, the situations in which they work, the nature of the working relationships involved and the connections between art, design and environment. The images contrast the work of artists in public art and students aged 5–18 in schools in relation to the nature of the work and the processes and working relationships involved. I raise questions about connections between art, design and environment:

- What is public art? What is art and design in schools? What are their functions?
- What is the relationship between art and design and the environment in public art and in schools?
- What working relationships are involved in public art and in schools?
- How can development take place in public art and in the art and design curriculum?
- What is public art?

Public art is notoriously ill-defined and can be interpreted in a variety of ways. It has been described as sculpture in the open air and art in public places. It is intended to be freely and physically accessible to the public. It may be owned by the community, though it can be located in private places and serve a community of interest. It can be permanent, static or object-based. It can also be temporary or ephemeral. It can involve artists or craftspeople working in the community, in performances, residencies, fellowships or exchanges. Public art claims to fulfil a wide range of functions, as monument, decoration, trace, narrative and poetry. Increasingly, public art has been used as an element in urban regeneration schemes and tourist development programmes. In many instances, it is intended to improve environmental quality and is used to upgrade and animate public spaces. It is used as an embellishment or decoration. It can symbolize civic pride or create a corporate image. It may alter a place temporarily or provide for an event or celebration and create a change in people's perceptions of that place. It can enhance their experience of a particular environment, or trigger a memory or association. It has been claimed that public art is a cultural investment, vital to the economic recovery of many cities, attracting companies, adding to land values, creating employment. It is said to contribute to local distinctiveness and create a sense of place or regional identity. It features in cultural tourism. Claims have been made that it can increase the use of open spaces, reduce wear and tear on buildings and reduce levels of vandalism by encouraging a sense of pride and ownership.

Tim Knowles, Brunel Shopping Centre, Swindon 1997. Social issues of wants, aspirations, consumerism and out-of-reach objects.

Some tensions are evident. Although art is used to embellish the environment, to celebrate people's experience of it and enhance their perceptions of it, there are artists who use it to challenge, disturb and shock people into a new awareness. Many artists are keen that public art should not just be seen merely as ameliorating urban decay, supposedly introducing a note of celebration or beauty into an otherwise hostile environment.

Nor do they want it viewed as an element in the heritage and tourist industries, an income-generating attraction in historic houses and theme parks. They want art to be valued as an end in itself, not as a service agent for something else [Guest 1994].

Art and environment

What is clear in public art is the special relationship between the work and the environment of which it is part. The artist takes account not only of the suitability of the venue as a place to site an artwork, but considers how each impacts on the other to form a certain experience which cannot be generated by the work alone. Change of venue affects not only the impact of the work, but also its meaning. Many artists look to the physical environment itself as a source of inspiration and an influence on their work. They are aware of the possible effects of climate, the action of wind and rain on their work, of the importance of the changing light and of varying wind force and the impact of weather on a particular location. The physical conditions in part determine the form of the work. Issues arise as to its value. Does placing art outside galleries make it any more accessible to a wider public? Is it the location, the ideas the work embodies, or the way in which it communicates them that makes it 'accessible'? Should the same kinds of judgements be made about public art as are made about art in gallery settings?

What needs to be considered perhaps is not whether public artworks would be successful in a gallery, but whether the projects succeed in the context for which they are created and for those for whom they are intended. The most successful outcome may not be a permanent piece of artwork – there may be less tangible and more long-term social, education and cultural benefits.

Art and design education in schools

How do these ideas apply to art and design in schools? Students might learn *about* art and design. They might learn *through* art and design. But what do they learn art and design for?

Is it to be able to appreciate art or design? Is it to be able to make or do it? Is it to develop certain skills and understandings through an involvement with the subject which can transfer to other settings? Why do teachers think it is important? Do the students share those views? Do they understand art and design as giving symbolic meaning to their lives? Does it improve the quality of their lives or their environment? Does it oblige them to be reflective about the human condition? Does it encourage them to dream dreams, envision the future and plan ahead?

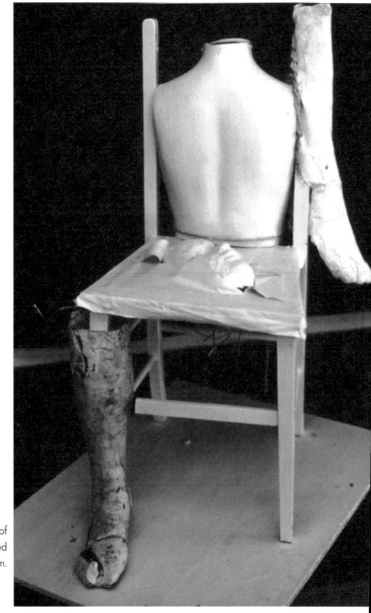

Student of 17 years at Banbury School, Oxfordshire, part of litterblitz' project using thrown away materials in a sculptor-led project on consumerism.

A monument to James Watt rejected by local people as 'not art' and now sited in Gourock, Scotland.

An outdoor acoustic laboratory at Kingswood Primary, North Carolina, and not intended as 'art'.

Does it enable them to realize their visions? Does it provide them with the means to shape and fashion their environment? Does it help them think, feel and take action? How does it impinge on their everyday lives?

The debate on 'visual literacy' initiated twenty-five years ago continues [Raney 1997]. Much of this is concerned with how art and design education in schools can influence the way young people experience, perceive and engage with their environment. Central to the idea of literacy is the notion of participation. How does art and design education enable young people to participate in the cultural life of their society, in shaping their being in the world and in impacting on their environment? In parallel with attempts to provide a liberal education in art and design, government diktat in the form of national curricula and examination requirements have acted to constrain the art and design curriculum. In the UK and in the work developed through the International Baccalaureate there is evidence which suggests that students' efforts are heavily influenced by a western fine art tradition, dominated by interests of the art establishment. Work can still be categorized using traditional labels such as 'portrait', 'still life', and interpretation of 'themes', though there is some evidence of 'installation' work in mixed media emerging. Traditional techniques and media continue to be popular, including painting, construction, collage, printing and photography. However, where students wish to explore and experiment further, in the use of video or computers, for instance, teachers are not always able to support their efforts. The work in the UK is particularly characterized by an emphasis on observational drawing, particularly 'nature' or 'natural' objects, and a line of research which requires students to study the work of other artists and rework ideas gleaned from that in their own efforts.

Art, design, environment, education
Over the past twenty years, particularly in the UK and in some other countries, a strand of development has emerged of work in schools which links art, design, environment and education. It relates to six areas:

- research and investigation;
- artwork, environmental perception,
- personal and emotional response;
- critical study, value judgements about
- aesthetic and design qualities;
- design activity, developing students'
- capabilities to deal with change;
- presentation and communication of ideas;
- realization (sometimes).

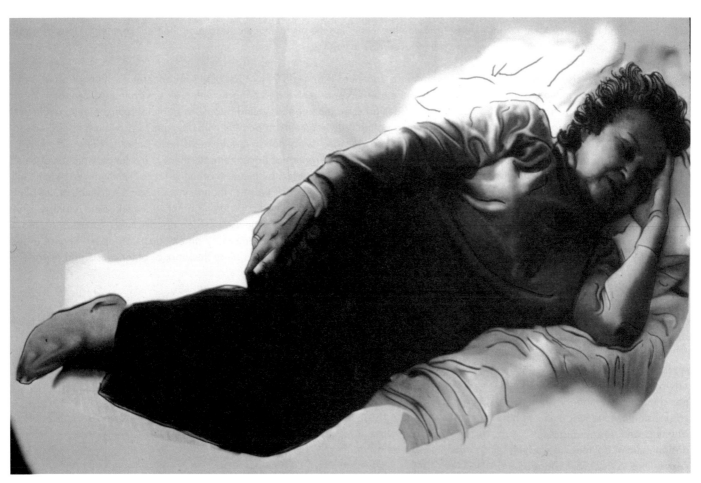

Art in health-care settings. Esther Rolinson using photography to document life on the wards with Brighton Healthcare Trust.

Pupils at Fairwater School, Cwmbran documenting life in various institutions to interpret 'hidden lives' of the community.

Research and investigation is developed through street work, based on direct experience, where students make use of the environment itself as an educational resource, rather than relying on secondary sources such as books, drawings, photographs, maps and plans. The local environment is a rich and varied resource, infinite in possibilities for study, constantly available and easily accessible. Artwork focuses on the aesthetic and design aspects of environmental study. It stresses the importance of visual language and spatial understanding. Used as a medium for perception, involvement in art enables students to explore, observe, record, interpret and analyze their environment. Used as expression, it enables them to communicate a personal, emotional response to place.

Critical study is primarily concerned with making judgements and the exploration of values. In art and design, critical study develops skills of connoisseurship, drawing on a knowledge of images and artefacts and the artistic and design processes which created them, as well as the historical, cultural and social contexts in which they were created. It requires them to work in groups, to compare and contrast their ideas, to formulate views and test out their opinions through argument and debate. It requires them to collect and weigh up evidence, develop their capacity for judgement and to explain or justify their opinions. Students share ideas, discuss and argue, revealing different viewpoints and differing values.

Underlying all the work is an appreciation that the environment is constantly changing. Change is the only certainty we have, the only thing of which we can be sure. How can young people deal with the experience of change positively and creatively? Design studies develop students' capacities to conceptualize, devise and create places. The work requires speculative and prepositional thinking, involving hypothesis, supposition and imaginative projection where students consider alternative or future urban design possibilities. Designing places creates not only experience of planning ahead, but also provides a vivid insight into the complexities of any decision-making involving people with different values, varied points of view and perhaps conflicting agendas.

Students gain experience in presenting their ideas through frequent, small-scale critiques to their peers during work in progress. They also present their work in more formal critiques with parents and professional designers by means of verbal presentations, exhibitions, booklets or video. Art and design work provides evidence of students' thinking. A verbal language is used to illuminate and justify their opinions [Adams in Guilfoil and Sandier 1997].

Students have been able to put their ideas into action to change an environment, most frequently that of their own school. The work evolves from developing a new awareness of a familiar environment, then proceeds through various stages of analysis, critique and design activity to proposals for change. These are debated by students and staff and, if accepted, an action plan is agreed. In many instances, students have also been involved in implementation. The cycle starts all over again as they monitor and evaluate the impact of their work and see possibilities for improvement [Adams 1994]. This work echoes many of the functions of certain types of public art. It is site-specific, concerned with environmental improvement. It develops a sense of place and aims to create a sense of identity and local distinctiveness. The involvement in changing their environment impacts on young people's perceptions of place and the meaning it has for them.

Working relationships
Participation is a key notion in public art. In the environmental work in schools, students have experience of different kinds and different levels of participation [Adams and Ingham 1997]. The long-term aim has been to develop their capabilities as active citizens in shaping the environment in the future. Public art projects also reveal different kinds of engagement and different levels of participation in the development of the work. Involving members of the public in a working contact with artists is generally a very exciting and satisfying experience. However, sometimes the 'feel good' factor is mistaken for good collaboration, which does not always result in good art.

Public art projects show artists at work in a variety of roles, many of them played out within the same project. They have sought financial support as applicants and supplicants and have had to learn the skills of the bureaucrat, filling in forms and attending meetings. As entrepreneurs or catalysts, they have had to make things happen. As dreamer and poet, the artist is seen to bring a particular sensitivity, sensibility and vision to the work. As researcher and investigator, the artist must generate ideas, then as a maker and technician, transform them into tangible outcomes. As interpreter and commentator, the artist's role is to illuminate and communicate.

The artist is working primarily in a social setting, with people as much as with expressive media. In public art, as well as being a maker, the artist works in the community, as animator, commentator and facilitator in creating objects and events, manipulating circumstances and situations to make something happen, working with a range of media which incorporate time and space as well as traditional materials, which take account of interactions between people and place. Acting as a visionary, as designer, a catalyst for change extending the traditional

Urban regeneration: local children from Pembroke Street estate (Portsmouth) primary school, working with tenants, artists and architects.

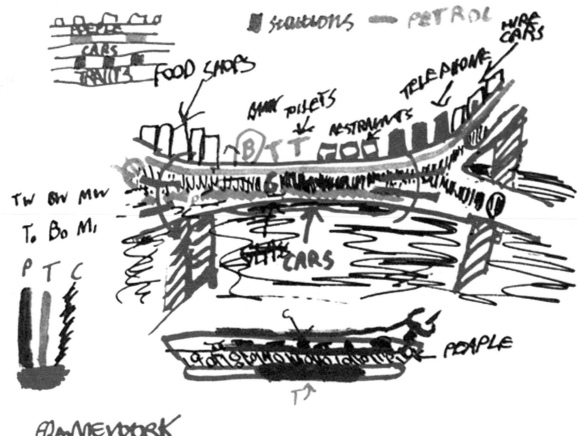

Nine-year-olds at Royal Academy workshops tackling ambitious projects such as a new Thames bridge. This study inspired by Richard Rogers.

Forest of Dean – artists using robust and biodegradable materials in a woodland setting.

Pupils at The Coombes Infant School, Arborfield, dig out and use clay to create temporary sculptures in the landscape.

roles of artist as reporter, holding a mirror up to the world. The artist no longer reflects what already exists, but helps to create a new vision or possibilities for change.

Artists are expected to work with other professionals as animators and facilitators, to involve the public. However, there are generally tensions in relationships across disciplines, departments and agencies and between individuals from different professional backgrounds. There are problems of communication, conflicting values and clashes possibly derived from differences in training, values, language, motivation and intent. As a member of a design team, what is the artist able to contribute in terms of conceptual thinking, symbolic meaning or imagery? How are different professionals able to communicate with each other and with their clients? There is a view that partnerships should not imply a blurring of roles, but create a discourse between separate but related disciplines. Successful collaborations are those where the participants have a personal and professional affinity as well as a shared vision.

Connections

In comparing recent and current work of artists in public art projects in the south of England with work in schools over the last twenty years, I have been struck by the resonances and echoes which exist between them. Pupils have sought to develop different modes of perception: those of the artists, the critic and the designer. Working in public art has required artists to adopt a range of viewpoints and roles. The notion of change has been central to both groups, whether changing people's perceptions of the environment or changing the physical environment itself. Both pupils and artists have had to learn strategies for visualizing possibilities for change, testing out ideas and anticipating how they might be realized. In schools, art was used as a conceptual tool to enable pupils to understand and think about the environment. Drawings, photographs, collage and models have been seen not as ends in themselves, but as a means of responding to analysing and appraising the environment and considering possibilities for change [Baynes 1982]. In public art, development of the artworks have gone hand in hand with other agendas, for social action, environmental change and commercial development, for example. Art has not necessarily been seen as an end in itself, but as a catalyst and support.

Conclusion

My original intention in writing this paper was to identify lessons to be learnt from the practice of public art which might be applied to work in schools. I suggest that as educators we need to expand our view of what art is and what it does, what making art might involve and certainly look for inspiration to current practice in public art. Artists are working increasingly in a variety of environments, not just the studio. They are working with a range of media and technical processes, so that labels such as art, craft or design may no longer be accurate. They are collaborating with other professionals. There is an increasing emphasis on process rather than product, with attention paid to outcomes over and above the production of artworks. Artists are impacting more readily and more directly on people's lives. The environment is no longer merely an inspiration for art – it is a setting for the development and location of art, a forum for debate about art and society, another clement in the artistic and design process. Artists are using art to change people's perceptions of place, their ability to respond to and impact on their environment, obliging them to engage in cultural issues.

On reflection, I see that work in schools has already recognized that. There is a wealth of experience in schools which links art, design and environment [Adams 1982, 1990, 1994, 1997, 1998]. Students have had experience of direct working contacts with different kinds of artists, craftspeople and designers. In addition to working on their own, trying to build up individual portfolios, students have welcomed exposure to interactive working, the experience of group creativity and the satisfactions and frustrations of shared endeavour. Teachers too have benefited from the experience of collaborating with other professionals on educational programmes. In the world outside school, art and design is increasingly developed as a result of collaborative working, whether in product, communications or environmental design or in fine art processes which require technical support. The model of the artist as lone genius perhaps needs to be reviewed and revised.

Instead of residencies in schools for artists to demonstrate processes of art-making, artists might join with teachers and their pupils in collaborative work focused on the environment. The need now is to make work in schools more visible, the learning methods and teaching strategies more accessible, and to share that experience and knowledge with the art community. Learning *through* art has always been a strength of art education in the UK, but there is a need to develop a wider social role for art and design, whether in schools or in the public realm. Some work will remain very private, imbued with personal feelings, experiences and perceptions, other work will be deliberately developed to support participation in community matters and intervention in the environment. Some work will appear part of the established tradition, while other approaches will deliberately challenge, disturb and confront.

In both art in schools and in the public realm, the need is not so much to try to confine art within existing categories, but to use it to allow greater scope for the way we experience places, the way we perceive and shape them. The need is not just to use art and design to learn to see what already exists, but to create alternative and future possibilities – to take art out of the gallery and into the street, move it out of the past and use it to shape the future.

This chapter was originally published in *The Journal of Art and Design Education*. Vol. 16. No. 3, pp. 231–239.

Bibliography

Adams, E. *Public Art: People, Projects and Process*. AN Publication, 1997.
Adams, E. and Ward, C. *Art and the Built Environment*, Longman, 1982.
Adams, E. Interprofessional Collaboration in Education, in *Issues in Art and Design Education*, (Ed.) Thistlewood D., Longman, 1990.
Adams, E. *Making the Playground*, Trentham Books, 1994.

Adams, E. Public Art Policy Review Seminar Series, report for the London Arts Board, 1994.

Adams, E. and Ingham, S. Changing Paces: Young People's Participation in Environmental Planning, to be published by The Children's Society, 1997.

Adams, E (1999) Art and the Built Environment: A Framework for School Programs in Built Environment Education. In *Built Environment Education in Art Education*. Guilfoil J. and Sandler A. (Eds.), Virginia, USA: National Art Education Association.

Boyden Southwood Associates, research into the application of new technologies and the arts, for the Arts Council of England, 1996.

Clifford, S. *Places: The City and The Invisible,* Public Art Development Trust, 1993.

Greene, L. *Commissioning Art Works,* Arts Council of England in collaboration with Public Art Forum, 1996.

Guest, A. and Smith, H. *The City is as Work of Art,* Scottish Sculpture Trust, 1994.

Miles, M. (Ed.) *Art for Public Places,* Winchester School of Art Press, 1989.

Raney, K. Visual Literacy, Issues and Debates. A Report on the Research Project Framing Visual and Verbal Experience, Middlesex University School of Education Reports and Evaluations, 1997.

Selwood, S. *Benefits of Public Art. The polemics of permanent art in public places.* Policy Studies Institute, 1995.

10

ART, DESIGN AND ENVIRONMENT: A PROGRAMME FOR TEACHER EDUCATION

Eileen Adams & Tony Chisholm

Background

The ideas which underpin the programme described here were derived from the Schools Council Project Art and the Built Environment, which sought to develop young people's perceptions of the built environment and enhance their capacity for criticism in relation to environmental appraisal. This curriculum development project in the 1970s & 1980s focused on learning methods and was directed primarily at practising teachers. In the 1980s, programmes with PGCE students were trialled at what were then Birmingham and Middlesex polytechnics. During the 90s, a short, intensive programme of study has been developed at Bretton Hall for PGCE Art and Design students. This has been possible through a collaboration between Tony Chisholm, the PGCE course leader, and Eileen Adams, an educator with wide experience of this area of work which links art, design, environment and education. The programme has evolved over the years, retaining the focus of links between art, design environment and education, but adjusting and adapting to current ideas, educational imperatives and changing circumstances.

Rationale

The programme is based on the use of the environment as an educational resource. It seeks to develop environmental perception and investigate issues related to different ways of seeing adopted by the artist, the critic and the designer. Students are introduced to the study of the environment, not as a historical, geographical or scientific study, but as a subject firmly set within the scope of art and design education. The experience of 'townscape', the 'urban landscape', might be compared to that of advertising. Both are primarily visual and emotional experiences, the appeal is to the senses and the emotions, not to the intellect or the rational being. Both affect us at a deeper level, influencing our perceptions, our feelings and our behaviour.

The programme also addresses pedagogical concerns. It gives students opportunities to consider what kinds of knowledge and understanding might link art, design and environment. It enables them to explore the learning methods and teaching strategies, which are appropriate for work in schools. It provides them with opportunities to develop resources for use in the classroom. It gives them a clear framework to develop approaches that they can use as a basis to inform their practice as teachers.

Programme

The programme is concerned with using art and design as a means of study to develop a sense of place, to make informed value judgements about aesthetic and design qualities of the townscape and to consider the impact of change on the environment. Although retaining the same aims, each year the programme has been modified, adapted and developed to suit changing circumstances as part of an increasingly condensed course of initial teacher-training. Various combinations of lectures, workshops and seminars, involving street work, studio sessions, presentations and critique have been tried and modified in the light of feedback from students.

The most successful course was that which involved an intense weekend workshop (16 hours), followed by an equivalent period of directed study. Students were invited to explore the idea of introducing a temporary change into a particular environment of their own choosing. They were asked to prepare three A1 panels: one to express a sense of the place of the chosen location (the artist's view); one analysing key elements and relationships, which identified the need or opportunity for change (the critic's view); and the last to show how their ideas for temporary change might impact on the environment (the designer's view). Students who wished to do so could use these panels as a stimulus for work in schools and develop a scheme of work to be carried out with pupils. This has created a useful source of research and reference material at the National Arts Education Archive at Bretton Hall.

In addition to the taught programme, students can choose to undertake a written assignment, which is formally assessed, where they are asked to explore environmental issues. They are expected to address a broader range of concerns than those which inform current orthodoxies and curriculum models in art and design education. They may also choose to create visual resources based on environmental reference in support of the school-based work.

Sadly, the amount of time available for the programme has been increasingly limited, a consequence of the reductive nature of initial teacher training. The allocation of time allows only for a half day of lectures, with little time left for street work sessions, workshops or critique, all necessary and valuable activities in this area of work. The techniques for study cannot be learnt through demonstration. They need to be experienced and practised. Ideas and opinions need to be discussed. Critical study and design activity need to be developed through group interaction.

Lectures

Lectures deal with the study of townscape, approaches to visual, spatial and critical analysis as well as learning methods and teaching strategies. Students are able to see examples of pupils' work from all age ranges, including examples from other countries. The ideas and approaches are discussed and students encouraged to make connections and comparisons with their own work or that which they have encountered in schools.

Perception

The programme seeks to extend students' perceptions, encouraging them not only to regard the environment merely as a source of inspiration and ideas for artwork, but to view it as critics and designers, extending the range of perceptions, analyses and critiques possible. This is made more interesting now that the yearly intake of students on the PGCE Art and Design course increasingly includes not only painters, but sculptors, designers and sometimes architects, landscape architects and students with skills in multimedia, time-based and installation work. Their varied backgrounds and previous professional training give rise to a range of different perceptions and values that feed and sustain the debate and create a fascinating critical dynamic.

A place is part of the environment that has been claimed by feelings. Our responses are dependent on our accumulated experiences and associations, our hopes and dreams and, perhaps, our fears and nightmares, as much as on the place itself. In their work with pupils, students are encouraged to use art and design as a means of engaging with a place, of achieving an enlarged emotional response as well as developing a greater awareness of its visual and spatial qualities. Art is used as a means of recording and analysing the experience of townscape, then reflecting upon and reworking that experience in order to make sense of it.

> The aim of teaching awareness of the environment through art is both to help children better understand the world around them and, through experience, the world within them. A major concern is to teach children to look and to see and to know. [Joicey 1995]

Fieldwork or, perhaps more accurately, 'street work', working directly from first-hand experience of the environment, has been an important feature of the programme. The park land at Bretton Hall has provided opportunities to explore ideas about landscape, not as a natural, but as a manufactured environment. The Yorkshire Sculpture Park has stimulated investigations about relationships between structures, spaces and people. The base at Powerhouse 2 in Wakefield offers the opportunity to explore the delights, surprises and problems of a townscape in transition. Students have drawn on their professional training as artists or designers to provide techniques for exploration, analysis and recording. Working together, they have shared their expertise and made visible techniques derived from the practice of art and design that can be applied to a study of the environment. They have developed a wider view of what might be suitable subjects for study and begun to see how the understandings and skills they learnt in the art or design studio can transfer to other settings and educational contexts.

What is challenging for many artists is the notion of 'space'. How is space created in the townscape? How is it defined? How is it contained? How is it divided? How is it used or abused? We are so used to seeing in terms of 'object' and 'ground' that it is hard to perceive space other than as background for objects in the landscape or a setting for people in the townscape. However, space is a key element, dynamic and powerful, in creating relationships between people and place. In views and vistas, it is the main element at work. How space is handled can make places seem safe or friendly, imposing or cosy, comfortable or claustrophobic. Students are helped to develop a vocabulary to describe the experience of space and other townscape features.

Critical study

This forms a basis for critical appraisal. It requires the use of visual and spatial 'languages' – and in addition, the use of a verbal language, in spoken or written form. Many former art students find this area of work quite challenging. It requires them to weigh evidence, to make informed value judgements about aesthetic and design qualities in the townscape, to explain and justify their views, show how they have arrived at them and consider, where appropriate, possibilities for change. This is done in the context of critiques or 'crits', where students present their work to others and respond to comments and questions.

This is an important experience for them, vital in the cycle of perception, evaluation and action. How will they talk about art, craft and design with their pupils in schools? What language is appropriate? What are the concepts involved? What are the skills required? What kinds of knowledge can be gained from direct experience of art and architecture and what understandings need to be developed through reading or talking? What skills come into play in critical study? The ability to compare and contrast, to contextualize a particular example in relation to the work of others, to locate it within a period of time or in relation to a set of ideas.

Design activity

Design is about shaping and controlling the environment. Design activity is primarily concerned with anticipating and visualizing change. It is about planning, requiring the consideration of possibilities and alternatives. It involves hypothesis and experiment. In considering ideas for temporary change, students from a variety of art and design backgrounds have been able to bring a variety of experience to bear. They have developed a design dimension that has a distinctive location in the realm of art and design.

Design/textile students, for instance, considered ideas using tensile structures, banners, fabric-covered constructions, transparent materials and the use of textiles to decorate and disguise. Other students considered the possibility of a change of use of a space, perhaps through performance art, requiring a temporary change in a particular environment. Some considered the use of landscaping to change an environment, while others looked to the use of different materials or colour, the introduction or removal of particular townscape elements to improve aesthetic and design quality.

Theoretical studies

Written assignments enabled students to consider the use of the environment as a resource for art and design education and to explore environmental issues that impact on art and design education. For instance, one student advocated the use of photography, video and digital imaging to develop an awareness of environmental issues, inspired by his own interest in landscape photography. His view was that

Students creating mud prints to record pattern and texture.

> introducing children to a considered form of photography will consequently demand a more considered view of what is around them. [Stott 1997]

The environment of the school grounds provides a useful focus for study. Another student suggested a study of land art to influence the development of sculptural pieces for the school grounds, but also to encourage young people to think about wider environmental issues of how the environment is shaped.

> Art should he used to stimulate thought about the environment, offering children a different stimulus to understand what is fundamentally their future. [Morgan 1997]

The work is future-oriented, focused on dealing with change.

Students discuss study techniques.

Critical session to reflect on the experience of street work.

Students were concerned about the balance of art and design studies, some stressing the importance of art to illuminate the human condition and the relationship between man and nature, while others chose to focus on the importance of design and designers in shaping and controlling the environment. Students readily understood the concept of 'reading' the environment.

> *It helps in developing comprehension of visual forms, crucial when exploring and deciphering our built urban and rural environment. It is a facility for helping nurture a responsive, visually literate child. [Maish 1994]*

Some students are able to relate the idea of 'literacy' to that of 'participation'.

> *...In addition to raising aesthetic awareness about specific aspects of the urban environment, I would consider the greatest value of the project lies in realising the relationship between environmental development and decisions made by individuals or groups. This relationship exemplifies the potential for pupils to take control and make changes to their environment through critical appraisal and design. [Carey 1995]*

School-based work

The programme seeks to extend young people's environmental experience and develop their perception and understanding of the townscape. It does not matter where students find themselves on teaching practice, the local area offers an inexhaustible source of inspiration and stimulus for art and design studies. In using environmental themes in their teaching practice, students are able to test out learning methods and teaching strategies which emphasize the importance of generating environmental experience, using it as a means of reflecting upon their experience and reworking it in order to make sense of it. They then build on this to develop interpretative and critical skills. Some, but not all, choose to take the work further into design activity. Some students see the importance of helping children to deal with the experience of change, particularly in being able to take a positive stance.

> *...most children feel that there is very little they can do to change anything. This project is much more localised and therefore accessible to pupils and they will feel much more able to solve any problems they encounter. [Macintosh 1995]*

Resources

Students are invited to create a small exhibition as a resource for their teaching practice. Some use photography, drawings, reproductions of paintings and sometimes original pieces of their own work to show how the environment can be used as a stimulus or subject for study. Images of found objects, patterns, textures and sculptural forms are selected as starting points and connections made with the work of artist and designers. Students use collections in museums and galleries as secondary reference material to enrich environmental study carried out first-hand.

Outcomes

Students are anxious to relate the work to the requirements of the National Curriculum. In analysing curriculum documents, they have found clear justification for work that links art, design and environment. They are able to clarify the contribution they can make as art and design teachers to environmental education or, conversely, see the place of built environment studies in the art and design curriculum. They are able to build on their previous experience, interests and expertise. The field of study is a broad one and all the students find that they can bring something from their previous experience and professional training to develop the work. The most fascinating outcome is to see how students are able to interpret ideas and methods developed nearly 25 years ago and to reinterpret them in the light of their experience, to shape them in relation to their interests and expertise and to relate them to differentiated needs and a general entitlement curriculum.

Evaluation

The setting of Bretton Hall in the Yorkshire Sculpture Park and nature reserve offers a wonderful resource to study art in landscape and landscape as art or design. The many fascinating built environments, small villages, suburban areas and towns provide an easily accessible resource for students to use as a basis for the study of townscape.

There is a value in group work for students to be able to compare experiences and perceptions, to share skills and understandings, to support each other's work and understand the importance of group work in the context of critical study and design activity. The programme reinforces and complements the range of teaching and learning enterprises in schools. Students value the opportunity to build on previous experience and expertise and to encounter subject matter which provides such a wide scope, distinctive challenges and possibilities for study.

The main problem is the lack of time available for such studies. This has an impact on the scope and quality of the work. However interested, enthusiastic or committed students are, the work requires time for exploration, field work, investigation, experimentation, studio development, discussion and debate. This is not possible in the present allocation of time within a PGCE course. However, creating options related to environmental study for workshops, written assignments, the preparation of teaching resources and schemes of work has created opportunities to develop the work. The main loss has been that of fieldwork and studio time to allow students to work together in teams. The result is that their experience of critical study and design activity has been diminished. Neither are the pedagogical implications sufficiently explored in group settings. It has been of great value to test out strategies for group work in the comparatively secure setting of an activity with fellow students before experimenting in schools.

Students do find some of the work challenging. Some are not used to critical study and have not mastered the conventions and skills of critique. Many are not used to verbalizing their ideas and opinions about art and design, yet as putative teachers, they will need to take on the role of professional communicators. Some see themselves primarily as fine artists, yet admit the necessity of extending their work to encompass design as part of their responsibilities as a teacher. Because of the immense scope of the subject, they sometimes find it difficult to focus and select appropriate areas of study.

For the tutors, the temptation is to reduce ideas and methods of working to formulaic prescription, to treat broad areas of study in a superficial manner and to expect students to understand complex subject matter without allowing them the time and opportunity to engage with it satisfactorily. Responsibility for supporting students has largely devolved to teachers who act as subject mentors. Students may also encounter studio environments with an ethos,

Resources for work in schools.

provision and some practices set in the mid-twentieth century rather than looking to the advent of the twenty-first century. These frustrations are of course not specific to this particular programme, but reflect the difficulties that are part of current practice in initial teacher-training.

Current developments

A recent action research project, 'Site Specific', has linked the work at Bretton Hall with initiatives in other teacher-training institutions. It has created a research network of colleagues, including tutors, teachers and students, interested in developing work which links art, design and the built environment. The research seeks to understand how the work of students with professional expertise as artists or designers might contribute to curriculum innovation. PGCE students from Bretton Hall are joined by PGCE students from University of Central England in Birmingham, University of Wales in Cardiff and Middlesex University together with BEd students from Andrews College and BA Community Arts students from the University of Strathclyde. The ideas and ways of working described in this paper are evident in the work of all the students. Other approaches are also being developed both as part of coursework and on school placements. Students are feeding off contemporary practice in art and design, particularly public art, and attempting to relate this to their developing practice as teachers. The research will explore how far the system of initial teacher-training is supportive of their efforts. It will examine how students' work can influence, extend and enrich teachers' practice. It will investigate how teachers can further develop the ideas and methods of working. This project attempts to support curriculum innovation and teachers' professional development.

This chapter was originally published in *The Journal of Art and Design Education*. Vol. 18. No. 3, pp. 338–344.

References

Adams, E. (1982). *Art and the Built Environment: A Teacher's, Approach* (with Colin Ward) Longman.

Adams, E. (1990). *Learning through Landscapes*. Learning through Landscapes Trust.

Adams, E. (1993). *Making the Playground*. Trentham Books.

Adams, E. (1997). Public Art: People, Projects and Processes, *Artists' Newsletter*.

Carey, P. (1996). The use of the urban environment to stimulate children's work and raise environmental awareness.*

Joicey, B. (1995). *Eye on the Environment*. WWF.

Joicey, B. (1995). Art and the Built Environment: Contemporary Concerns and Future Developments, Symposium at University College Bretton Hall, May.

Macintosh, S. (1995). Decorative Features of Buildings Focusing on Tiles and Mosaics.*

Maish, N. (1994). Environmental Issues.*

Morgan, M. (1997). The use of visual material in a project to aid pupils' work and raise awareness of environmental issues.*

Stott, R. (1997). Using photography as the introduction to a scheme that will help develop children's observation of their own environment.*

* Where no publisher is mentioned, these refer to students' unpublished assignments. Site-specific info sheets may be had from Eileen Adams.

11

Training Community Artists in Scotland

Julie Austin

The community arts movement in Scotland began in the late 1960s. A White Paper from the Secretary of State for Scotland, *A Policy for the Arts – The First Steps*,[1] encouraged local authorities to establish arts centres and consider how the arts could be developed through collaboration with voluntary organizations and agencies by sharing of expertise and resources. With the introduction of *The Local Government and Planning (Scotland) Act 1982*,[2] also referred to as the *Stuart Report*, Scottish local authorities were required to 'ensure the adequate provision of facilities for recreational, sporting, cultural and social activities.'.[3]

Following two national conferences in 1988 hosted by the Arts Council, the Local Government Training Board and the Calouste Gulbenkian Foundation, exploring *The Future for Community Arts Training*,[4] key skills were identified:

> These included evaluation and assessment skills, fundraising skills research and report writing, negotiating skills, interpersonal group skills, teaching and co-production skills, celebratory skills and resource management. Other skills which were considered to be essential included an understanding of council procedures and awareness of local government administrative systems, planning, policy development and execution, arts and design skills.[5]

One year on, in 1989, the Bachelor of Arts Degree at the then Jordanhill College of Education in Glasgow was validated, offering three pathways for learning:

- Sport in the Community
- Outdoor Education in the Community
- Community Arts

By the time of its second revalidation (in 1999 – also the year that the Scottish Parliament and Scottish Executive were established) Community Arts had become a 'stand alone' honours degree (BA (Hons) in Community Arts), awarded by the University of Strathclyde and delivered by the Faculty of Education, previously Jordanhill College. It retains its unique position as the sole provider of Community Arts study at undergraduate level in Scotland.

Defining community arts

> We are firmly of the opinion that the arts has the potential to help to transform the lives of individuals and the well being of communities.[6]

Essential to community arts practice is the ability to engage and support clients in arts disciplines with a view to fostering change and achieving empowerment. Through this active participation, individuals, groups and communities are provided with opportunities to enhance self-esteem, create identity and find expression to effect personal, social, cultural or political change. The overriding aim is to improve quality of life.

Art disciplines include art and design, dance, drama, media and music, but this list is by no means exhaustive. They encompass a variety of creative activities within a range of contexts, be it samba drumming as part of a gala or carnival procession, or a devised theatre piece in a young offenders' institution:

> ...activities are often in the form of projects and (though not exclusively) consist of workshops that lead towards an end event or end product.[7]

This feature is central to the training of those who deliver community arts and will be looked at later in the chapter.

There is often confusion between the terminologies of community arts and performing arts. While both forms practise arts specialisms, performing arts strives to achieve the 'best quality performances'[8] in the represented art discipline, and focuses on the training of the individual to be the best exponent of his or her craft. By contrast, community arts promotes the principle that everyone can be creative regardless of any perceived talent or skill. It has as its premise that process has precedence over product, and that activity is client-led – designed to facilitate

A first year community arts student facilitating a drumming workshop with primary school students. *Photograph by Glen Coutts*

the needs and wants of the individual or group. It also *'tends to be recognisable in terms of the process leading up to a form of artistic expression, rather than through the medium in which art is expressed.'*[9] Pre-defined standards of achievement, therefore, are not the main concern for community arts practitioners. Rather, an evaluation of skills attained and abilities progressed is considered a preferable indicator of success.

Defining community artists

Community artists exercise their skills for the benefit of others:

> *Community Arts workers have a huge responsibility to their participants, audience and funders. There is a distinct difference between an artist and an arts worker – the former has a duty to bring the best out in himself, the latter a duty to bring the best out in others.*[10]

In broad terms there are two categories of worker: those who facilitate and deliver the art activities with clients – a 'hands-on' approach – and those who are the strategic planners, managers or administrators for projects and initiatives – for example, Cultural Links Officers, Cultural Co-ordinators, Arts Development Officers and Outreach and Education Officers. These categories, however, are not mutually exclusive, and functions may vary depending on the work and the community being served.

The term 'community' covers a diverse range of groups identified normally by a common characteristic or purpose: children and young people, young offenders, school refusers, the elderly, ethnic minorities, asylum seekers, substance abusers, people with physical disabilities or mental health issues and the unemployed. Serving such a wide and extensive list, the community artist can expect to work in an array of physical and geographical contexts, delivering a range of projects from small to large scale. Engagement in community arts activities is not confined to arts centres, but takes place wherever need and purpose have been identified. This could involve a worker in settings such as residential care homes, prisons, young offenders' institutions, hospitals, community centres, adult learning centres, libraries, schools and public spaces – wherever people gather.

Given the variety of potential clients and spaces, collaboration is key to the community artist's practice – collaboration not only with end service users, but also with the agency or organization which provides access to them. In the *public sector*, examples include social work and community education departments, health boards, the prison service and local authority education departments. There have been partnerships in the *voluntary sector* with organizations such as *Age Concern Scotland*,[11] *Youthlink Scotland*[12] and the *Scottish Drugs Forum*,[13] and in the *commercial sector* with companies like *Impact Arts Limited*[14] and *Nuarts Ltd*.[15] Initiatives like these require the community artist to network and build capacity, and effective training is key to delivering this agenda.

Describing the training programme

The BA (Hons) in Community Arts has evolved from its first incarnation in 1989 through three full revisions (1993, 1999 and 2004). Each version was developed through consultation with students past and present, industry representatives (including arts agencies) and local authorities and academics in further and higher education. Importantly, it has been informed indirectly through dialogue with clients themselves. In its current specification the degree is 'designed to provide graduates with sufficient skill, knowledge and understanding to enable them to enrich the lives of people in the community through their ability to create opportunities for involvement in the arts.'[16]

Programme content, therefore, must offer suitable and relevant areas of study to allow the student to acquire the necessary skills, knowledge and understanding to achieve this objective. This is done through a coherent and progressive modular structure that spans four years of learning in arts management and art forms. As the students proceed they elect to specialize in dance, drama, music or visual arts, with the emphasis on the application of the form. With reference to the skills identified by Brooks at the start of the chapter, there is provision for 'fundraising skills', 'research and report writing', 'resource management' and 'planning, policy development and execution', through compulsory dedicated modules in Arts Funding, Monitoring and Evaluation, Enquiry and Research Methods and Dissertation, Management in the Leisure Industry and Cultural Theory. For the other skills, 'evaluation and assessment', 'negotiating', 'interpersonal group' and 'teaching and co- production', inclusion is evidenced within modules appropriate to each level of study, where they are incorporated in descriptors as 'Key Transferable Skills'. In line with all undergraduate degree programmes taught in the Faculty of Education, there is a requirement to address a range of four key topics.

- Human Learning and Development
- Societal Context of Professional Roles
- Collaborative Practice
- Personal and Professional Development Planning[17]

Implementing the training programme

It is recognized that training must develop the student as both an independent learner and scholar, and a community arts practitioner with all the requisite skills for delivery. Teaching and learning methods, therefore, reflect this in the balance of lectures, workshops and tutorials they deploy.

Significantly, group work and placement experience make a major contribution to the student's learning, with practical engagement valued highly. This is primarily the domain of the four previously cited arts disciplines, where experiential learning is underpinned by theory. Borzak (1981) acknowledges that experiential learning involves 'a direct encounter with the phenomena being studied rather than merely thinking about the encounter, or only considering the possibility of doing something about it.'[18]

A young client engages with dance. *Photograph by Glen Coutts*

In year one, when all four arts disciplines are compulsory elements of study, students are introduced to the concept of workshop facilitation. It is considered reasonable to assume that when students embark on the Community Arts Degree, they will have particular academic experience or achievement in one or perhaps two of the disciplines. Often, students will perceive themselves as having no ability in disciplines of which they have no previous experience. As the philosophy underlying community arts practice promotes the belief that everyone should have access to arts experience, it is the responsibility of each subject leader – the academic member of staff responsible for a specific arts discipline – to create and structure a learning environment which nurtures and empowers each participant, regardless of their preconceptions of the subject or themselves within it. As Robinson opines: *'everyone has creative capacities, but they often do not know what they are.'*[19]

Throughout the programme students are taught in a variety of ways, including lectures, tutorials and workshops. The workshop format allows the student to function on two levels:

- The student as client where the lecturer or tutor operates as facilitator
- The student as potential facilitator

This process is consonant with Schon's (1983) concept of the *Reflective Practitioner*, where he identified two types of reflection: reflection-*in*-action and reflection-*on*-action. When students are engaged as participants in the workshop, they are reflecting-in-action as they are responding and reacting to the activities and tasks on which they are working as they unfold. In potential facilitator mode, they will be reflecting-on-action as they think about what has taken place. The intervention of the tutor is important during this phase. Students are asked how they felt when engaged in the activities, and then to consider how this experience might transfer to other client groups and what impact it might have. The key reflection is on how the students were facilitated and why it was done in this way. They are encouraged to make connections between the practical workshop content and its effect, and to project how this might be applied in other situations or contexts. Once students have progressed through a series of tutor-led workshops, they have the opportunity to test their learning and understanding by implementing practical activity with peers as participants. This might involve, for example, leading a drama session or piece of choreography in dance and collaborating with peers as facilitators in a team project designed for, and delivered to, a specific client group. This approach correlates directly with Kolb's (1975) experiential learning circle comprising four elements:[20]

The tutor facilitates her students as clients in a drama workshop. *Photograph by Glen Coutts*

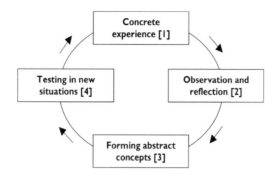

Experiential learning circle

Mapping the workshop training demonstrates this concept in practice:

- **Concrete experience –** student engaged practically as client
- **Observation and reflection –** student assimilates the experience as potential facilitator
- **Forming abstract concepts –** student makes connections for future contexts
- **Testing in new situations –** student tries out ideas and implements own activity as facilitator

To appreciate the skills involved in facilitation it is necessary to understand the roles and responsibilities of the facilitator. Johnston (2005) in *House of Games* groups responsibilities and tasks under five headings:

A. Safety (p. 61) – physical and emotional
B. Managing relationships, methodology and time (p. 66)

- client group, staff, carers or volunteers
- form, content, objectives and strategies
- length and number of sessions

Students collaborate with peers to create a piece of choreography. *Photograph by Brian Lochrin*

C. Building the group (p. 71) – giving attention, reading the group, mythologization
D. Developing the articulacy of the group (p. 75)
E. Troubleshooting (p. 80) – lateness, offensive behaviour, splits within the group

While this list was originally created in relation to animating drama, the skills areas it promotes are transferable to all practical facilitation regardless of topic. Clifford and Hermann (2002) in *The Facilitator's Guide* ask the perhaps obvious but important question – why facilitate? They discuss lone and co- facilitation and offer a set of fifteen *'Golden Rules'* to *'assist you with your work.'*[21] These include advice on planning and implementation and how to give instructions and use appropriate questioning to elicit client response. The guide provides a procedure for dealing with mistakes and addresses 'scapegoating', where the group places responsibility on the facilitator for anything they perceive to have gone 'wrong'.

For the student in training as facilitator, there is much to learn and put into practice. The Team Project mentioned earlier is an important case in point.

Exemplifying practice
The Team Project is undertaken in the student's first year and is the last activity conducted before embarking on Placement. Placement will be discussed in more detail later in the chapter. Having undertaken 36 hours of practical contact in each of the subject areas – art and design, dance, drama, media and music – the entire year group, numbering between 20 and 25 students, must design, devise and deliver a multimedia brief to a client group of their choosing. Within the delivery, each student has to facilitate and lead two of the four arts disciplines with the clients. The students have only fourteen hours of timetabled sessions (two hours per week for seven weeks) in which to carry out their planning and preparation, including the process of identifying the client group.

During the eighth week, the project has to be delivered over one or two full days. A small budget is provided, but is not sufficient to cover all potential costs, and students are advised to seek help in kind. All the learning gained in the course of first year classes is put into practice through this project. From the first two-hour session, the team has to establish how it will conduct its meetings, who will chair and take minutes of those meetings, and what the agenda for discussion will be. At the end of each meeting, the next week's chairperson, minute secretary and agenda are agreed. Although two lecturing members of staff support the students, it is the responsibility of the team to create the project and establish ways of communicating and working. For the project to succeed, cooperation and collaboration are essential.

During the academic session 2006–07, the team decided to work with 60 Primary Seven (11- 12–year-old) students from a primary school within easy reach of the University. Letters were sent and phone calls made to four schools, with team members delegated as designated

Second year community arts students rehearsing performance in drama. *Photograph by Julie Austin*

contacts to follow up on which schools might be interested and able to participate. One school was finally identified as suitable, and visits were made with the aim of gathering information about any specific pupil needs, and clearing parental permissions and consents. It was agreed that the venue for the project would be on the University campus, which meant that specialist accommodation had to be booked and consideration given to where lunches could be eaten and suitable toilets accessed.

The team used as their stimulus the International Year of Planet Earth[22] and focused on the topic of global warming. Their challenge was to structure a full day's activities that would allow every child to participate in four workshops, each covering the four arts disciplines. They divided the pupils into four groups of fifteen, each with the name of one of the traditional 'four elements', earth, wind, fire and water. To facilitate travel from one workshop to the next, timetables and maps were constructed and distributed to show which group should be where at what time. Leaders and facilitators for each phase of each workshop were named, and workshop plans giving a full breakdown of activities and timings were circulated to the team. For the purposes of client evaluation at the end of each workshop, the children placed a sticker on a wall chart depicting a temperature gauge. Where the pupils put the sticker depended on how they rated the workshop. The culmination of the event was a 'sharing' where all the children and students reflected on the project's activities and viewed the completed art installation that had been created by each visual arts workshop during the course of the day.

Using Johnston's template, it is possible to see that the Team Project as a tool for learning provides the opportunity for students to demonstrate the skills of facilitation and relate them to a live client group.

Across all arts disciplines and throughout all years of the course, experience is valued as fundamental to learning. It is generated, recorded and evaluated within a variety of modules, two of which permeate the first three years of the course:

• Placement
• Personal and Professional Development Planning

Placement is designed to give students 'first-hand experience across a range of Community Arts work'[23] and is carried out full-time in blocks whose length varies according to the year group. In first year, four weeks are scheduled, and this increases to six weeks in years two and three. Over the three years, this amounts to sixteen weeks, representing approximately one-fifth of the programme. A considerable allocation of time, therefore, is dedicated to practice in the field, where students are expected to relate, and make connections, to what they have learned on campus.

They must also display a range of eighteen competencies, six in each year, where the level of difficulty rises incrementally. These are grouped under three headings:[24]

A section of the Team Project art installation. *Photograph by Sharon Smyth*

- Planning, Practice and Delivery
- Strategic Planning and Management
- Professionalism and Evaluation

In addition, students must reflect on and analyse the experience gained while on placement by submitting a written report. This process contributes to the student's understanding of the Societal Context of Professional Roles, one of the four key topics mentioned earlier when describing the training programme. Collaboration, another key topic, is integral to Placement.

The partnership between the University and the Placement Agency is of vital importance. The diversity of agencies mirrors the provision of activities that already exist and incorporates a range of sectors and organizations, both formal and informal, and of differing scale. The common feature is their contribution to the professional development of the student by providing relevant, challenging experience. This is valued very highly by both the University and the student.

A second important factor is cooperation between the student and the agency. The student has to negotiate the programme of work to be undertaken and reach consensus with the agency with regard to schedule, while the agency must endeavour to enable the student to access appropriate activity and client groups. Just as the student is required to contribute effectively to the work of the agency and respond sensitively and positively to the agency's needs, so does the agency need to offer support in helping the student acquire the requisite skills.

A further crucial dimension is the relationship between the student and the University. Students should liaise with their allocated tutors to inform on progress and facilitate contact. The tutor's responsibility is to advise, guide and support the student throughout the experience and to monitor and ultimately report on progress.

The student has one further requirement in relation to client groups. To comply with statutory legislation designed to protect vulnerable adults, young people and children, the student must be in possession of a full Disclosure Scotland Certificate[25] administered through the Scottish Criminal Records Office.[26]

The purpose of Placement is to ensure that the student develops 'knowledge, understanding and skills in the practice, management and organisation of Community Arts.'[27] This, as well as other areas of development, can be tracked through the fourth key topic, the student's commitment to Personal and Professional Development Planning.

Personal and Professional Development Planning allows the student to create a personal development portfolio which can be added to throughout years one to three of the degree. The aim is to help students recognize and reflect on six key skills:[28]

- Communication and Presentation skills
- Analytical and Numerical skills
- Information Technology skills
- Planning and Organizing
- Team Working and Collaboration
- Creativity and Innovation

Students create a 'personal log', or journal, whereby they can rate their individual skills and identify which of them need improving or developing. Based on this, they construct a development plan outlining how improvement might be effected. They record a review of their learning in diary entries, and specific tasks are set for each of the three years of the process. One such task is the creation of a curriculum vitae, which can be revised and adapted in the course of the student's professional career.

All this is done using a Virtual Learning Environment (VLE) which allows students to upload and maintain personal progress files and completed tasks. Each student is allocated a counsellor from the teaching staff, who is responsible for monitoring and providing feedback on student progress. Using the VLE, the counsellor can access the student's work and offer supportive commentary via e-mail.

Through participation in the Personal and Professional Development Planning Process, students will ultimately be able to demonstrate their ability to operate as self-monitoring professionals, and it is hoped that this will continue as a process of lifelong learning.

Concluding the training

The teaching programme undertaken by Community Arts graduates is of considerable professional relevance. Those who complete it successfully and are awarded the degree will have demonstrated a range of professional and practical skills in a variety of contexts. They will have displayed competence in at least two arts disciplines, and will have a working knowledge of the sector they wish to enter, be it local government or the private sector. The Scottish Executive's commitment to local cultural entitlements[29] has provided a tangible opportunity to expand arts provision and increase the community artist's employability:[30]

> It is important that those fortunate enough to have been encouraged to sample and enjoy culture should ensure that the same good fortune is available to others.

As reflective practitioners, community artists are well placed to do this.

Student teams working and collaborating. *Photograph by Glen Coutts*

Notes and references

1. Great Britain. (1965). *A policy for the arts; the first steps*. London: HM Stationery Office.

2. Available from URL: www.scotland.gov.uk/Publications/ (accessed 3rd April 2007).

3. Community Development Foundation (1992). *Arts and Communities*, the report of the national inquiry into arts and the community, p. 62.

4. Brooks, 1988, cited in Clinton, L. (1994). Community Development and the Arts, 2nd Edn., London: Community Development Foundation.

5. *Ibid.*, p. 16.

6. The Scottish Parliament (2005). Enterprise and Culture Committee Report SP Paper 302 Report on Arts in the Community, Edinburgh: Scottish Parliament, p. 1.

7. Webster, M. & Buglass, G. (2005). *Finding Voices, Making Choices*, Nottingham: Educational Heretics Press, p. 2.

8. Scottish Executive (2006). *Scotland's Culture*, Edinburgh, Scottish Executive, p. 48.

9. See URL: http://www.culturalprofiles.net/scotland/Directories/Scotland_Cultural_Profile/-113.html (accessed 2nd April 2007).

10. Fuller, K. and Hale, S., Can you tell what it is yet? In Webster, M. and Buglass, G., *Finding Voices, Making Choices*, Nottingham: Educational Heretics Press, p. 54.

11. See URL: www.ageconcernscotland.org.uk (accessed 12th February 2008).

12. See URL: www.youthlink.co.uk (accessed 3rd April 2007).

13. See URL: www.sdf.org.uk (accessed 3rd April 2007).

14. See URL: www.impactarts.co.uk/ (accessed 3rd April 2007).

15. See URL: http://nuarts.co.uk/ (accessed 3rd April 2007).

16. Department of Sport, Culture and the Arts (2004). BA (Hons) Community Arts Definitive Course Document, Glasgow: University of Strathclyde, p. 20.

17. Faculty Shared Learning Group paper, (2004). Internal paper, Glasgow: University of Strathclyde.

18. Borzak (1981), p. 9 quoted in Brookfield 1983, p.16 as cited by Smith, 2005, p. 1 Smith, M. K., David A. Kolb on Experiential Learning, The encyclopedia of informal education. See URL: http://www.infed.org/b-explrn.htm (accessed 3rd April 2007).

19. Robinson, K. Out of Our Minds Oxford: Capstone Publishing, 2001, p. 3.

20. Borzak, *op. cit.*

21. Clifford, S. & Hermann, A. (2002). *Making a Leap- Theatre of Empowerment*, London, Jessica Kingsley, p. 23.

22. SEE URL: www.yearofplanetearth.org (accessed, 3rd April 2007).

23. BA Community Arts Placement Policy, 2006–07, p. 1. Department of Sport, Culture and the Arts, BA Community Arts Placement Policy, 2006–07, University of Strathclyde, 2006.

24. *Ibid.*

25. See URL: www.disclosurescotland.co.uk (accessed 3rd April 2007).

26. See URL: www.scro.police.uk, (Accessed 3rd April 2007).

27. BA Community Arts Placement Policy, *op. cit.*, p. 1.

28. BA Community Arts Definitive Document, *op. cit.*, appendix 2, ePPDP Module Descriptor.

29. Scottish Executive, *op. cit.*

30. *Ibid.*, p. 19.

12

Community Art: What's the Use?

Glen Coutts

Glasgow's art in public spaces

To set some of the complex issues surrounding community art in context, it may be useful to first consider an area of art practice with a much longer tradition: public art. Glasgow is a city filled, some might say littered, with public art. Examples of public art and urban design in the city range from 'traditional' sculptures commemorating past heroes[1] and historical events to the magnificent architectural detail of Glasgow's Victorian and Georgian buildings, an enduring testament to the stonemason's and sculptor's craft.

However, Glasgow's public art also echoes its imperial and industrial past, reflects on current developments and challenges the viewer to consider its future.[2] Public sculpture in particular covers a vast spectrum of purpose and style from the commemorative to the whimsical – a sculpture in Woodlands Road, featuring the well-loved cartoon character Lobey Dosser, is thought to be the only two-legged equestrian statue in the world. Nor are the citizens of Glasgow, who are well known for their sense of humour, averse to adding their own embellishments. A centrally located equestrian statue depicting the Duke of Wellington acquires unconventional headgear in the course of most weekends.

Over the past forty years or so, Glasgow has been in a state of constant regeneration, re-inventing itself first as City of Culture (1990) and then as City of Architecture and Design (1999).[3] More recently, the redevelopment of the waterfront area along the River Clyde,[4] which flows through the centre of the city, has been the focus of a number of art-related projects.

Overall, however, there has been uneven support for the arts in the city and, as Harding pointed out,[5] no clear policy for public art. Perhaps there has been even less of a policy for community art. The distinctions between 'public' and 'community' art are becoming increasingly

Lobey Dosser, Tony Morrow and Nick Gillon, bronze, 1992, junction of Woodlands Road and Woodlands Gate, Glasgow. *Photograph by Brian Lochrin*

Monument to the Duke of Wellington, Carlo Marochetti, bronze, 1844, Royal Exchange Square, Glasgow. *Photograph by Brian Lochrin*

sgow Skyline. *Photograph by Brian Lochrin*

Monument to Robert Burns, George Edwin Ewing, bronze, 1877, George Square, Glasgow. Photograph by Brian Lochrin

Citizen Firefighter, Kenny Hunter, bronze, 2001, Central Station, Glasgow. *Photograph by Brian Lochrin*

Untitled: Girl with a Rucksack, Kenny Hunter, 2004, Cumberland Street and Jane Place, Glasgow. *Photograph by Brian Lochrin*

Smokestack, Rita McGurn and Russell Lamb, fibreglass and steel, 1994, Old Rutherglen Road, Glasgow. *Photograph by Brian Lochrin*

The Heavy Horse, Andrew Scott, galvanised steel, 1999, M8 motorway, Glasgow. Photograph by Brian Lochrin

blurred, and, as a result, the urban landscape is shifting. The changing face of public art can be clearly seen in the course of a walk of a couple of miles from the bronze statue of Robert Burns in George Square,[6] past *Citizen Firefighter*[7] outside Central railway station, and across the Clyde to *Untitled: Girl with Rucksack*.

In the course of about thirty minutes, the walker has spanned over 100 years of public art history. Over that period the focus has shifted from the commemoration of specific individuals, like Scotland's national poet, to something more generic, like Kenny Hunter's tribute to firefighters. *Untitled: Girl With Rucksack*, also by Hunter, is sited in the Gorbals, an area of the city that has seen more change than most over the years, with art playing a prominent role in its regeneration.[8] Is the girl arriving or leaving? Who is she? Where has she come from? What does she hope to find or leave behind? Are these questions that even occur to our walker? What impact does all this public art have on the citizens of today? Does the statue of the Duke of Wellington have the same relevance and meaning now as it did when it was unveiled in 1844? Is the regular addition of the traffic cone something more than just a light-hearted gesture?

Public art interventions do not produce neutral objects and events. Many artists, for instance, have used architectural or industrial 'markers' to make a statement about Glasgow's industrial past. *Smokestack* by Rita McGurn and Russell Lamb is one striking example of this. Andrew Scott's *Heavy Horse* at the entrance to Glasgow Business Park in the east of the city is another.

The *Duke of Wellington*, *Lobey Dosser*, *Citizen Firefighter* and *Robert Burns* represent the very obvious and visible side of public art in Glasgow[9] – high-profile and relatively expensive commissioned art that cannot be avoided in the street, and which contributes to the city's wealth through what has become known as 'cultural tourism'. But what about other kinds of public and community art, which involve the direct participation of local communities, young people and, increasingly, formal and informal educational establishments? Over the past 25 years there has been a significant rise in the number of 'artist-in-residence' projects taking place in Scotland, and in the employment of various 'community art' and 'arts development officers' by local councils. This points to an increasing interest in community-focused and community-driven arts.

Community art: Whose art is it anyway?

Political statements,[10] rhetoric about 'cultural entitlement' and an emphasis on education from national arts funding bodies, such as the Scottish Arts Council, show that the process-led model, which has come to characterize community art, is becoming more widely understood and accepted. Of course, artists still exhibit in galleries and work in a wide variety of contexts, but many also work in both public art and community art, as well as in education. Scottish art schools offer degree programmes for the training of artists and designers, there is a vibrant artistic community and the boundaries between gallery-based art, public art, education and community art are becoming less clearly discernible.

It was during the 1970s, as Braden[11] and Dickson[12] remind us, that there was a resurgence in the UK of interest in what has become known as 'community art'. These days, it is widely accepted that much can be learned from the participative, collaborative or, as Harding calls it, 'socially engaged' approach that characterizes the very best practice in this field. Back in the 1960s and 70s, however, things were very different. This was a time of high unemployment and major political and social upheaval in the inner cities, a time when the arts in general were under serious threat. Many artists, particularly young graduates from UK art schools, became increasingly disenchanted with the gallery system and looked towards the kind of art being produced in countries like Mexico or North American cities such as Chicago. There was a move away from individualism and self-expression, or 'art for art's sake', towards social relevance and participation:[13]

> While APG (Artists Placement Group) placed artists in institutions, businesses and government departments, other artists were committing themselves to sharing their art practice with those most excluded from the world of art. This came to be known as 'community art' and the term has been one of the most contentious issues at the core of this art practice.[14]

Although the term has come into wider use only in the past 30 years, it could be argued that community art has always existed in Scotland. Perhaps social, political and cultural conditions in Scotland have been particularly conducive. However, the evolution of the movement has not been linear. In the early days of 'new towns', such as Livingston or Glenrothes, the local councils employed 'Town Artists', who were expected to work alongside architects and planners – a role pioneered by Victor Pasmore during the 1950s in Peterlee in County Durham. The new towns were designed with the idea of easing the housing problems of neighbouring traditional cities like Edinburgh and Dundee, and had significant budgets dedicated to making them attractive to new residents. It was an innovative and imaginative but short-lived experiment, and by the end of the 1980s, there were no more town artists in Scotland.[15] As so often happens, when budgets need to be trimmed, the arts are amongst the first casualties.

The seeds had been sown, however, and many artists continued to look at new ways of interacting with the built environment and at ways of involving communities in producing art. Community art as we now know it was on its way, and this has gone hand in hand with recent renewed interest in public art and urban design. Although commemorative statues, fountains and elaborate street furniture have always been prominent features of the Glaswegian landscape, many of these artworks were the product of a traditional commissioning process, whereby an individual artist would be approached, or there would be a competition for the commission. The active participation of a community, the public, the people who would live with the artwork, was very rare. These days, the artistic input into initiatives like the Clyde Regeneration Project, with its new museums, housing and walkways, is recognized as having a vital social role:

> From community art projects to bold architecture, creative concepts are central to regeneration initiatives, and artistic events and projects are a pivotal factor in the creation of stimulating, attractive and safe environments.[16]

However, just as the purpose, meanings and values embedded in these new public artworks have changed, so have the communities who live with them:

> Historically, public art had always been a part of the fabric of cities and one of the main ways in which societies have publicly expressed values.[17]

Art and design education in Scotland

Perhaps one reason for the abundance of public and community art activity in Scotland lies in the way that the art education system has developed. In Scottish schools, the arts (art and design, music and drama – there is no separate subject of dance) have a secure place. Art and design is commonly thought of as a practical subject with students engaged in 'hands-on' activities using the media and processes of art: still life, drawing and painting or sculpture. For many years that was true, but art and design now places a much greater emphasis on developing creative thinking, aesthetic judgement, collaborative working and problem-solving skills. The art curriculum, originally designed to improve hand and eye co-ordination for future factory workers, these days promotes awareness of the influence of art and design on young people's lives at home, in school and within the wider community.

Reforms to the school curriculum have had, and continue to have, a significant impact on art education. The introduction of Standard Grade (the national syllabus guidelines for 14- 16-year-olds) in the late 1980s marked a paradigm shift – for the first time, Design was accorded equal status to Art, and Standard Grade consists of three equally weighted elements: Design Activity, Expressive Activity and Critical Activity. Students follow units of work that are either 'Expressive' or 'Design' in focus; within each unit Critical Activity is embedded and closely related to the practical work.[18] Teachers' work has been supplemented by a variety of initiatives and partnerships, like cultural coordinators, creative links officers[19] and artist-in-residence schemes.[20] The ambition to increase participation in and understanding of the arts is implicit in the aims of many such initiatives, aims that clearly resonate with the values of community art. Links between universities and schools also provide fruitful partnerships. Increasingly, 'boundaries' are being crossed between primary and secondary schools and the formal and informal sectors of art education. For instance, art students or community artists might work with art teachers in secondary (high) or primary (elementary) schools to focus on an environmental design problem, as happened in a project outlined by Coutts and Rusling,[21] which sought to develop solutions to real issues of local concern.

Projects like these represent exciting opportunities for art education to develop creativity in young people and will have an increasingly important role in making the arts accessible to a wider audience. Given the numbers of artists now choosing to work in the public arena and the political drive for wider participation in the arts, it might seem certain that community art has a bright future. That remains to be seen.

Different perspectives

Perhaps it is time to look at community art from a different perspective, time for a critical examination of the pedagogic potential of community art practice and an appraisal of how it might relate to the more 'traditional' models of artists working in the public domain described at the start of this chapter. What are the distinctive features, qualities and benefits of community art? How might these characteristics inform practice in our education system for the arts in schools and beyond? How might these qualities be researched, documented and evaluated?

At the core of community art practice lie the notions of participation, engagement, collaboration and empowerment. A community artist is not an artist first and foremost, in the traditional individualist 'self-expressive' sense; rather, the artist acts as a *facilitator*, enabling communities to arrive at solutions over which they have a sense of 'ownership'. Essentially, to work in community art means taking a step back, handing over some control and allowing the artwork to emerge from the group. Artists adopting this model of practice must constantly refine and develop their own skills, not just those required to create artwork, but also those necessary for understanding community issues and problems. Community artists must work in close partnership with the people who will have to live with the results of the process, and need excellent communication, interpersonal, motivational and organizational skills to facilitate effective art projects. It is not an easy career option.

The formal education community in Scotland has been slow to recognize the potential of community art, but there are some positive signs. Although the majority of artists in Scotland are still trained in one of the Schools of Art in either a design or fine art discipline, there are other options, like the ground-breaking department of 'Environmental Art', now known as *Sculpture and Environmental Arts*, established by Scotland's first 'town artist', David Harding, at Glasgow School of Art.[22] In 1987 a new degree course was established at the University of Strathclyde, the *BA (Hons) in Community Arts*. This unique course is aimed specifically at using a range of art forms as a means of working with groups and individuals,[23] with the emphasis on the role of the community artist as facilitator or *animateur*. This changing pattern of training has produced a new generation of artists who are making a distinctive contribution to community art projects.

What's Your Problem? was the title of an initiative funded during Glasgow's year as City of Architecture and Design in 1999. The project took place in the Milton area of Glasgow and involved twenty young people and two art students. In consultation with a number of community agencies, they worked for a short, intensive period to create proposals for the redevelopment of a local play area. In this way, the users of the playground were empowered to become designers. The young people were all members of an 'after-school' group, a less formal educational situation than a school, and this was an important dimension to the project that was used to the full.

The *What's Your Problem?* project. Students investigate the site. *Photograph by Brian Lochrin*

School students work together as a design team. *Photograph by Brian Lochrin*

A school student concentrates on her design ideas. *Photograph by Brian Lochrin*

A school student designs her ideal bus shelter. *Photograph by Brian Lochrin*

This design-based arts intervention is an example of what can be achieved outwith the 'formal' school curriculum. It provided a workshop model refreshingly free of guidelines, rules, measuring instruments or 'attainment targets'. This is not to say that it lacked structure or rigour, but it did emphasize participation, enjoyment, problem solving, creativity and working as a team. It is also a good example of how the distinctions between the formal and informal sectors of Scottish education are becoming less marked. National Guidelines for Scottish schools[24] urge artists and designers to make more direct contributions to the school curriculum, while the National Cultural Strategy,[25] the National Policy for Architecture[26] and research by Matarasso,[27] Allan[28] and Dougall, Coutts and Dawes[29] have all examined the role of the artist collaborating with communities and the impacts and educational potential of such collaborations.

The informal sector has not as yet been subject to the kind of rigorous analysis and testing seen in the formal educational sector in the United Kingdom, which is overseen by the National Curriculum in England and Wales,[30] the National Guidelines for Expressive Arts 5 – 14[31] and the Effective Learning and Teaching publications[32] in Scotland.[33] Teachers are obliged to plan, review and test their learning outcomes against national standards, and the 'buzzwords' are league tables, performance indicators and learning audits. There are no equivalents in the growing informal sector, and while this offers a measure of autonomy and flexibility during 'workshop' sessions, there is a danger that too much autonomy could lead to a lack of structure and focus. There needs to be a balance between 'process' and 'product'. Too much emphasis on process at the expense of product can be disastrous, particularly in the visual arts.

In one project that succeeded in achieving this balance, the artist and writer, Mark Dawes,[34] aided by four arts students, worked in collaboration with two primary schools and one secondary school in Glasgow. The project looked at organic forms in architecture and street furniture, and allowed the students to address both curricular and non-curricular concerns relevant to the 10 – 14 age group. The workshops explored a wide diversity of materials and allowed the participants to experience the process of collating and presenting the results for an exhibition at the Tramway exhibition space in the city. Central to this project was the idea that pupils were being invited to become directly involved in designing and making a plan for an actual building, rather than merely accepting the architecture and urban design handed down by previous generations. The active, experiential learning model adopted during these sessions encouraged the young people to think of themselves as designers proposing solutions to real design problems. Informal evaluations amongst teachers indicated a positive attitude towards the presence of artists and students in the classroom. Artists and teachers working together is clearly an area worthy of further research in itself, given the number of such projects that there have been in the UK alone.[35]

The results of another successful project involving the active participation of young people can be seen in Taransay Street in the Govan area of Glasgow, which for many years was the centre of the shipbuilding industry. The ceramic artists Marion Brandis and Nick Martin worked with pupils from two local primary schools and Govan Housing Association to transform the dull brick façade of Kvaerner Shipyards' walls with a series of six mosaics depicting the shipbuilding industry and the massive cranes that dominate the local skyline. The two artists designed

One student particularly enjoys a 'hands-on' approach to art. *Photograph by Brian Lochrin*

Taransay Street Mosaic, Marion Brandis and Nick Martin, 1993, Taransay Street, Govan, Glasgow. Photograph by Brian Lochrin

street level photoworks

| Home | About Us | Diary | Education | Courses | Downloads | Archive | Links |

Archive | New Horizons

New Horizons

The work was developed in weekly sessions over 3 months with refugees and asylum seekers and explored the notion of an 'orientation' guide to Glasgow, but one that explored emotional orientation as much as any map.

The CD-ROM offers a poignant profile of Glasgow and features photographs, video interviews, arrival stories, personal experiences and orientation information that has been developed

Scroll Up   Scroll Down

Click on thumbnails for larger images

Back to Education Main Page

Related links: multi-story

The New Horizons Project web pages. Screenshot

the two larger ones at either end, and the primary pupils the four smaller ones. The designs were digitized from the children's drawings, each pixel representing one mosaic tile.

The use of digital media is becoming increasingly common in community-driven arts projects, and a particularly effective example is the innovative 'multi-story' project coordinated by *Streetlevel Photoworks*.[36] Supplementing digital input with photography and creative writing, this involved artists working with some of Glasgow's numerous refugees and asylum seekers over a period of fourteen weeks and resulted in a CD-ROM and a website.[37]

Another project coordinated by Streetlevel, *New Horizons*,

> ...offers a poignant profile of Glasgow and features photographs, video interviews, arrival stories, personal experiences and orientation information that has been developed with artist Lindsay Perth and photographer Iseult Timmermans of Street Level.[38]

What all these projects have in common is a genuine community focus. Whether that community is a class of primary school pupils or a group of asylum seekers is immaterial.

The benefits of community art: The problem of evaluation

As a lot of public money is devoted to supporting public and community art, it is reasonable to ask how we know what is effective. What are the benefits? Is the short-term nature of some projects a strength or a weakness? What can be learned from the interdisciplinary and participative approach central to community art, and how do we extrapolate the features that make for good practice? What are the implications for artists wishing to work in this arena? With the distinctions between 'community',' mainstream', 'formal' and 'informal' education becoming increasingly blurred, we need more research into such questions.

So what might be the main benefits of community art projects? In addition to specific learning in art and design, collaborative projects might promote the development of 'core' or 'key' skills.[39] In the Scottish curriculum these skills include: communication (verbal and written); working together; literacy and numeracy; presentation and negotiation; using Information and Communications Technology (ICT); problem solving and creative thinking. It is a predictable list – who would argue with these as essential skills for our young people on leaving school? Unfortunately, the way that students currently learn, particularly in secondary schools, is still quite traditional, formal and passive. The model of community art I have described here, on the other hand, favours an active, experiential learning style; key characteristics are an emphasis on collaboration, inclusiveness and empowerment, on process rather than product, on active rather than passive learning styles. Also, unlike a lot of traditional public art, community art projects have an outcome that is often temporary, which raises the important issue of sustainability.

In some cases participants in a project are just beginning to get really involved when the funding ends or the artist has to move on to something else.

There has been literature reporting improved social inclusion and increased participation in arts activity as a result of artists' residencies in the field of education and artist-led community initiatives,[40] but measuring these benefits is no straightforward task, and statistics alone do not tell the full story.[41] Some UK literature[42] suggests that such programmes can raise self-esteem and promote understanding of the arts, but we cannot take this for granted – there is still a degree of misunderstanding of the mechanisms through which these 'social impacts'[43] are allegedly imparted. International literature on this subject is quite extensive, and there have been a number of research studies in England,[44] but in Scotland there is a need for more precise information about how community art projects might bring about tangible benefits for both artist and 'client'. In short: what's the use?

From the seminal work of Read[45] and Dewey[46] to the more recent writings of Matarasso,[47] Carey[48] and Clements[49] the relationship between the arts, social climate, effective education and evaluation has periodically fascinated policy makers, academics, social commentators and, occasionally, politicians. Over the past 25 years or so, there has been a shift of emphasis in the type of community art project taking place in Scotland, away from artists based in educational establishments or writers in residence towards, for example, health programmes with an artistic component but with wider aims.[50] The focus has, however, tended to be primarily on the artistic activity itself – projects are rarely well documented and hardly ever critically evaluated. The evidence base suggests that while there is quite a lot of activity aimed at developing participation in the arts,[51] there is little quality research into effectiveness. There are notable exceptions, of course, such as Artlink, ArtFull and Projectability,[52] but clearly these shortfalls need to be addressed.

In England, meanwhile, the Arts Council England (ACE) has recently examined[53] the role of the arts in four key areas: employment, education, health and crime; and Creative Partnerships, the Artist Teacher Scheme[54] and Making it Work[55] have been promoting the potential benefits of arts practice in education and the wider community with the support of ACE, the National Society for Education in Art and Design (NSEAD) and the Department for Education.

Most of what documentation there is on the many residence projects that have taken place over the last twenty years or more[56] applies to small-scale examples. Some projects, however, have had the ambitious aim of not only acting as vehicles for increasing participation in the arts, but also encouraging a wide range of 'non-arts' organizations to host their own residencies.[57] It is important that these initiatives should be properly documented and critically analysed, and that funds should be put in place to make this possible.

At the beginning of the twenty-first century, the Scottish Arts Council is making artists' residencies a priority and encouraging artists to fulfil their creative and business potential. Placing arts, culture and creativity at the heart of learning has become its central mission, and a new national cultural development agency, *Creative Scotland*, has been proposed with this in mind. The agency's key objectives are as follows:

- To promote understanding, appreciation and enjoyment of the arts and culture to people in Scotland, and in particular to seek to increase the number and diversity of people accessing and enjoying them;
- To identify, support and develop talent and excellence in the arts and culture;
- To seek to realize the benefits of the arts and culture; and
- To help to support the success of the creative industries.[58]

These aims are entirely in accord with the broad philosophy of community art. The SAC's priorities[59] and the National Cultural Strategy[60] lay great emphasis on participation in and access and entitlement to the arts, and this arts-infused approach to social inclusion explicitly recognizes the centrality of culture and creativity to a well-balanced life.

Perhaps that is the real use of community art.

Notes and references

1. They usually are heroes; very few are heroines. Glasgow's main civic space, George Square, for instance, is home to no less than twelve monuments. One is the Cenotaph, of the others, ten are men, only one woman is represented, Queen Victoria. For an excellent sculpture in Glasgow see, for example, McKenzie, R. (2005). *Public Sculpture of Glasgow*, Liverpool: Liverpool University Press.
2. For an exploration of Glasgow Sculpture, see: http://www.glasgowsculpture.com/ (accessed 12 February 2008).
3. For an overview of Glasgow's cultural renaissance during the 1980s and 1990s, see: http://www.glasgow.gov.uk/en/AboutGlasgow/History/Cultural+Renaissance.htm (accessed 12th February 2008).
4. Creative Clyde. For details about the cultural dimensions of the Clyde Waterfront project, see: http://www.clydewaterfront.com/publicationdownloads.aspx (accessed 10 February 2008).
5. Harding, D. (1997). The ill clad city: Glasgow turns its back on public art. *Journal of Art and Design Education*, vol. 16, no.1, pp. 35–45.
6. McKenzie, R. op. cit., p. 140.
7. For background to Hunter's Citizen Firefighter, see: http://www.strathclydefire.org/about/citizen.asp (accessed 3rd April 2007).
8. Warwick, R. (Ed.) (2006). *Arcade: Artists and Place-making*, London: Black Dog Publishing.
9. It should be noted that there was an element of public participation, at least in funding most of this era of Glasgow's public art. In the case of the monument to Burns, for instance, money was raised by 'shilling subscription' open to all sections of the community and not restricted to Glasgow.

10. See, for example, the First Minister Jack McConnell's (2003) St Andrew's Day speech available at: http://www.scotland.gov.uk/News/News-Extras/176 (accessed 12th February 2008).

11. Braden, S. (1978). *Artists and People*, London: Routledge and Kegan Paul.

12. Dickson, M. (Ed.) (1995). *Art with People*, Sunderland: AN Publications.

13. *Ibid.*, p. 28.

14. *Ibid.*, p. 30.

15. For more detail on the relationship between public art and new towns, see: http://www.davidharding.net/article04/index.php (accessed 8th March 2007).

16. Creative Clyde. *op. cit.*, p. 3.

17. Harding, D. (1997). *op. cit.*, p. 35.

18. Scottish Examinations Board (SEB) (1985–87). Standard Grade: Revised Arrangements in Art and Design at Foundation, General and Credit Level, Dalkeith: SEB.

19. For more information about Creative Links Officers and Cultural Coordinators, see: http://www.sac.org.uk/1/information/publications/educationandlifelong learning.aspx (accessed: 8th March 2007).

20. For more information about the Scottish Arts Council Partners programme, see: http://www.scottisharts.org.uk/1/artsinscotland/artsandcommunities/partners.aspx (accessed 8th March 2007).

21. Coutts, G. & Rusling, L. (2002). Design, Environment and Community Arts: What's Your Problem? *Art Education*, vol. 55, no. 6, pp. 41–47.

22. Harding, D. & Buchler, P. (Eds.) (1997). *Decadent: Public Art: Contentious Term and Contested Practice*, Glasgow: Fowlis Press. For information about Sculpture and Environmental Art at Glasgow School of Art, see: GSA Environmental Art http://www.gsa.ac.uk/gsa.cfm?pid=7&nid=0&sid=0&criteria=&version=html (accessed 5th May 2007).

23. For information about Community Arts at the University of Strathclyde, see: http://www.strath.ac.uk/sca/courses/bahonsincommunityarts/ (accessed 5th May 2007).

24. Scottish Office Education and Industry Department (1992). *Curriculum and Assessment in Scotland: National Guidelines: Expressive Arts 5–14: Art and Design*, Edinburgh: SOEID.

25. Scottish Executive (1999a). *Creating our Future...Minding our past: A national cultural strategy*, Edinburgh: Scottish Executive Education Department.

26. Scottish Executive (1999b). *The Development of a Policy on Architecture for Scotland*, Consultation Document, Edinburgh: SEED.

27. Matarasso, F. (1997). *Use or ornament? The social impact of participation in the arts*. Stroud: Comedia.

28. Allan, J. (1997). The Sow's Ear, the Ivory Tower and the Enlightened Benefactor. *Journal of Art and Design Education*, vol.16, no. 1, pp. 33–43.

29. Dougall, P., Coutts, G. & Dawes, M. (1999). *Scanning the City: A Virtual Journey around Public Art and Urban Design in the City of Glasgow*, Glasgow: University of Strathclyde, DEG@S [CD-ROM].

30. Department for Education (1995). *The National Curriculum in England and Wales*, London, HMSO.

31. Scottish Office Education and Industry Department, *op. cit.*

32. HMIE (1998). *Effective learning and teaching in Scottish secondary schools (art & design)*. A report by HM Inspectors of Schools, Edinburgh: HMSO.

33. It should be noted that things are changing; curricular reform during 2007 and 2008 is leading to massive reform in both England and Scotland. See, for example, http://www.curriculumforexcellencescotland.gov.uk/ and: http://www.qca.org.uk/qca_13575.aspx (accessed 12 February 2008).

34. Coutts, G. & Dawes, M. (1998). Drawing on the Artist Outside: Towards 1999. *Journal of Art and Design Education*, vol. 17, no. 2, pp. 191–196.

35. See, for example, Arts Council England (2004). *The impact of the arts: some research evidence*. London: ACE; Sharp, C. (2006) *The longer-term impact of Creative Partnerships on the attainment of young people*, Slough, NFER.

36. For more information about Streetlevel, see: http://www.streetlevelphotoworks.org/ (accessed 12th February 2008).

37. The Multi-Story project can be explored at: http://www.multi-story.org/ (accessed 12th February 2008).

38. Statement from the New Horizons project web pages. More information about the New Horizons project can be found at: http://www.streetlevelphotoworks.org/education/education-archive/newhorizons/newhorizons.html (accessed 5th May 2007).

39. More information about Core Skills can be found at: http://www.ltscotland.org.uk/nq/coreskills/index.asp or http://www.sqa.org.uk/sqa/servlet/controller?p_service=Content.show&p_applic=CCC&pContentID=1518 (accessed 3rd April 2007).

40. See, for example, Comedia (2002). *Releasing the Cultural Potential of our Core Cities*, London: Core Group; Harland, J. & Kinder, K. (1995) *The Arts in Their View*. Slough: NFER; Harland, J. et al. (2005) *The Arts-Education Interface: a Mutual Learning Triangle?* Slough: NFER; Jermyn H. (2001) *The Arts and Social Exclusion: A review prepared for the Arts Council of England*, London: Arts Council of England; Landry, C. et al. (1996) *The Art of Regeneration: Urban Renewal through Cultural Activity*, London: Comedia; Manser, S., & Wilmot, H. (1995) *Artists in Residence*. London: London Arts Board; Marceau, J. (2004) *Social Impacts or Participation in Arts and Cultural Activities, Stage Two Report: Evidence, Issues and Recommendations*. The Cultural Ministers Council Statistics Working Group and University of Western Sydney; Social Impact of the Arts Project (SIAP) (2005). Available at: http://www.sp2.upenn.edu/SIAP/ (accessed 8th March 2007).

41. Selwood, S. (2002). *Measuring Culture*. Available at: http://www.spiked-online.com/Articles/00000006DBAF.htm (accessed 9th March 2007).

42. See, for example, Sharp, C. (2006). *The longer-term impact of Creative Partnerships on the attainment of young people*, Slough, NFER; Harland & Kinder, *op. cit.*; Harland et al., *op. cit.*

43. Arts Council England (2003). *Artists working in Partnership with Schools*. London: Arts Council England; Matararasso, F. *op. cit.*; Marceau, J. *op. cit.*

44. Harland & Kinder, *op. cit.*; Matarasso, F. *op. cit.*; Harland et al., *op. cit.*; Sharp, *op. cit.*

45. Read, H. (1943). *Education Through Art*. London: Random House.

46. Dewey J. (1934). *Art as Experience*, New York: Penguin.

47. Matarrasso, F. *op. cit.*

48. Carey, J. (2006). *What Good Are The Arts?* London: Faber.

49. Clements, P. (2007). The Evaluation of Community Arts Projects and the Problems with Social Impact Methodology, *International Journal of Art and Design Education*, vol. 26, no. 3, pp. 325–335.

50. See, for example, Art in Hospital (2007). Available at: http://www.artinhospital.org/ (accessed 8th March 2007); Engage (2005) Scotland Visual Arts Education Awards (Sponsored by Scottish Executive's National Programme for Improving Mental Health and Well-Being). Available from Engage Scotland at http://www.engage.org/scotland.aspx (accessed 8th March 2007); Creative Interventions in Health (Glasgow City Council and SAC). Available at: http://www.glasgow.gov.uk/en/Residents/ArtsDevelopment/Newsletter/artsandsocialinclusion.htm (accessed 8th March 2007).

51. Ruiz, J. (2004). *A literature review of the evidence base for culture, the arts and sport policy.* Research and Economic Unit, Scottish Executive Education Department, Edinburgh: Scottish Executive.

52. Artfull: Arts Mental Health and Well-Being (2007). Available at: http://www.artfull.org/content/view/147// (accessed 8th March 2007); Artlink available at http://www.lds4b.com/What+we+do/Training+partners/In+your+area/Forth+Valley/Artlink+Central/Artlink+Central.htm (accessed 8th March 2007); Projectability. Available at: http://www.project-ability.co.uk/ (accessed 8th March 2007).

53. Arts Council England, *op. cit.*

54. Artist Teacher Scheme (ATS) (2005). Available at: http://www.nsead.org/cpd/ats.aspx (accessed 4th March 2007).

55. Making it Work [MiW] (2006). Available at: http://www.nsead.org (accessed 8th March 2007).

56. Coutts & Dawes, *op. cit.*; Latham, G. (1983). Artist in Residence at Drumcroon: an Educational Experience, *Journal of Art and Design Education*, vol. 2, no. 1, pp. 50 -59; Pascal, G. (2006), Educating Art in a Globalizing World. The University of Ideas: A Sociological Case Study, International Journal of Art & Design Education, vol. 25, no.1, pp. 5–15; Sheridan, H. (2006), Inspiration into Installation: An Exploration of Contemporary Experience through Art, *International Journal of Art & Design Education*, vol. 25, no. 2, pp. 134–146: Taylor, R. (1991) *Artists in Wigan Schools*. London: Calouste Gulbenkian Foundation.

57. The refugee council in partnership with Streetlevel is a good example.

58. Culture (Scotland) Bill (2006). Consultation document available at: http://www.scotland.gov.uk/Publications/2006/12/14095224/0 (accessed 6th March 2007). See also: http://www.scotland.gov.uk/Topics/Arts-Culture/19347/18411 (accessed 12th February 2008).

59. Scottish Arts Council [SAC] (2005). Available at: http://www.scottisharts.org.uk/1/artsinscotland/education/development.aspx (accessed 8th March 2007).

60. Scottish Executive 1999. *op. cit.*; Culture (Scotland) Bill, *op. cit.*

13

COLLABORATIVE PROJECT-BASED STUDIES IN ART TEACHER EDUCATION: AN ENVIRONMENTAL PERSPECTIVE

Timo Jokela

The challenges of contemporary art

According to modernist theory, art is a universal phenomenon. In environmental and community art, however, this idea is problematic. In his analysis of the basics of environmental design education, Neperud[1] states that art educators have adopted their methods directly from artists and deluded themselves into believing that creating archetypal forms in nature could somehow promote both the sustainable objectives of environmental design education and environmental responsibility.

The modernists also saw art as something autonomous, essentially independent of other social sectors. Art was the concern of art institutions and was not regionally, locally or politically engaged. Shusterman (2001), Lacy (1995), Gablik (1991) and Kester (2004) have described how this view came under challenge with the emergence of postmodernism,[2] and in Finland this has been discussed by Sederholm (1998), Hiltunen (2006) and Jokela (2005, 2006) among others.[3] In contemporary art, especially community and environmental art, the emphasis is on how art connects with everyday life, actions and places. This does not imply any form of regionalist or nationalist political programme, but is, as Hautamäki[4] points out, a new way of seeing and understanding relationships between people – spontaneous networks and joint goals and objectives as opposed to overemphasized individuality, consumerism and globalization.

In contemporary art, environmentality and communality are seen as natural, multi-layered bonds that are part of the essence of human life. Each individual is part of several different communities and environments, sometimes simultaneously, in the course of a lifetime. Moreover,

River Project. 1995. Project explored the environment and community of the river Ounas. Art students and the men of the village of Köngäs participated in building the raft. The traditional and familiar work becomes community art in which the roles of the artist and audience are mixed. It could be asked who is making the work of art, who is the performer and who is the audience? *Photograph by Timo Jokela*

River Project. 1995. Piece of community art – a raft of logs floating over 200-kilometer journey down the River Ounasjoki from Köngäs to Rovaniemi. *Photograph by Timo Jokela*

communities and environments are inseparable. A home, a village, a suburb, a school and a meeting point for young people are all both communities and environments that tie our culture and our entire existence firmly to time and place.[5] The people who live in them, however, are constantly changing them through their actions, and this is a fruitful starting point for artistic activity.[6]

Environmental and community art are targeted at the environment of the practitioner and the participating audience, and realized in the form of activities within it. This requires the intertwining of art in the traditional sense and what the modernists referred to as 'non-art' – popular culture, folk art, entertainment, local customs and so on. It also makes it possible to move beyond an institution-centred conception of art towards the kind of thinking that emphasizes art as a creative event in line with the principles of the aesthetics of pragmatism[7] and sociocultural animation,[8] and connects it to the kind of active citizenship called for in critical pedagogy.[9] Artists and audience are often seen not as separate but, in Lacy's words,[10] jointly involved as both creator and recipient of the artistic experience.

We cannot expect to achieve this outcome from traditional studio-centred learning or classroom-centred teacher training. A critical stance towards the world surrounding us and the need for collaboration with our peers in other social sectors has become a cornerstone of modern educational practice, and the teaching of contemporary art must be no exception. Art educators have to be able to analyse their own position not only as teachers, but also as cultural workers and mediators of cultural values.

Art education as cultural work
Since the Age of Enlightenment, western society has been dominated by the idea that the emergence and dissemination of new cultural phenomena is always a change for the better, radiating from centre to periphery and normally from West to East and South to North. It has also been assumed that art educators make a significant contribution to this process.

According to Häyrynen, these attitudes started to attract criticism from the Council of Europe and UNESCO in the 1970s. In their insistence on attempting to impose universal cultural values, they were seen as a relic of colonialism. A number of marginal groups had already lost their cultural autonomy, and this had led to a slow burn of resistance as people began to wake up to the idea that there are many equally valid cultures, each of which has been shaped by a unique environment and way of life. In due course the preservation of cultural diversity in all its forms became the new general objective of European cultural policy,[11] and the European Union has instructed its Member States to adhere to the 'principle of subsidiarity'. This means that cultural matters should be handled by the lowest competent authority, and a higher authority should intervene only when it is clear that the lower authority is not properly fulfilling its role. In Finland, the art teacher is often one of the few cultural workers in a municipality and, therefore, has both the power and the responsibility to maintain the cultural diversity of the local environment.

Kurtakko Project. Art students building willow sculptures connected to a culture trail, 2005. Photograph by Maria Huhmarniemi

Kurtakko Project. 2005. Willow sculptures – cattle of the 'Mistress of the Water on the Meadow'. *Photograph by Timo Jokela*

The return of regional and local culture to the cultural policy agenda has been accompanied by a number of changes in EU regulations on regional and national policy and finance.[12] Staff have been required to adjust to a raft of new practices, and the shift to the new system has not been entirely trouble free. In several EU Member States, cultural initiatives take the form of projects that take place over predefined programming periods. In theory, regional development organizations (provincial federations, employment and economic development centres, county administrative boards and municipalities) are responsible for coordination, strategic planning and development, as well as financing and implementation. In practice, the programmes are realized by local authorities, art and culture institutions, research institutes, social service workers, industry and commerce and, increasingly, schools and other educational establishments. Funding is now more accessible at a local level, and some art educators with the requisite skills have been able to find a role in the regional development process and to attract support for their activities. This has been particularly true of basic art education, museum pedagogy and the sectors of visual art teaching that have hitherto been more flexible than schools in moving towards project-based activities. There are also, however, some good examples of schools that have proved their competency in acting as regional activity centres.[13]

New Finnish law, which defines regional impact and development of social relationships as primary objectives of universities,[14] has been a decisive factor in the development of art education as an academic discipline and of teacher-training in general. For the University of Lapland this has meant consideration of the role of art education in developing the University's Northern expertise, cooperation between research and art, and the creation of social relationships for the purposes of teacher-training. Finding new action models was, especially in the 1990s when the University was facing serious financial difficulties, of vital importance to this new field of study. It had to prove both its effectiveness outside the University and its ability to attract funding.

The changing face of the school

The Finnish school system has been praised for its success in the OECD's Programme for International Students Assessment (PISA) study.[15] However, the results achieved in mathematics and foreign languages do not convince everyone, and there is pressure for change. According to Tomperi & Piattoeva,[16] the basic role of the school is twofold and reflects an age-old paradox: to acclimatize its students to accepted social norms, but at the same time to promote critical thinking. It has also been widely seen as the role of the school to promote awareness of cultural tradition. Now, however, representatives of the commercial and financial sectors are proposing new additions to the school curriculum, including education in entrepreneurship, with a view to training pupils to become successful performers with the skills to meet the needs of a competitive society.[17] This has provoked a response from various strands of critical pedagogy,[18] and Paulo Freire's[19] view of education as a means of improving the world through egalitarian dialogue is regaining currency in some quarters.

In the end, teachers are responsible for what goes on in schools. They have to walk a fine line between contradictory expectations, but this aspect of their work is often absent from their training. Tomperi & Piattoeva[20] point to the often-noted fact that current teacher-training strategies

Land of Forest Spirits – a natural experience path. 2004. Art students working with the materials of the nature and creating small scale of environmental art. *Photograph by Timo Jokela*

produce teachers who are largely unaware of their wider role in society, and are unable to identify the impact of the school's operating parameters on either the pupils' learning outcomes or their own world-view. Lacking an understanding of the relationships between teaching and socio-political factors, the teacher sees the world and mediates it to the pupils, as a ready-made construction in which every subject taught in the school is in a separate category. Seen from this perspective, visual art struggles with the same problems as other subjects, the distribution of lesson hours and availability of equipment and tools, and this has a negative effect on the motivation of both pupils and teacher.

The Finnish school system already has the potential to offer a much better framework for the development of an active and open participatory community. In the final report on the National Board of Education's OPEPRO project, the purpose of which was to identify teachers' initial and continuing training needs, Luukkainen concludes that

> Communality, leadership, encountering and embracing differences, cooperation skills, opening and changing learning environments, and social consciousness are central development needs regarding the content of today's teacher education.[21]

As Rinne and Salmi put it, the school's ability to open out towards the world is seen as a decisive factor:

> If learning possibilities and the concept of learning are to be widened, the surrounding world has to be able to enter the world of the schools and other educational establishments, and the concept of learning has to be opened in such a way that it can encompass not only the domain of the school, but also the world around it. These are the necessary prerequisites.[22]

It is perhaps time that we took the context-bound nature of contemporary art into consideration when looking at possible new models for visual arts teacher education.

Essential and applied art: Walking a fine line

Change always faces resistance, and in the domain of art and culture this has manifested itself as the modernist conception of art as an autonomous activity. In the context of art education, this leads to the insistence that the learning and creation of art has sufficient educational value as an objective in itself. Proponents of this 'essentialist' view see the use of art for other purposes – social work, cultural travel, industry and commerce – as destruction or exploitation of the essence of art.[23].

This is a view that no longer enjoys widespread support. It is now commonly accepted that art is an important economic resource, a significant contributor to sustainable development and general well-being, and even a promoter of health. Investing in art and culture is thought to prevent social isolation, unemployment and regional decay. According to Häyrynen, the threat posed by globalization to local and national identities

This page and opposite. The *Spirit of Särestö Project*. 2001. The project's objective was to develop teaching material and working methods for the Reidar Särestöniemi Art and Heritage Museum. In developing the material, the expertise of the Department of Art Education in combining nature, Lappish culture, art pedagogy, and culture-oriented travel proved invaluable. *Photograph by Timo Jokela*

underlies discussion of the strengthening of civic ties and the informal sector, and this inevitably foregrounds the aims and ideas of community art education.[24] It also raises questions about who should be in charge of the development process, under what conditions it should be carried out, and what should be the role of visual art education, either as an academic research discipline or as an educator of professionals.

There is pressure from several directions to change practices and to come up with new ways of making the bond between art, the community and the environment more visible. If we adopt this approach, we will need to put in place tools for the critical evaluation of its impact. In addition to good organizational skills, the art educator needs knowledge of the nature of particular communities and environments, and an understanding of what kinds of process are reasonable and feasible in those settings. Art and art education cannot operate as separate and autonomous agencies, they have to be able to establish connections to other disciplines and social sectors, and to develop new forms of collaboration in which the art educator, the artist, the social worker, the cultural worker and the environment planner can work in ever-closer cooperation with local communities. In this kind of collaboration, art educators need a new kind of expertise, or at least the ability to prove their competency in project-based activities. The essential quality of art does not disappear, but, rather, it can be argued, comes to life when it acquires meaning from the immediate social context of its creation.

Collaborative project-based studies in art education

In response to this pressure for change, the University of Lapland's visual arts education programme initiated pedagogical project-based studies in the latter part of the 1990s. The incorporation of visual art education into the University's existing Northern expertise was one of the central goals of these studies. This enabled collaboration with other disciplines and provided a basis for applying for external development finance and for looking for collaborative partners outwith the campus. Environmental and community art were the chosen areas of study, both because they embody the ideal of social renewal that underpins contemporary art, and because they require project-based collaboration between the disciplines of art and science as well as a range of social sectors.

Anttila[25] defines a 'project' as a combination of coordinated activities aimed at developing and creating processes, strategies and events that activate the communities involved, improve the aesthetic qualities of the environment and, above all, make it possible for future visual art teachers to become familiar with work that brings different sectors together. A project's objective can be one or more of the following:

- To incorporate art into the regular activities of the community;
- To use art as an instrument for change;
- To develop new ways of collaborating to realize artistic activities;
- To test theories in practical situations;
- To collect data through artistic activities for the purposes of visual art education research.

Trans Barents Highway Symposion of Art. Workshop at Salla village. 2003. Willow installation made by art students, artists from Finland, Sweden, Norway and Russian villagers of Salla. *Photograph by Timo Jokela*

This page and opposite. Trans Barents Highway Symposion of Art. Workshop at border of Finland and Sweden. 2003. Art students, artists from four countries and local people working together with hay installation. The material, straw, was given to the project by a local farming organisation. *Photograph by Kenneth Mikko*

In the projects initiated by the University of Lapland, students, art educators, artists and scientists from different fields worked together around a common environmental theme. Representatives of artistic and cultural institutions, the tourist industry, commercial enterprises and the local community have also played their part. The common objective of the projects is to develop pedagogical models through which existence in a Northern environment can be examined, and artistic knowledge and insights from other disciplines can be combined in an experiential learning process. The results can then be incorporated into existing project models in order to create truly artistic and reflective learning processes. Instead of a single individual's subjective experiences, these processes centre on the collective experiences of an entire community and the cultural and aesthetic bond between the community and the environment. At the same time. the participation of a range of interest groups encourages dialectical interaction and polyphony.[26]

In the Fells and in the hearts of towns

The projects have included a wide range of different activities: village artworks and art events, creating environment artworks with communities, exhibitions in galleries and museums, publications, art camps for young people, children's events, and motivating local people to examine their own environment, identity and stories. Most of them have concentrated on the special qualities of the Northern environment and culture. Among the most noteworthy are the *Joki* (River) project that took place in the River Ounasjoki area,[27] The *Tunturi* (Fell) project[28] and the *Ultima Thule* project that was staged in the villages on the shores of the Arctic Ocean in northern Norway.[29] Also worthy of mention are the Utsjoki-based *Tulikettu* (Fire Fox) project[30] and the Pelkosenniemi-based *Tunturin Taidepaja* art workshop (a labour market political project for young people), whose objectives were to broaden community art education.[31]

As well as these multidimensional long-term projects, dozens of small-scale ventures on a wide variety of themes have been undertaken. Among them have been snow construction projects aimed at making town and travel environments more attractive, the collaborative artistic development of schoolyards and the playgrounds of children's day-care centres, art events in the suburbs, art school camps organized by village communities, wandering art realized in the wilderness, street performances and puppet theatres. Pupils and teachers from local schools have participated in all these projects, which has enabled direct evaluation of the suitability of the activities involved and of their impact in terms of the set objectives. This has often been realized in the form of the final master's theses of art education students.

These initiatives have established new art events in Lapland. Interest in the collaborative activities between Finland, Sweden, Norway and Russia on issues of further education for artists and the development of sources of livelihood in the Barents region has been especially gratifying.[32] These activities have resulted in work that stands out both nationally and internationally, and can truly be called 'the art of art education that takes Northern conditions into consideration'. The most recent example was the *The Snow Show*, a three-year Winter Art Education Project[33] financed by the European Social Fund and organized by the University of Lapland's Department of Art Education. A meeting of the 'High Art' of international art institutions, regional development work and art education for schools, this was persuasive evidence of the value and potential of visual art education.

The cycles of an artistic action research project

Over the years, project-based studies have combined research, pedagogy and the various ways of creating art in a manner that suits the nature and objectives of art education. It is appropriate, therefore, to refer to these activities as artistic action research. Since the activities are always bound to a specific place, work should always start from investigation of that place and its sociocultural circumstances. Only projects based on a profound knowledge and understanding of the working environment and participating community have a permanent and positive outcome.

The analysis of artistic action research combines methods from the fields of cultural history, natural history, the social sciences and contemporary art. In particular, discussion of place and identity in the field of humanistic geography has contributed to the formulation of the theory of place used in the context of art education. According to Jokela & Huhmarniemi[34] and Jokela et al.,[35] investigations of places explore a place as an objective, subjective and textual entity as well as considering the local community's sociocultural situation. Surveying a place's objective aspects involves observing and describing forms, materials and distances, while subjective experience of a place is gained by spending time there and participating in community activities. This is a multi-sensory activity involving first-hand perception and analysis by an artist-researcher. It can recover past memories associated with a place, or examine personal conceptions and assumptions about it. The textual attributes of a place refer to the stories and communal perceptions associated with it. Place names, travel stories, books and conversations with local people can all serve as source material. The artistic process encourages more sensitive and accurate observation, and can also be used to evoke personal and collective memories and inspire discussion. According to Kurki,[36] the sociocultural circumstances of a place are central to increasing awareness of community needs and problems, understanding the special characteristics of the local community and finding resources and partners to collaborate with. It is vital to become familiar with local practices in order to ensure the successful execution of a project.

Heikkinen & Syrjälä[37] have pointed out that action research always takes place in a specific historical, political and ideological framework, from which both possibilities and restrictions in relation to the action emerge. However, an analysis of the place and community in which the action is to take place is not a sufficient basis for artistic activities. The instructors on the project also have to familiarize themselves with the history of the working, artistic and pedagogic methods they intend to use. They have to be able to understand and explain why the activities are the way they are before they can be developed. Although action research is situational, the researcher needs to become familiar with literature and previous research on the subject as well as artistic solutions related to it. In this way, a foundation is laid for the planned activities at a conceptual level.

Once the initial investigation and conceptualization stages have been completed, the project proceeds in cycles in much the same way as traditional forms of action research. This involves a planning stage, an art activity stage, an evaluation stage and an improvement stage. It is

Tower Project at the centre of Rovaniemi. This small-scale project focused on perceiving and analysing the built environment and recognizing symbolical meanings in the environment. *Photograph by Timo Jokela*

important to form a task force or research team to motivate the participants and discuss the division of tasks and responsibilities and to make a detailed plan about how the reflective data are to be collected and processed. The researcher may be able to discern the contours of the artistic dimension of the project during the acting and evaluation stages more clearly by collecting two different kinds of reflective data: data concerning the activity itself and data concerning the artistic experiences related to it. This is a good way to collect research data for the purpose of phenomenological analysis of art education processes, an approach which is useful when trying to understand the experiences and changes in thinking that the artistic activities trigger in the people involved.

The art that is created during these projects is a direct indicator of how successful and empowering they have been to the creators and the participating audience. The primary sharing and evaluation of this work takes place during the action, in its immediate context. This alone, however, is not enough; the development process needs to be reported on the basis of analysis of the reflective material, and development suggestions for the next action cycle must be put forward. In practice, it has proved fruitful to analyse the action-related and artistic experience-related reflective data as separate but parallel processes.

Evaluation of artistic action research

Research on art projects, until recently mainly the preserve of students' master's theses, is now becoming increasingly interesting to postgraduate researchers. Field practice is laying an empirical foundation for art education theory and helping to clarify visual art education as an academic discipline. As a relatively new discipline, art education frames its research questions from its own perspective, and seeks to answer them on the basis of its own research data without having to resort to the methods of other disciplines. Only in this way can art education create its own research tradition and, as Varto puts it, 'form a new discipline in the ontological sense'.[38] It is important to bear in mind that visual art education as both a science and an art is more far-reaching than its most immediate pragmatic application, the art teacher degree programme. It simultaneously embraces art, research and education, and the traditional criteria of academic study, for example, the ideal of objectivity, are unable to do justice to this. Moreover, narrativity, which is often associated with artistic action research, emphasizes relativism and subjectivity, and without any deeper insight into the subject matter can easily lead to the conclusion that 'anything is possible in art'. If we are to accept Varto's[39] ideas about the development of art education into an independent discipline, we must understand that we need to develop evaluative criteria that take the ontological character of art education into consideration.

Heikkinen & Syrjälä,[40] following Steinar Kvale,[41] suggest that in evaluating action research we should move from 'validity' to 'validation'. Validity refers to a stable truth or set of facts that a researcher seeks to describe, whereas validation refers to a process of gradual understanding. This kind of truth requires constant negotiation and dialogue and is never complete. Heikkinen & Syrjälä, drawing on the ideas of Kvale and Winter,[42] suggest five principles for the evaluation of action research: historical continuity, reflectivity, dialecticism, functionality and evocativeness.

The *Spirit of Särestö Project*. 2001. Environmental performance at the Särestö Art and Heritage Museum. In addition to the museum and the department of art education, two high schools also took part. From the Toppila high school of Oulu and the high school of Kittilä art teachers, Finnish and history teachers also participated in the project. *Photograph by Timo Jokela*

The principle of evocativeness is particularly interesting. Following Patton,[43] Heikkinen & Syrjälä[44] suggest that artistic criteria should be used for the purposes of evaluation of narrative research. According to these criteria good research works in the same way as good art does – it evokes new thoughts and feelings and makes people think differently:

> *The author has to be able to breathe life into the research report, and therefore he or she needs to have a better command of his or her mother tongue than what is required in traditional types of research.*[45]

The principle of evocativeness, however, is connected with the research report and not the artistic activity. When evaluating artistic action research, there has to be the possibility, for example, of examining the actual empowerment engendered by a village festival during the festival itself. Although according to the principle of evocativeness a well-written research report may be 'art', it is not adequate for the purposes of evaluation. A good community or environmental art project, on the other hand, can be seen as research.

Mind-broadening experiences

In this chapter, I have described how the development of pedagogical project-based studies, and the artistic action research related to them, has evolved into an important element of art teacher-training and community and environmental art. This work is still in progress, but the results are already visible. The work of art educators has been concretized in visible events that have had an immediate impact on their participants, and become a part of everyday life. We are still discovering new areas where art education has a role to play, and this feeds back into the art education work taking place in schools. The work we have done has also been presented at several international events, where the response has been extremely enthusiastic.

Over all, then, the outcome of these projects has been very encouraging. Students have been motivated to produce both artistic work and research and, perhaps, even more importantly, have gained extensive experience of practical work with a wide range of interest groups. The success of the projects has also improved the self-esteem of teachers, raised the profile of the field of art education and imparted the confidence to engage with even the most complicated questions. And, of course, the benefits do not stop there – an art education system that places community and environmental values at its centre has a positive influence on other disciplines across the entire social spectrum.

Notes and references

1. Neperud, R. (1995). Texture of Community. An Environmental Design Education. In Neperud R. (Ed.) *Context, Content and Community in Art Education.* New York: Teachers college, pp. 222–245.
2. See Gablik, S. (1991). *Reenchantment of art.* London: Thames and Hudson and Gablik, S. (1995) Connective aesthetics: art after individualism. In S. Lacy (Ed.) *Mapping the Terrain. New Genre Public Art.* Seattle: Bay Press, pp. 74–87. See also Kester, G. (2004) *Conversation pieces. Community +*

communication in modern art. London: University of California Press; Lacy, S. (Ed.) (1995) *Mapping the Terrain. New Genre Public Art.* Seattle: Bay Press. See also Lippard, L. (1997) *The Lure of the Local. Senses of Place in a Multicentered Society.* New York: New Press and Shusterman, R. (2001) *Taide, elämä ja estetiikka. Pragmatistisen filosofian näkökulma estetiikkaan.* Finish translation V. Mujunen. Tampere: Gaudeamus.

3. See Sederholm, H. (1998). *Starting to play with Arts Education. Study of Ways to Approach experiential and Social Modes of Contemporary Art.* Studies in the Arts 63. Jyväskylä: Jyväskylän yliopisto and Sederholm, H. (2000) *Tämäkö taidetta?* Porvoo: WSOY. See also Hiltunen, M. (2006) Elettyä taidetta – yhteistä toimintaa. In Kettunen, K., Hiltunen, M., Laitinen, S. & Rastas, M., (Eds.) *Kuvien keskellä – Kuvataideopettajaliitto 100 vuotta,* pp. 25–37; Jokela, T. (2006) Nurkasta ulos – kuvataiteen opettajakoulutuksen uusia suuntia. In Kettunen, K., Hiltunen, M., Laitinen, S. & Rastas, M., (Eds.) *Kuvien keskellä – Kuvataideopettajaliitto 100 vuotta,* pp. 71–85.

4. Hautamäki, A. (2005). Johdanto. In A. Hautamäki, T. Lehtonen, J. Sihvola, I. Tuomi, H. Vaaranen & S. Veijola. *Yhteisöllisyyden paluu.* Helsinki: Gaudeamus, pp. 7–13.

5. See Rauhala, N. (2005). *Ihminen kulttuurissa – kulttuuri ihmisessä.* Helsinki: Yliopistopaino.

6. See Hiltunen, M. & Jokela, T. (2001). *Täälläkö taidetta? Johdatus yhteisölliseen taidekasvatukseen.* Lapin yliopiston taiteiden tiedekunnan julkaisuja D 4. Rovaniemi:Yliopistopaino.

7. See Shusterman, R. op. cit.

8. See Kurki, L. (2000). *Sosiokulttuurinen innostaminen. Muutoksen pedagogiikka.* Tampere: Vastapaino and Kurki, L. (2005) Sosiokulttuurinen innostaminen yhteisöllisyyden rakentajan. In T. Kiilakoski, T. Tomperi & M. Vuorikoski (Eds.) *Kenen kasvatus? Kriittinen pedagogiikka ja toisinkasvatuksen mahdollisuus.* Tampere: Vastapaino, pp. 335–357.

9. See Giroux, H. A. & McLaren, P. (2001). *Kriittinen pedagogiikka.* Suomentaja J. Vainonen. T. Aittokoski & J. Suoranta (Eds.) Tampere: Vastapaino. See also Suoranta, J. (2005) *Radikaali kasvatus.* Helsinki: Gaudeamus.

10. Lacy, S. (1995). Debated Territory: Towards a Critical Language for Public Art. In Lacy S. (Ed.) *Mapping the Terrain. New Genre Public Art.* Seattle: Bay Press, pp. 171–185.

11. Häyrynen, S. (2006). *Suomalaisen yhteiskunnan kulttuuripolitiikka.* Jyväskylä: SoPhi.

12. See Lakso, T. & Kainulainen, K. (2001). Sivusta aluekehitystyön ytimeen. Kulttuuriala strategisen ohjelmatyön osa-alueena. In S. Riukulehto (Eds.) *Perinnettä vai bisnestä? Kulttuurin paikalliset ulottuvuudet.* Jyväskylä: Atena Kustannus Oy, pp. 32–51.

13. See Lindroos, K. (2004). Koulu alueellisena toimintakeskuksena. In Launinen, Leevi & Pulkkinen, Lea (Eds.) *Koulu kasvuyhteisönä.* Jyväskylä: PS-kustannus, pp. 201–212.

14. See, for example, University of Lapland – Strategy for 2010. Available from URL: http://www.ulapland.fi/english (accessed 20th May 2007). University of Lapland has an important role in regional development policy and it works in close connection on local area and research and education in university are strongly emphasizes northern issues. An objective of the University of Lapland is to promote knowledge of the Northern regions of the world, their social and cultural development and the welfare of the people living in the Northern regions.

15. OECD. (2002). *Reading for Change: Performance and engagement across countries: results from PISA 2000.* Paris: OECD.

16. Tomperi, T. & Piattoeva, N. (2005). Demokraattisten juurten kasvattaminen. In T. Kiilakoski, T. Tomperi & M. Vuorikoski (Eds.) *Kenen kasvatus? Kriittinen pedagogiikka ja toisinkasvatuksen mahdollisuus.* Tampere: Vastapaino, pp. 247–286.

17. See Launonen, L. & Pulkkinen, L. (2004). Koulu kasvuyhteisönä. In L. Launonen & L. Pulkkinen (Eds.) 2004. *Koulu kasvuyhteisönä.* Jyväskylä: PS-kustannus, pp. 13–75.

18. Giroux, H. A. & McLaren, P. op. cit. and Suoranta, J. op. cit. and Kiilakoski, T. (2005). Koululaitos ja toiveet kehityksestä. In T. Kiilakoski, T. Tomperi & M. Vuorikoski (Eds.) *Kenen kasvatus? Kriittinen pedagogiikka ja toisinkasvatuksen mahdollisuus.* Tampere: Vastapaino, pp. 139–196.

19. Freire, P. (2005). Sorrettujen pedagogiikka. Suomentaja J. Kuortti. T. Tomperi (Eds.) Tampere: Vastapaino.

20. Tomperi, T. & Piattoeva, N. (2005). Demokraattisten juurten kasvattaminen. In T. Kiilakoski, T. Tomperi & M. Vuorikoski (Eds.) *Kenen kasvatus? Kriittinen pedagogiikka ja toisinkasvatuksen mahdollisuus.* Tampere: Vastapaino, pp. 247–286.

21. Luukkainen, O. (2000). *Opettaja vuonna 2010. Opettajien perus- ja täydennyskoulutuksen ennakointihankeen (OPEPRO) selvitys 15. Loppuraportti.* Helsinki: Opetushallitus.

22. Rinne, R. & Salmi, E. (2000). *Oppimisen uusi järjestys.* Tampere: Vastapaino, p. 48.

23. See Eisner, E. W. (1972). Educating artistic vision. New York:Macmillan. The questions of the essence of art education (essential art education) have been discussed since Elliot Eisner's publications in the 1970s; Efland, A., Freedman, K. & Stuhr, P. (1996) Postmodern Art Education: An Approach to Curriculum. The National Art Education Association: Reston, Virginia.

24. See Häyrynen, S. op. cit.

25. Anttila, P. (2001) *Se on projekti – vai onko? Kulttuurialan tuotanto-ja palveluprojektien hallinta.* Artefakta 10. Hamina: Akatiimi.

26. Heikkinen, H. L.T. & Syrjälä, L. (2006). Tutkimuksen arviointi. In Heikkinen, H. L. T., Rovio, E. & Syrjälä, L. (Eds.) *Toiminnasta tietoon. Toimintatutkimuksen menetelmät ja lähestymistavat.* Helsinki: Kansanvalistusseura, pp.143–161.

27. Jokela, T. (1996). Ympäristöstä paikaksi – paikasta taiteeksi. In A. Huhtala, (Ed.) *Ympäristö – arvot? Heijastuksia pohjoiseen.* Lapin yliopiston hallintoviraston julkaisuja 35. Rovaniemi: Lapin yliopistopaino, pp. 161–178; Jokela, T. & Lohiniva, L. (Eds.) (1996) *Joki–the River. Ympäristötaidetapahtuma Ounasjoen alkulähteiltä Ounasjokisuulle.* Lapin yliopiston taiteiden tiedekunnan julkaisuja, sarja C. Rovaniemi: Sevenprint.

28. Jokela, T. [ed.] 1999. *Tunturi taiteen ja tieteen maisemassa.* Taiteiden tiedekunnan julkaisuja C 12. Rovaniemi: Lapin yliopistopaino.

29. Jokela, T. & Kuuri, E. (Ed.) 1999. *Ultima Thule. Northern Environment and Art Education Project.* University of Lapland publications in visual arts and design C 14. Rovaniemi: Lapin yliopistopaino.

30. Hiltunen, M. (2005). The Fire Fox. Multisensory approach to Art Education in Lapland. International Journal of Education through Art. 1:2, pp. 161–177.

31. Hiltunen, M. (2004). Erämaa opettaa. Kehollisesti ympäristön, taiteen ja yhteisön maisemissa. Aikuiskasvatus. 1/2004, 54 -59. Helsinki: Like, 25–37.

32. See Jokela, T., Mikko, K. & Kynman, F. (2004). *The Trans Barents Highway Symposium of Art.* Umeå: Nyheternas Tryckeri.

33. See Jokela, T. (2007). Winter Art as an Experince. In Kylänen M., Häkkinen A. (Eds.) *Articles on Experiences 5 – Arts & Experiences.* Rovaniemi: Lapland Centre of Expertise for Experience Industry, pp. 114–135. Huhmarniemi, M., Jokela, T. & Vuorjoki, S. (Eds.) (2003) *Talven taidetta. Puheenvuoroja talven*

kulttuurista, talvitaiteesta ja lumirakentamisesta/Winter art. Statement on Winter Art and Snow Construction. Käännös/Translation R. Foley. Lapin yliopiston taiteiden tiedekunnan julkaisuja D 6. Rovaniemi: Sevenprint. Huhmarniemi, M., Jokela, T. & Vuorjoki, S. (Eds.) (2003) *Talven taito. Puheenvuoroja talven kulttuurista, talvitaiteesta ja lumirakentamisesta/Winter Skills. A Guidebook for Snow and Ice Sculpting.* Käännös/Translation V. Välimaa-Hill Lapin yliopiston taiteiden tiedekunnan julkaisuja D 7. Rovaniemi: Sevenprint. Huhmarniemi, M., Jokela, T. & Vuorjoki, S. (Eds.) (2004) *Talven tuntemus. Puheenvuoroja talvesta ja talvitaiteesta/Sense of Winter. Statements on Winter and Winter and Art.* Käännös/Translation V. Välimaa-Hill. Lapin yliopiston taiteiden tiedekunnan julkaisuja D 9. Rovaniemi: Sevenprint. Huhmarniemi, M., Jokela, T. & Vuorjoki, S. (Eds.) (2004) *Talven toimintaa. Koulujen talvitaideprojekteja/Winter Activities. Winter Art Projects in Schools.* CD-ROM. Käännös/Translation M. Narbough, A. Nieminen & V. Välimaa-Hill. Lapin yliopiston taiteiden tiedekunnan julkaisuja D 11. Rovaniemi.

34. Jokela T. & Huhmarniemi, M. (2007). Environmental art and community art in northern places. In Mason, R. & Eça, T. (Eds.) *Intercultural Dialogues in Art Education.* London: Intellect Books.

35. Jokela, T., Hiltunen, M., Huhmarniemi, M. & Valkonen, V. (2006). *Taide, yhteisö & ympäristö/Art, Community & Environment,* Rovaniemi, Lapin yliopisto. Available from URL: http://ace.ulapland.fi/yty/english.html (accessed 7th May 2007).

36. Kurki, L. (2000). Op.cit.

37. Heikkinen, H. L. T. & Syrjälä, L. op.cit. pp. 143–161.

38. Varto, J. (2001). *Uutta tietoa. Värityskirja tieteen filosofiaan.* Tampere: Tampereen Yliopistopaino.

39. *Ibid.*

40. Heikkinen, H. L. T. & Syrjälä, L. op.cit., pp. 143–161.

41. Kvale, S. (1996). *InterViews: An Introduction to Qualitative Research Interviewing.* Thousand Oaks: Sage.

42. Winter, R. (2002). Truth or fiction: problems of validity and authenticity in narratives of action research. *Educational Action Research* 10 (1), pp. 143–154.

43. Patton, M. (2002). *Qualitative Research and Evaluation Methods.* 3rd ed. London: SAGE.

44. Heikkinen, H. L. T. & Syrjälä, L. op. cit., pp. 143–161.

45. Heikkinen, H. L. T. & Syrjälä, L. op. cit., p. 160.

14

HARD LESSONS: PUBLIC SCULPTURE AND THE EDUCATION SYSTEM IN NINETEENTH-CENTURY GLASGOW

Ray McKenzie

Like most British cities that underwent rapid expansion as a result of the Industrial Revolution, Glasgow began to embrace the practice of erecting monuments in the decades following the Napoleonic Wars, subsequently developing a rich tradition of public art that flourished throughout the Victorian period. Focused largely on the achievements of 'great individuals', the statues that were to become such a conspicuous feature of the city's streets and open spaces were designed to satisfy a variety of cultural needs, including the celebration of national achievement in the arts and commerce (see, for example, statues to Robert Burns and William Pearce), the acknowledgement of political debt (the Duke of Wellington) and the expression of patriotic duty (Queen Victoria). None of this, of course, conflicted with the more general belief that they should, as objects of visual beauty, contribute to the aestheticization of urban space. But underpinning all of these functions, and in a sense providing their ideological grounding, there was also an expectation that such monuments should have an implicitly didactic role. According to one late-nineteenth-century commentator, reporting on the unveiling of the monument to the great Govan shipbuilder William Pearce, the statue was not just a 'beautiful thing', but also 'an incentive and an encouragement to every passing apprentice to do what he could to emulate the professional career of the great founder of the Fairfield Yard.'[1] Set up as models for our admiration, historic monuments are thus intended to instil in us a sense of what it means to live a useful and productive life. They are literally a lesson to us all.

The degree to which works of this kind really are capable of transmitting an educational content has recently become the focus of much critical debate, and the claim that they can perform effectively as mediators of ideological value is now recognized as deeply problematic.[2] Purely on the level of common sense it would appear to be absurd to describe an inanimate object as a carrier of didactic meaning. Carlo

Carlo Marochetti, *Monument to the Duke of Wellington*, bronze, 1844, Royal Exchange Square, Glasgow. *Photograph by Ray McKenzie*

Marochetti's *Monument to the Duke of Wellington* (1844), with its accompanying depiction of the Battle of Waterloo, may well provide a vivid illustration of the great man's military achievement, and it is not difficult to see how it could be used to stimulate an interest in the events of his time. But it scarcely *explains* those events in any meaningful sense. Statues cannot in themselves teach us anything. However authoritative they might appear as public statements, the experiences they engender bear no relation to the discursive engagement with ideas that is required for learning to occur. The best that can be said of them is that they act as a confirmation of collective memory – as reminders of what is already known.

Before we dismiss out of hand any idea that monuments might have a legitimate didactic role, it is however worth considering two factors that are relevant to nineteenth-century monuments and the cultural operations in which they are embedded. Firstly, the belief that historic monuments are intrinsically problematic is very much a modern invention. If we are troubled by the appearance of imperialist assertiveness in the *Duke of Wellington* it is because we do not share the values of the society that erected it, and because the 'collective memory' embodied in it is no longer accessible to us as a direct experience. It is unlikely that Marochetti's generation, many of whom would have been alive at the time of the Napoleonic Wars, were troubled by any such anxieties. In common with almost every other public monument raised in Glasgow in the nineteenth century, the statue of Wellington was funded entirely by public subscription, so in a very real sense its presence on the pavement of Queen Street signifies what was at the time a widespread consensus of opinion.[3] Far from being imposed on an ignorant or indifferent public, it was in fact put there because the public demanded that it should be there. Under such circumstances its limited educational value could hardly have been perceived as a drawback. Its role was not to teach something new, but to reaffirm a lesson that was already well understood.

The second factor is that the growth of public monument culture in Glasgow coincided with a massive expansion in educational opportunities, particularly for the 'artisan classes' on whose skills the success of the Industrial Revolution depended. The early nineteenth century was the era of the Mechanics' Institute, the Working Men's College and the multitude of Schools of Arts and Sciences that proliferated in all the manufacturing centres where there was a need for a well-trained labour force. It was also the era of mass literacy, with a corresponding explosion in cheap publications, including newspapers and illustrated weeklies, all of which fed an increasingly voracious appetite for information mediated by print. It is probably fair to say that the many thousands of Glasgow citizens who turned out to witness the inauguration of the *Monument to the Duke of Wellington* on 8 October 1844 were better educated, and better informed about the world, than any previous generation in history.

How do we assess the didactic function of public sculpture in the light of these facts? One way to answer this question is to consider the kinds of sculpture that were produced within the context of the nineteenth-century education system itself, in particular the use of statues and relief carving as an enrichment of the buildings in which the business of education was actually carried out. As will be shown, not only was this a more varied practice than one might suppose, but the willingness of educational establishments to make use of sculpture in defining their public identity was also widespread enough to suggest a belief that it could play more than a merely decorative role. I would like to suggest that, far from being an ornamental appendage, the architectural sculptures commissioned for display on educational buildings were the product of a much more ambitious intention – that they were in fact meant to be read as a visual embodiment of the principles of pedagogic practice in action. This was the real lesson they were designed to teach. My intention in this paper is to test this claim by examining a group of sculptures that were made in response to a range of educational aspirations, and to explore the insights this might give us into the operations of Victorian public art as a whole. Most of the examples will be drawn from Glasgow, but it will be necessary from to time to include works from other local centres of sculptural production, such as Paisley and Greenock.

Although the University of Glasgow has a record of commissioning statues that stretches back to the seventeenth century,[4] it was not until the 1820s that sculpture began to play a fully public role in the context of a specifically educational project. The earliest recorded example of such a work is John Greenshields' life-size statue of James Watt leaning on a steam cylinder, which was commissioned by the Glasgow Mechanics' Institute in 1824 for their premises on Shuttle Street, and which now stands in the foyer of the University of Strathclyde's Royal College building. The Mechanics' Institute itself had been established in the previous year after a number of members of the staff of the existing Andersonian Institute found themselves in dispute with their employers and seceded to form an independent technical college.[5] It was an immediate success, with over 1,000 students enrolling in the first year, many of them no doubt attracted by the apparently 'democratic' management style that allowed students to vote lecturers on or off the payroll according to their popularity.[6] It was also the prototype from which George Birkbeck, a former professor at the Andersonian, developed his vision of the Mechanics' Institute movement that later made technical education accessible to working men across the entire country.[7]

Something of the populist egalitarianism that motivated the creation of the college is evident in the circumstances that led to the commissioning of the statue. According to the Institute's historian Humboldt Sexton, there was in the academic year 1823–24:

> ...an agitation for the erection of a statue to the memory of James Watt. In aid of this, Dr Ure gave a lecture at the Andersonian, and he was followed at the "Mechanics" by James Longstaff, who gave a public lecture on the "Steam-engine". On the lecture-table he had working models of Newcomen's and Watt's engines.[8]

He goes on to record that the charge for admission to the lectures was one shilling, and that £30 was raised in this way. The urgency suggested by Sexton's use of the word 'agitation' is probably explained by the fact that although Watt had died four years earlier, in 1819, there was still no public monument to him anywhere in the city, or indeed anywhere in the UK. What more appropriate way for the Institute to announce its arrival than by being the first organization in the world to pay public tribute to 'the great benefactor of mankind'.[9] Watt's reputation as a

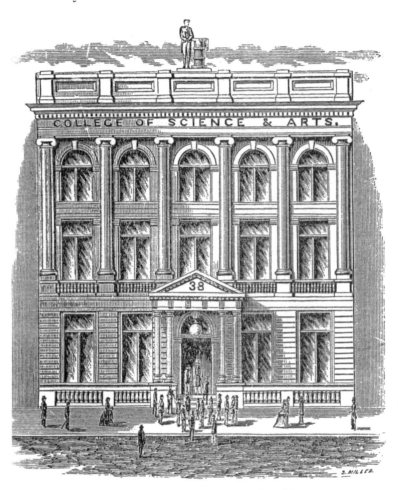

John Greenshields, *Monument to James Watt*, sandstone, c.1824, University Strathclyde, former Royal College, 204 George Street, entrance hall. Photograph by Brian Lochrin

J. Miller, *College of Science and Arts, 38 Bath Street, Glasgow*, woodcut c.1881, from A Humboldt Sexton, *The First Technical College*, p.78. (Private collection)

FIG. 41.—The Mechanics' Institute, 38, Bath Street.

technological genius who had risen from relatively humble origins, and whose early success was almost entirely due to his association with the University of Glasgow, also made him a natural choice for a new college anxious to convince fledgling artisans of the attractions of a technical education.[10] He was, in short, the paradigm of everything the Institute was trying to achieve.

There is much that remains unclear about the commission: we do not know, for example, when the completed statue was delivered, or precisely how it was first displayed. What is clear, however, is that by 1831, when the Institute moved to its bespoke new premises on North Hanover Street, the statue had been given a fully public profile by being hoisted on to the pediment of the main street frontage – the presiding genius, figuratively speaking, over the educational objectives being pursued in the lecture halls below.[11] We also know that when the Institute relocated in 1859 to an entirely new building at 38 Bath Street, and changed its name to the College of Science & Arts, the statue went with it, retaining its prominence by being placed on the attic balustrade, where it probably stayed until it was moved to its present site in the early years of the twentieth century. So for the best part of 70 years, Greenshields' statue of Watt, leaning nonchalantly against one of the critical technological breakthroughs of the Industrial Revolution, acted as a visible symbol of what is now recognized as one of the nineteenth-century education system's most distinctive initiatives.

If there was no public acknowledgement of Watt's contribution at the time when the Institute opened in 1823, it was not long before a veritable spate of similar monuments began to make an appearance, many of them directly linked with seats of learning. The portrait sculptor Sir Francis Chantrey alone was to produce five versions of a colossal seated effigy of him over the next fifteen years, including one in marble for the University of Glasgow (1830), now in the Hunterian Museum,[12] and a bronze copy for George Square, Glasgow (1832), for which the Mechanics' Institute also managed to raise £30.[13] Edinburgh was a little slower off the mark, but in 1854, to celebrate the amalgamation of the Watt Institute and the School of Technical Arts, Peter Slater was commissioned to make a copy of the Chantrey prototype to be placed on the pavement in front of their building on Adam Square. This was moved to their new premises on Chambers Street in 1872, and is now located in the main campus of Heriot-Watt University at Riccarton.[14]

Not surprisingly, Watt's own home town played an important part in commemorating the great man, and it is significant that the two major statues of him in Greenock were commissioned as part of educational initiatives. On the ground floor of the Watt Monument Library on Union Street, directly in front of the main public entrance, is yet another marble version of Chantrey's image of the inventor (1838), seated meditatively with a pair of dividers and a large sheet of paper, as if in the act of thinking through a technical problem. In this case the context is as important as the statue, not simply because part of the function of the building was to provide a protective enclosure for it, but because the library largely owes its existence to a gesture by Watt himself. On a visit to the town in 1815, he enquired of his friend Andrew Anderson – the brother of John Anderson, after whom the Andersonian Institute was named – if there were any 'talented young people in Greenock in need of encouragement'. On learning that indeed there were, he donated £100 towards the establishment of a scientific library, containing books

Sir Francis Chantrey, *Monument to James Watt*, marble, 1838, Watt Monument Library, Union Street, Greenock. *Photograph by Ray McKenzie*

Henry Charles Fehr, *Monument to James Watt*, bronze, 1908, former Watt Navigation College, Dalrymple Street, Greenock. *Photograph by Ray McKenzie*

on subjects ranging from the properties of fluids to shipbuilding.[15] This was later amalgamated with several other specialist libraries to form the core of the present collection, for which the building that now houses them was commissioned. With the statue forming the centrepiece of the entire conception, the Watt Monument Library pays tribute to the memory of Greenock's most illustrious son in a way that comes very close to fulfilling the elusive Victorian ideal of a 'living memorial' – a commemoration that is educationally productive as well as visually imposing. The fact that it is still in use today – apparently the oldest surviving subscription library in Scotland – testifies to the effectiveness of the initiative.[16]

The same desire to combine visual commemoration with social usefulness is evident in the second major tribute to Watt by his home town, the bronze statue by Henry Fehr on the exterior of the Watt Navigation College, dating from the early part of the twentieth century. Although the 'artisan classes' of Greenock had been pressing for a more publicly visible tribute to their hero since the 1880s,[17] no positive action was taken until 1903, when the expatriate Scots philanthropist Andrew Carnegie announced his intention to contribute £10,000 towards such a scheme.[18] Carnegie himself was at the time writing a biography of Watt for a series of books on 'Famous Scots',[19] and as an industrialist who had made his fortune through steel production he clearly saw the creation of a public monument to Watt as a further means of acknowledging the degree to which he owed his personal success to the work of the great inventor. What is most interesting about his offer, however, is that he made no stipulations as to the form the monument should take. This was decided through public debate, much of which was focused on the question of whether it should be a 'monument pure and simple', or one 'with a soul in it' – that is to say, a statue to commemorate his achievement, or an institution to perpetuate it.[20] In the event it was resolved to do both, and the Watt Navigation College, with a bronze statue of Watt by Fehr raised on a specially designed corner projection, was opened to its first cohort of students in June 1908[21] The decision to commission both a school and a statue evidently put a strain on the project's finances, and this precluded the commissioning of a completely new statue. As a result Fehr was asked to make a second cast of the monument he had recently erected in City Square in Leeds, which shows Watt in period costume, gesturing with an almost balletic grace as he prepares to bring a pair of dividers onto an open notebook in his left hand. The Greenock version, however, differs from the original in one important detail. Here the dividers and notebook have been replaced by a piece of equipment that has recently been identified as a 'steam engine indicator', a specialist instrument invented by Watt to calculate the efficiency of engines fitted to steamships.[22] It is the only known monument to Watt that departs from the conventional practice of signifying his achievement through one of three common and easily recognized attributes – a pair of dividers, a steam cylinder or a governor mechanism – and thus relates directly to the business of the school to which it is attached. It is a fine statue, and speaks eloquently to Watt's continued relevance in the context of technical education at the start of the twentieth century.

If we return now to Glasgow, we find that during the period when Greenshields' statue of Watt presided over the North Hanover and Bath Street premises of the Mechanics' Institute, a number of other educational establishments found it desirable to invoke the image of the great man as a way of embodying their pedagogic philosophy in symbolic form. He appears, for example, as one of four monumental statues by

John Mossman, *James Watt*, sandstone, 1878, former Glasgow Academy, Elmbank Street, Glasgow. *Photograph by Ray McKenzie*

John Mossman raised on channelled ashlar buttresses on the main façade of Glasgow Academy on Elmbank Street, designed by Charles Wilson in 1846. As a 'private school for young gentlemen',[23] the Academy no doubt had access to the necessary resources to indulge in such an unusually high degree of architectural enrichment. But it was also committed to a broader range of educational goals than any of the buildings where Watt had appeared so far, and no doubt chose the four historical figures – from the left, Cicero, Galileo, Watt and Homer – as emblems of the principal components of a balanced curriculum: science and technology, bracketed by the study of Latin and Greek.[24]

Figurative sculpture by John Mossman is used to express an even more diverse range of educational goals on the façade of the Athenæum Building in Nelson Mandela Place, designed in a slightly more austere classical idiom by J. J. Burnet, and opened in 1886. James Watt makes a further appearance here, this time seated at first-floor level beside a steam cylinder and with a governor mechanism in his hand, the function of which he appears to be explaining to a young boy. The fact that the boy holds a pair of dividers and a scroll, in a manner recalling the way Watt himself is depicted by Chantrey in George Square and Greenock, suggests that the statue is not so much a portrait of the scientist himself as a symbolic representation of 'Scientific Education' in general. The Athenæum is, of course, a very special institution in terms of the educational role that it played. As much a gentlemen's club as a seat of learning, it was designed to cater to the needs of the 'commercial classes of Glasgow',[25] attracting students who could not afford to attend the University but required a more liberal education than was provided by the Mechanics' Institute. It was, in effect, a miniature free university, committed to the *dissemination of a Knowledge of Science and the Arts, by the agency of which a nation is enriched and ennobled*.[26] In keeping with this broad and liberal pedagogic mission, we find Watt and his pupil balanced at the opposite end of the façade by a similar group representing 'Literature'. The scheme is completed by a row of standing portraits on the attic storey signifying the four principal arts: John Flaxman (sculpture), Sir Christopher Wren (architecture), Henry Purcell (music) and Sir Joshua Reynolds (painting).[27]

The Athenæum is typical of the buildings that have so far been mentioned in this study in its use of sculpture as a vehicle to project its own educational ideals into the public domain, and this in turn conforms to the established architectural practice of using the exterior of a public building to express the essence of what goes on inside. But the two groups on the first storey represent a departure from mainstream practice in one important respect. Until then, Watt had been presented as a paradigm of everything the process of education is directed towards – as one among many heroes, whose achievements are invoked as exemplars of what the education system is able to accomplish. In this case, however, we see him in the company of one of the beneficiaries of that system who is in the process of undergoing a learning experience. The two pairs of figures are representations, in other words, of the active transmission of knowledge itself.

Nor is this the only case in which architectural sculpture has been used to express an educational ideal in this way, and variations on this strategy are to be found across a range of nineteenth-century school buildings. The specialist teaching practices of the Anderson College of Medicine, for example, are illustrated on its Dumbarton Road façade by a carved lunette by James Pittendrigh Macgillivray of the pioneering

John Mossman, *Scientific Education*, sandstone, 1888, former Athenæum, Nelson Mandela Place, Glasgow. *Photograph by Ray McKenzie*

John Mossman, *Literary Education*, sandstone, 1888, former Athenæum, Nelson Mandela Place, Glasgow. *Photograph by Ray McKenzie*

John James Burnet, *former Athenæum*, 1886-88, Nelson Mandela Place, Glasgow. *Photograph by Ray McKenzie*

Glasgow surgeon Peter Lowe demonstrating how to take a pulse to a class of trainee doctors. One student, with his sleeve rolled up, plays the role of the patient, while another takes charge of the hourglass on a table nearby.[28] At the opposite end of the spectrum, we find a similar use of relief sculpture on the exterior of the so-called Half-Timers' School in Paisley, built in 1887 by the philanthropist Sir Peter Coates to provide a basic education for the young girls who worked for the other half of the week in the thread mills that generated his vast personal fortune.[29] Though the building today is in an almost ruinous condition, with one of its two narrative relief panels lying in fragments among the rubble on the ground, enough survives for us to gain a sense of what the sculptor wanted us to believe went on in the classrooms within. In the panel that remains *in situ* we see a young female teacher conducting a geography lesson to a class of girls whose apparent attentiveness corresponds well with a statement in the school log book that *'no drones were allowed to exist in this Educational hive.'*[30] Among the surviving fragments of the second panel we can make out the figure of a senior pupil with her arm placed protectively round the shoulder of a younger girl, an image of companionship that suggests a school that was committed as much to the social and moral development of its pupils as it was to delivering a purely academic curriculum.

It is tempting to dismiss such a vision of classroom harmony as unrealistically sanitised, and there is little doubt that the sculptors employed to make work of this kind were expected to depict school life in a favourable light, with all the more authoritarian aspects of the educational regime tactfully suppressed. And yet there is evidence elsewhere to suggest that the Dickensian cliché of the classroom as an internment camp patrolled by cane-wielding Gradgrinds was far from true of every Victorian school. In Greenock Cemetery, for example, there is a finely carved relief by George Mossman on a *stele* marking the grave of the schoolmaster James Lockhart Brown, who died in 1847 having spent 24 years as Rector of Greenock Grammar School. Once again we see a suspiciously idyllic-looking representation of the interior of a schoolroom, with model pupils attending dutifully to their studies, the older boys providing assistance to their junior colleagues. What makes this image special, however, is that it may have been commissioned by the pupils themselves as a tribute to their former master. So popular was Brown with his boys, and so effective was he as a teacher, that his work was continued after his death by the formation among pupils and alumni of a 'Brown Society', which organized debates and prize competitions for essays in Latin and Greek, as well as fund-raising events such as *gaudeamus* dinners, some of the proceeds of which were used to have his monument repaired and maintained on a regular basis.[31] As it happens, the tallest pupil on the right is Norman Macbeth, who later emerged as a distinguished portrait painter, and it may well be that he advised Mossman on the composition of the relief and the likenesses of the boys depicted in it.[32] Far from being a falsely idealized representation of Victorian school life, the relief corresponds to the pupils' recollection of it from their own experience.

Of all the sculptural representations of the learning process that were produced in this period, however, one of the most memorable is the statue of a young scholar sitting, chalk and slate in hand, on the pediment of the former Buchanan Institute for Destitute Children, on Greenhead Street, opposite Glasgow Green.[33] Carved from freestone by William Brodie in 1873, this larger-than-life-size figure is of a boy *'whose*

James Pittendrigh Macgillivray, *Peter Lowe conducting a medical class*, freestone, 1889,
Anderson College of Medicine, Dumbarton Road, Glasgow. *Photograph by Ray McKenzie*

Unknown sculptor, *Geography Lesson*, marble, 1887, former Ferguslie Half-Timers' School, Maxwellton Street, Paisley. *Photograph by Ray McKenzie*

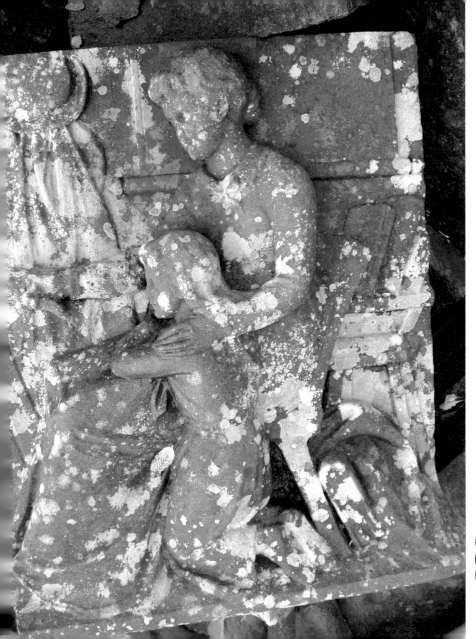

Unknown sculptor, *Geography Lesson*, marble, 1887, former Ferguslie Half-Timers' School, Maxwellton Street, Paisley. *Photograph by Ray McKenzie*

George Mossman, *Monument to James Lockhart Brown*, sandstone, c.1847, Greenock Cemetery, compartment E. *Photograph by Ray McKenzie*

garments bespeak him as one of the humble class which the foundation was intended to benefit',[34] but whose expression of absorbed concentration provides us with a poignant reminder that the act of learning is always an internal and purely private affair. Brodie produced a small marble version of the statue, which he entitled *The Mathematician*,[35] so we may deduce that the symbols he is writing or is about to write on the slate are numbers rather than words, while the jack plane at his feet suggests that the calculation in which he is engrossed may have a practical rather than a purely theoretical outcome. Brodie himself had good reason to appreciate the generosity of the Institute's founder, James Buchanan, who in addition to commissioning him to make several earlier works sponsored the trip he made to Rome in 1853 in order to complete his own theoretical and practical education.[36] What gives the work its special meaning in the present context, however, is the remarkable similarity of its treatment to the *Monument to Thomas Graham* in George Square, which Brodie had completed the year before. One of the most distinguished chemists of his day, Graham was the author of two groundbreaking publications and the inventor of 'Graham's Law' on the diffusion of gases. But he was also an inspiring teacher, working as a lecturer at both the Mechanics' and the Andersonian Institutes – where his pupils included David Livingstone and the industrialist James 'Paraffin' Kelly – before leaving for London to become Professor of Chemistry at University College.[37] The poses of Graham and the destitute boy are not identical, but the resemblance is too striking to be a coincidence. Both are shown in a reflective attitude, with the chin resting on the right hand and the left supporting an emblem of education – a slate for the boy, an edition of one of his books for the professor.

Between them, these two statues embrace the entire spectrum of educational achievement as it unfolded in the nineteenth century – from the earnest beginner, struggling to master the rudiments of an intellectual discipline, to the mature academic with the fruits of lifelong success propped on his knee. They are proof of the subtle pattern of connections that runs through that greatest of Victorian enterprises, the drive to make education accessible to everybody, regardless of their means or class background. But they also confirm the degree to which the education system depended on artists such as Greenshields, Mossman and Brodie to give the lofty ideals that motivated it a concrete, three-dimensional form. The handful of examples of their work that have been discussed in this brief survey give some measure of how effective sculpture was as a means of broadcasting those ideals, in some cases literally from the rooftops, for all the world to see.

William Brodie, *Monument to Thomas Graham*, bronze, 1871, George Square, Glasgow. *Photograph by Brian Lochrin*

William Brodie, *Monument to Thomas Graham*, bronze, 1871, George Square, Glasgow. *Photograph by Brian Lochrin*

Notes

1. 'Sir William Pearce. Memorial Supplement', *Govan Press*, 13 October 1894, p. 2c.

2. See, e.g., Andreas Huyssen, 'Monument and Memory in a Postmodern Age', in James E Young (Ed.), *The Art of Memory: holocaust memorials in history*, Munich and New York, Prestel, 1994, pp. 9–17.

3. For a fuller discussion, see R. McKenzie, *Public Sculpture of Glasgow*, Liverpool, Liverpool University Press, 2002, pp. 36–39; see also, Philip Ward-Jackson, 'Carlo Marochetti and the Glasgow Wellington Monument', *Burlington Magazine*, 132:1053 (December 1990), pp. 851–61.

4. For example, Robert Erskine's marble bust of Zachary Boyd, c. 1657, now in the Hunterian Museum (GLAHA 44157). This was originally placed in a niche in the inner quadrangle of the Old College on the high street and, therefore, accessible to staff and students but not to the general public. See http://www.huntsearch.gla.ac.uk (accessed 10 February 2008).

5. A. Humboldt Sexton, *'The First Technical College' A Sketch of 'The Andersonian' and the Institution Descended from it: 1796–1894*, London, Chapman & Hall, 1894, p. 69. The Andersonian had been set up in Glasgow in 1796 with a bequest from John Anderson, Professor of Natural Philosophy at the University of Glasgow.

6. *Ibid.*, p. 72.

7. *Ibid.*, pp. 69–70.

8. *Ibid.*, pp. 73–74.

9. *Glasgow Herald*, 18 June 1832, p. 2d.

10. Sexton, *op. cit.*, p. 13.

11. *Ibid.*, p. 75. See also illustration '[f]rom an old print', p. 756.

12. McKenzie, *op. cit.*, pp. 393–94.

13. *Ibid.*, pp. 122–24.

14. Anon., *Inauguration of the statue of James Watt in connection with the Watt Institute and the Edinburgh School of Arts*, Edinburgh, Sutherland & Knox, 1854.

15. George Williamson, *Letters Respecting the Watt Family*, Greenock, G. Williamson, 1840, pp. 40–43.

16. 'Literary treasures at Scotland's oldest subscription library', *Greenock Telegraph*, 27 April 1964, p. 3.

17. 'Argus' and the James Watt Monument Scheme', *Greenock Telegraph*, 24 October 1881, p. 4b.

18. 'Carnegie Watt Memorial Scheme. Meeting in Greenock To-Day', *Greenock Telegraph*, 5 January 1903.

19. Andrew Carnegie, *James Watt*, Edinburgh and London, Oliphant Anderson & Ferrier, 1905.

20. 'The Proposed Watt Memorial', *Greenock Telegraph*, 11 September 1903, p. 2d.

21. 'The Watt Statue on Memorial Building', *Greenock Telegraph*, 1 June 1908, p. 2e-f.

22. Correspondence with Rowan Julia Brown, National Museums of Scotland, 9 June 2006.

23. Charles McKean, David Walker and Frank Walker, *Central Glasgow: an illustrated architectural guide*, Edinburgh, RIAS, p. 152.

24. McKenzie, *op. cit.*, pp. 107–09.

25. James Lauder, *The Glasgow Athenæum: a sketch of fifty years' work, 1847–1897*, Glasgow, St Mungo's Press, 1897, p. 7.

26. *Glasgow Athenæm. First Soiree*, printed handbill, 28 December 1847, inserted in *ibid.*, between p. 17 & p. 18.

27. McKenzie, *op. cit.*, pp. 305–06.

28. *Ibid.*, p. 90. It is worth noting that although the present building was erected in 1889, the college itself is descended from the medical faculty of the Andersonian Institute, mentioned above in connection with the Mechanics' Institute.

29. David Rowand, *Golden Threads*, Paisley, *Paisley Daily Express*, 1999, pp. 101–03.

30. Paisley Central Library, *School Log Book, 1887–1908* (Ferguslie Half-Timers' School), p. 225.

31. 'Brown Society', *Greenock Advertiser*, 24 April 1860, p. 2e.

32. 'Artist on Tombstone', *Greenock Telegraph*, 19 September 1978, p. 5d-e.

33. McKenzie, *op. cit.*, p. 155.

34. *Building News*, 4 September 1874, p. 300a.

35. City Art Gallery, Dundee. The statuette is 60cm high.

36. G. M. Fraser, 'William and Alexander Brodie, Sculptors', *Scottish Notes and Queries*, vol. 1, 3rd series, January 1923, p. 8. It is worth noting that Brodie began his artistic training at the Aberdeen Mechanics' Institute (*ibid.*, p. 5).

37. *Ibid.*, pp. 139–40; see also Sexton, *op. cit.*, pp. 41–45. Kelly provided the funds for erecting Brodie's statue of Graham, as well as John Mossman's *Monument to David Livingstone* (1879), which was also originally in George Square.

15

Living City: An Experiment in Urban Design Education

Les Hooper and Peter Boyle

Brisbane is a sub-tropical city in the south-east corner of a state experiencing rapid urban growth. Predictions of a 200 kilometre conurbation stretching north and south of the city are rapidly being realized, and along with growth come huge challenges for planning, management of resources and provision of imaginative, equitably shared urban spaces.

For the first time in human history more than half of the global population is estimated to live in cities. Future cities may continue to nurture creativity and civilised human interaction, or be overwhelmed by inequity, unplanned growth and alienation of public space. Investigating the urban environment, and building critical literacy about planning, public design and public space, seems, therefore, urgent and legitimate goals for education.

Living City is an attempt to create a programme that builds awareness of urban environments while at the same giving a voice to the younger communities who use, consume, share and take pleasure in the city. It is an educational experiment on a relatively modest scale but with important implications, we hope to show, for visual arts pedagogy. The *Living City* planning team of three, Genevieve Searle, Peter Boyle and Les Hooper, has managed to sustain the project over seven years from the inaugural event at the 1999 InSEA Congress.[1] Each event is themed on an active urban development, and withdraws student participants from regular classes to spend three days of intensive on-site workshopping and inquiry into the challenges of the target site, and into the wider themes of sustainability, ownership, cultural values and contested city visions.

While each workshop builds dialogue with expert designers and stakeholders, it also seeks to give voice to young peoples' ideas about the way they experience the city, and to represent their ideas to developers and decision-makers. Hence the empowerment of future citizens is a

Site mapping during the 2006 Watershed event at Brisbane's Howard Smith Wharves. *Photograph by Hamish Lancaster*

Watershed workshop. *Photograph by Peter Boyle*

Brisbane City from the air. *Photograph by Richard Brecknock*

Mentor and group at work. *Photograph by Hamish Lancaster*

key, if implicit, goal of the programme. Partly for this reason, and partly because the *Living City* constituency is drawn from visual art students, each event includes artists' residencies that explore the 'poetic' layers of city experience, and encourage students to express responses that are nuanced and individual as well as collective.

The *Living City* project is also very much the story of a partnership, a partnership of diverse interests but shared vision among the three core members of the planning team. We have invested considerable energy in sustaining this partnership and through these efforts many others – professionals, educators, artists – have been drawn into the orbit of particular events, and have invested in one way or another (not least financially) in its continuation and growth. More about partnerships later. We will begin with the designer's perspective of the programme and what he sees as its benefits, not only for the student participants and the wider community, but for the other designers and mentors who bring the authority of their professional knowledge and practice to the discussion.

The designer and mentor's perspective

The primary focus of the *Living City* programme is not to teach design, architecture, urban design, town planning, landscape architecture or art, but to crystallize experiences and insights that already exist among the students and can be drawn out through debate and discussion.

In this setting, professionals are able to share insights into their own way of working, their approach to design or a site of interest, or their ways of identifying and dealing with challenges and opportunities that ensue from their understanding of a site. They can offer different ways of looking at a site that lie outside of the experience of the average young person. These may be drawn from principles, practices or techniques from their own professions, but may also derive from experiences they have had through interaction with various stakeholder groups or individuals within the broader community, for example, developers, people with disabilities, unemployed people and business owners.

Since the *Living City* programme tends to deal with sites and projects that are significant in the public realm, it is also important to introduce the concept that the community may be viewed as a 'client' – the stakeholder group as the ultimate end-user of the project. Student participants engage with this idea not only as an important group within the community, but also as potential advocates for other sectors of the community. The latter may be inspired by the communication of related experience by mentors or by direct discussion with representatives of the 'community' invited into workshops.

While participants have the opportunity to take on board information provided by professional and community mentors in the exploration of ideas for a site under study, the programme critically emphasises the need for students to engage in the exploration of their own ideas and to find their own voices.

Team presentation at Watershed 2006. *Photograph by Peter Boyle*

Presenting team designs at Watershed, 2006. *Photograph by Peter Boyle*

Presenting team designs at Watershed, 2006. Photograph by Peter Boyle

Pitching a 'Carnival' concept at Watershed 2006. *Photograph by Peter Boyle*

The studio setting of each *Living City* workshop provides a platform for participants – students, design professionals, artists, teachers and community representatives – to communicate and share their own experiences and their own views on the project at hand. In this milieu, there is potential to develop an understanding of different kinds of knowledge, including technical, scientific, local and personal, with no particular form of knowledge privileged over the other.

Collective knowledge and input often manifest themselves not in the initial ideas put forward, which come from individuals and groups, but in the way they are developed, connected with other ideas and communicated, both graphically and orally.

The contribution of diverse 'knowledge' allows for the possibility for it to be discussed and challenged, hopefully understood in the context of the project or, at the very least, mutually respected by the group.

The programme not only stimulates the student participants to seek their own voices and negotiate their own visions for a future for a particular site or their city, it also forces the design professionals involved to acknowledge 'other' experience and input. This may challenge their own form of knowledge to some degree, but it also provides a great opportunity to understand the community they ultimately design for, and offers the potential for that understanding to enrich their own design processes.

The educators' perspective: *Living City*, pedagogy and visual art

This chapter is framed by the different perspectives of its co-planners. The designer's discussion of the intrinsic value of the programme, and his assertion that it is not primarily about the education of students in built design or any of the specific disciplines he enumerates, moves us on to considering its wider implications for pedagogy. I hope this will allow me to show that the programme's value resides partly in its resistance to some of the qualities and norms of the conventional educational experience. As an art teacher I also like to think that our way of dealing with student knowledge and creativity has something to offer in the search for new learning approaches. I believe that the central challenge in most of our projects – responding to complex multi-faceted problems in the real world that require discussion and debate across multiple fields of knowledge – sits well within a particular curriculum framework known, in this part of the world at least, as the 'New Basics'.[2] Hopefully, I can draw some of these threads together through this discussion.

Firstly, what is the educational power of the event for students? How can it be measured when, as I have pointed out, it lies outside normal curriculum and assessment? We have had seven years to think about this question, and while we haven't had the resources for any detailed study of the impact of the programme, the subsequent tertiary and professional pathways of participants and feedback from student surveys indicate that for many it is a formative and inspiring experience. Although anecdotal evidence is unscientific, one bus conversation on the way back from the city with a student who had just finished her first day of workshops was revealing: '*This is so different, I loved every minute of it. For the first time in my life I know what I want to do when I leave school.*'

The question of evaluation of programmes like *Living City* is a bit of a distraction of course. Not all valid educational experiences need to be assessed in the ways that individual disciplines presently require or demand. There is, moreover, a move in our State of Queensland to re-frame exit statements of student achievement to include a wider range of valid information, reflecting, for example, participation in enrichment programmes or contribution to community events. Student knowledge and experience gained through the programme could also be readily quantified through the assessment of mainstream subjects, or through independent senior projects undertaken by the students (and even required through programmes such as the International Baccalaureate). In the Queensland context it is something of an anomaly that these more flexible models of certification for students exiting at year 12 sit side by side with much more intensive testing regimes in the 'core curriculum' for students in the junior and middle schools.

Assuming for the moment that the event and the experience is authentic, valid and powerful, what can visual arts educators take out of it with respect to curriculum design and leadership within their schools?

Essentially the pedagogical and practical challenges of visual arts are strongly linked. Without strong representation in schools the arts will weaken over time in favour of a more aggressive or fashionable curriculum with fewer resourcing issues. The challenge for visual arts is to maintain relevance and attract excellent students while persuading school planners and parents to view their subject offerings as intellectually challenging. Pressures building within the 'back to basics' debate are re-marginalizing visual arts, and visual arts educators need to continue to build diverse and challenging curriculum experiences as a response to this dynamic.

After seven years of the programme, involving some 250 student participants from around 30 schools, we have developed some confidence in the impact of both the programme and the model. I will now outline some of the reasons why I feel the *Living City* model has the potential to inject new energy into the visual arts curriculum.

First, however, some of the familiar arguments against the model: that it is a 'tacked on' experience; that it is not embedded in the visual arts curriculum; that, as it is based on withdrawal of students on a volunteer or self-nominating basis, it deals only with elite students and would not succeed in the 'normal' classroom environment; that it does not contribute to formal assessment; that the logistics of sustaining networks and partners is too difficult; that cross-curriculum or rich learning experiments are impractical if not supported structurally; and, finally, that the core of visual arts education is imaginative and creative individual production, not cross-curriculum, team-based projects.

Without answering all these objections, some of which are valid, I would argue that we have responded to many of them through the actual practice of the programme over its seven years. I can also frame a more general response in two ways. Firstly, through two rhetorical questions: Can the visual arts curriculum afford not to innovate and experiment? Can it afford not to lead curriculum and structural change if the alternative is subservience to other models and other curriculum agendas? And, secondly, by challenging the claim that art students would not respond to cross-curriculum design or team-based projects. Certainly visual art provides a space in the curriculum where students have the greatest

On the workshop trail at Howard Smith Wharves. *Photograph by Hamish Lancaster*

Walking through the site. *Photograph by Hamish Lancaster*

freedom to explore issues of individual identity and destiny. It can also, however, be the time and the place where they measure their identity against communal culture and the wider web of human relations. We in art departments may believe that art education is all about uniquely creative individual and personal expression, but perhaps we need to focus just as sharply on the public realm and shared meanings as senior students move with increasing confidence from private expression to public debate and contested visions.

So what does this programme offer as a model to visual arts educators fighting for their place in the sun? Firstly, it is a model for the power of partnerships. The students who are involved in the programme are engaged with real-life issues of complexity and urgency, and their discussion is framed by the professionals and the stakeholders who will contribute to decision-making. The *Living City* partners are not teachers trying to work through curriculum content, but passionate voices for alternative visions of the city. The project outcomes developed in design teams are respected at the level of ideas, and may be reflected in the decision-making in active developments, not graded and forgotten.

Secondly, the very fact that the project transcends curriculum boundaries is an opportunity for the visual arts to show curriculum leadership. The arts are often relegated to supporting roles in curriculum projects; it is important to demonstrate to the learning community that there are qualities of creative thinking and visual awareness that will inform an approach to the built environment, for example, or to design in the public realm, and that will enrich the perspectives of other disciplines.

Thirdly, there is an opportunity through the programme to rescue the much abused and hijacked curriculum domain of 'design' from other areas, including Information Technology, the Social Sciences, and the Manual Arts, and to make rich design education an essential part of the curriculum mix within or alongside visual art education. Design education brings with it the opportunity to seriously explore new modes of work and assessment – team projects, professional mentorships and placements for young designers, oral presentations and team charettes.

In this context, I'll briefly refer to two observations from the draft report of the National Review of Visual Education developed for the Australian Government by Murdoch University. The report first suggests that while young people are highly sophisticated users and consumers of technology, their mastery is not often matched by high-order critical literacy or awareness:

> *The digitised production of high quality multi-modal images has made positions in music, cinema and the graphic arts accessible to young people who possess only vernacular levels of technical skill in these disciplines. Equally, young employees across many fields are required to capture images and design presentations in which the skill and the technology used is high, but the ethical, aesthetic and communicative judgment is correspondingly banal.*[3]

The report goes on to suggest that where 'design' education is devolved to empirical curriculum models, students may miss opportunities for deeper engagement with design thinking:

Design is increasingly more associated with design practices and valued for its vocational ends rather than for its hermeneutic value and its unique thinking processes. Design in visual education curriculum and current educational practices needs to be reexamined within the current debates around vocational education, aesthetic understandings, historical, contemporary and cultural design and arts practice.[4]

Design and design 'process' are frequently appropriated with limited understanding by curriculum areas outside the arts, and, therefore, the arts should actively advocate for design thinking and explain and reclaim design as a unique way of seeing, rather than a one-dimensional methodology. And if the 'aesthetic, ethical and communicative judgment'(s) exhibited by young people are 'banal', where better to hone critical thinking than an immersion event incorporating high-level design thinking and evaluation of the consequences of design decisions?

Fourthly, there is the opportunity, demonstrated in the *Living City* experience over seven years, to gradually build relationships – with the design and built environment faculties of universities for example – and to build networks across schools and with professional associations. Partnerships in these areas are always empowering for staff and students and help persuade school administrations that the visual arts provide clear tertiary and professional pathways for students.

Finally, in this brief assessment of opportunities, there is the ready transferability of the model to other curriculum contexts. In Kelvin Grove State College middle school, for example, visual arts leads a cross-curriculum team to deliver one of the year eight 'rich tasks' concerned with designing a structure in the built environment. For the past two years, our neighbouring university, the Queensland University of Technology, has hosted three-day workshops for the whole year-eight cohort at Kelvin Grove State College (200 students) and for specially selected excellence students, in which they are able to work with industry mentors to design structures and present design concepts to panels of professionals. Through the success of these events, QUT has committed to supporting the programme into the future. Visual arts faculties in several other schools participating in the programme have also integrated the model into group projects or encouraged participating students to present team concepts to professional panels.

This is probably the moment to return to the notion of the 'New Basics' curriculum and why it makes a good fit with the kind of learning offered in the *Living City* programme. The New Basics curriculum sets out a series of rich tasks for students progressing through the middle school, including the built environment task outlined above, that share a problem-based, cross-curriculum focus. New Basics itself as a curriculum idea evolved out of an investigation of, among other things, our competitive advantage in the knowledge economy, and the perception that traditional curriculum frameworks were beginning to fail students preparing for a world of rapidly changing knowledge priorities. It proposed and prioritized a set of learning elements or 'productive pedagogies' that were intended to raise the level of critical thinking, communication and connectedness to real world issues. Naturally it is an experiment that continues to evolve and, in the case of Queensland schools, is becoming enmeshed with more traditional curriculum approaches. It has, however, offered many schools (and universities) a platform for new thinking about curriculum structures. Its rethinking of the middle school curriculum has been succeeded by a review of secondary curriculum in Queensland[5] that seeks to set out new overarching knowledge 'domains' (including, interestingly, design) that encompass traditional disciplines and, once again, address priorities in future education. The idea appears to be, on the one hand, to thin out a curriculum that has become crowded with a complicated array of subject offerings that differ markedly in quality and, on the other, to encourage schools to offer subject groups that help students make connections across knowledge areas, and that once again create opportunities for cross-curriculum learning and the construction of independent projects in the final years of schooling.

In this context, it seems to me, *Living City* offers a model for the kind of learning that innovative schools are engaging with. It certainly gave me the confidence to develop the collaborative project in urban design for year-eight students that took them from their familiar schooling environment to round-table workshops with engineers, planners and architects, and that had them confidently communicating their design concepts to expert panels in the space of just a couple of days.

I would like to conclude with some thoughts on the power of partnerships. Partnerships are about networks that enlarge understanding, about meetings with professionals and stakeholders in other disciplines that take individuals out of their comfort zone and challenge established assumptions. As such, they are of enormous value in personal and professional growth. They are also quite difficult to maintain over the long term and very demanding of time and energy, as involvement in them often leads to ever heavier professional commitments. The three co-planners have sustained our event by personal commitment to the integrity of the idea, but as the event has developed, a network of government bodies, participating schools, tertiary educators, artists, professional designers and professional associations has grown to support and help develop it. This development has been the result partly of opportunities that have arisen as sites of interest become available, partly of the coincidence of interests of designers, educators and local government, and partly of a conscious effort on our part to push the event in new directions while maintaining a fairly simple process and scale. I feel that the effort to create and sustain partnerships and relationships outside, in my case, the immediate context of classroom teaching has been personally enriching and given me both a wider range of tools for teaching and a wider perspective on pedagogy.

Earlier in the chapter, I undertook to frame my contribution to the project through visual arts pedagogy and curriculum. I hope I have shown why I think the visual arts curriculum needs to demonstrate leadership in cross-curriculum inquiry and why I think the city, our focus, has a place in such inquiry. It is a big enough theme to accommodate any number of approaches and curriculum frames, but the imaginative sensibility has always been central to a critique of where we have been and where we are going, and this seems more than appropriate in a world where we all run the risk of living in someone else's city or being excluded from a creative city future through a failure of imagination.

Future

For each event we have generated considerable documentation and resources, including videos, CD-ROMs, exhibitions and educational materials, mainly disseminated to participating schools. We have now established a Web presence for the project[6] with the intention of drawing together its thematic threads, documenting past events, developing resources accessible to a wider community and educational audience and inviting further interaction, particularly from young people.

Responding to the design challenges: teams draw their concepts on site at Howard Smith Wharves. *Photograph by Hamish Lancaster*

udio drawing process at Watershed. *Photograph by Peter Boyle*

Teams at work – mapping responses to the site. *Photograph by Peter Boyle*

The Living City program explores the ways in which young people relate to the city. They don't have to be an "expert" designer or prospective architect or town planner but need to be curious about how cities work and what makes particular spaces interesting, and to think about fresh, creative ways of making and using city spaces.

Brisbane/Ljubljana student photos/messages

LIVING CITY

home >   intro >   lc past >   lc next >   link >   interact >

LIVING CITY LIVING CITY LIVING CITY LIVING CITY LIVING CITY LIVING CITY

Home page of the *Living City* web site. Peter Boyle, Verge Urban Landscape Architecture Pty Ltd

Notes and references

Living City co-planners: Les Hooper, Head of Visual Art, Kelvin Grove State College; Peter Boyle, Co-Director, Verge Urban Landscape Architecture; Genevieve Searle, Public Art Officer, City Planning, Brisbane City Council; We are grateful to our co-planner, Genevieve Searle, for her energy, commitment and insights over the years.

1. The World Congress of the International Society for Education through Art was held in Brisbane in September 1999. *Living City* was first conceived as an event to engage secondary students with the Congress, and supported by international delegates including Dipak Lahiri of Sweden and Glen Coutts from Scotland.
2. The 'New Basics' was developed by a curriculum team in Education Queensland under the leadership of Dr Alan Luke through the late nineties and began to be implemented in some Queensland schools from around 2000. The New Basics attempts to identify the critical literacies and pedagogies that underpin education for the future and deliver them through a suite of 'rich tasks' to be undertaken by all students at junctures through the junior and middle phase of learning (yrs 1–9). All rich tasks require an interdisciplinary learning approach, and were to be co-planned and delivered across different subject disciplines. The New Basics has co-existed with an outcomes-based curriculum model maintained in most schools since 2000 and is to some extent being merged with the mainstream through a new assessment and reporting framework for yrs 1–9, QCAR (Queensland Curriculum, Assessment and Reporting) being introduced in 2007/8. http://www.qsa.qld.edu.au/qcar/index.html (accessed 5th May 2007).
3. Stankievicz, M. (2004). *Quoted in: National Review of Education in Visual Arts, Craft, Design and Visual Communication*, pp. 88–91. Centre for Learning Change and Development (CLCD), Murdoch University, Western Australia.
4. *National Review of Education in Visual Arts, Craft, Design and Visual Communication*. Centre for Learning Change and Development (CLCD), Western Australia: Murdoch University, p. 3.
5. The review of Senior Schooling in Queensland is currently being undertaken by the Queensland Studies Authority, a statutory body reporting to the Queensland Government. The review sets out to reform the curriculum framework for the senior years of schooling. Among other things the review recommends that the existing range of senior subjects be re-organized into around fifteen learning domains. This would, in the present draft, position Visual Arts in a domain with subjects such as Media, Home Economics, Engineering and Technology. Http://www.qsa.qld.edu.au/syllabus_review/index.html (accessed 5th May 2007).
6. See: http://www.livingcity.net.au/ (accessed 5th May 2007).

16

Using Multimedia to Teach Young People about Public Art in Glasgow

Glen Coutts

It would be a misinterpretation to assume that the CD-ROM *Scanning the City*[1] is a simple catalogue of public art and built structures in the city of Glasgow, since the dynamic of any cityscape is infused as much by social archaeology and anthropology as it is by architectural constituents.

The precise remit placed on the writer and his team was to create a framework that could be interrogated by school students in the age range 10–14, and the design features had to be customized to the needs of that particular client group. However, the author will suggest that there are a number of alternative, perhaps more specialized, lines of interrogation that could be addressed with regard to the visual data and text contained on the CD-ROM. For instance, undergraduate students of community arts are using the publication as part of their own research into public art practice. Creating a body of data without an interrogative framework would have resulted in a mere index that ignored the central requirement of the commission to stimulate discourse relating to the metaphysical as well as the physical terrain. The title *Scanning the City* was selected to evoke both an overview of the range of public art and urban design within the city boundary, and to suggest more of a rigorous analysis of public art and urban space. Public art in Glasgow can act as metaphors of the city's imperial and industrial past and its, possibly, ephemeral present and as an indicator of its future.

The last decade of the twentieth century has seen the re-invention of Glasgow as a recognized City of Culture (1990) and a City of Architecture and Design (1999). During the intervening years, however, there has been uneven support for the arts in the city and, as Harding[2] pointed

The Gorbals Urban Trail, screenshot from *Scanning the City* [CDROM]. DEG@S, University of Strathclyde, Glasgow, design: Mark Dawes.

out, no clear policy for public art. Perhaps there has been even less of a policy for community arts, which transfers the locus of discourse and empowerment over the built environment to the citizenry.

It is hoped that the design of the CD-ROM will offer such empowerment and act as a template for similar lines of enquiry in other cities by challenging the notion that public art or interventions by artists are neutral objects and events rather than cultural resonators in the narrative life of a city. Defining and assessing the resonance of particular items of public art is the central impulse that informs the interactive possibilities contained in *Scanning the City*. The software affords opportunities for users (who might as legitimately be tourists to the city as school students living within the city) to negotiate their way around the urban terrain graphically and culturally.

Design of the software

The first priority in the design framework of *Scanning the City* was to make a multimedia record of what public art and urban design existed within the city boundaries. The second priority was to locate and differentiate distinctive sectors in terms of a more precise urban geography. This gave rise to the central 'chapter' in the software entitled 'Urban Trails'. The electronic text is not a definitive account of public art in the city because of the resources and timescale of the project. Instead, the CD-ROM sets out to stimulate debate about public art.

A rich heritage of cultural activity, particularly public art, surrounds students in Glasgow schools, but is there a place for exploration of that heritage in the crowded curriculum in Scottish schools? *Scanning the City* seeks to engage the young people of Glasgow in active debate about the role of artists working in urban spaces and the Scottish National Guidelines applaud such activity.

> *Pupils should increase their understanding and appreciation of technical processes of the past, of other cultures, and of those required for the future. This can be supported by research, viewing electronic and printed media, practical experiments and demonstration.*[3]

Over the last decade, the writer has been involved in numerous public and community art projects with undergraduate and postgraduate students and this experience suggests that public art and built environment education has real potential for learning in a variety of contexts and across subject disciplines. In one particular undergraduate project, which provided impetus for the CD-ROM, students in three city schools (aged between 11 and 14 years) examined street furniture and formulated alternative designs as reported by Coutts and Dawes.[4] Parallel to this work, the writer had been developing a CD-ROM for students to engage in an interactive examination of artists' work in the classroom.[5] The sharp perceptions and enthusiasm of the young students involved in both projects helped crystallize the proposal to undertake a larger scale study that eventually resulted in the multimedia essay now discussed here.

The 'Armadillo', Concert and Conference Centre, the Clyde Auditorium. *Photograph by Brian Lochrin*

Theoretical underpinning

Although it is not the aim of *Scanning the City* to explicitly interrogate the city in terms of its social history or urban geography, the images, text and video sequences within each urban trail afford those alternative lines of enquiry. The city as a living and changing organism is implicitly addressed through a focus on the ways in which different elements of each urban trail have, through time, accreted formal and informal public art. In the Clydeside and Govan Urban Trail, for instance, Norman Foster's concert and conference centre (known locally as the 'Armadillo') is situated near to where the Finnieston crane used to load locomotives for export, thus, demonstrating how Glasgow's changing employment patterns and lifestyles have impacted on the urban landscape.

Exploration of the role of artists in a public context is contained throughout the CD-ROM at a level consistent with the curriculum requirements for the age group. *Scanning the City* is currently being used in Scottish schools and initial feedback has shown the design to be appropriate for the intended target group and effective in the purpose it was created for. The narrative of the electronic text explores many of the themes relating to public art and built environment education examined in the writings of Adams and Ward,[6] Adams[7] and Harding.[8] Issues raised by these writers informed the development of *Scanning the City* in the sense that the user is encouraged to reflect on the variety of interventions made by artists in the built environment. The eclectic selection of public artworks in each urban trail or case study in the 'Public Art Catalogue' creates opportunities for teachers to engage school students in debate about the role and function of public art in Glasgow. Undergraduate students using the software are currently comparing and contrasting a variety of artists' methods of operating in the built environment context.

Teachers and student-teachers are exploring other questions with students in schools, for example:

- What are the critical factors impacting on an artist working in the public context?
- What do artists provide that is unique to the urban or built environment?
- What conditions maximize the learning and teaching benefits of artists working in a specific context?

The process of researching the CD-ROM by Dougall, Coutts and Dawes[9] convinced the team that the time is right for further investigation of the 'added value' that artists, particularly when working in collaboration with communities, bring to the built environment. It is hoped that after using *Scanning the City*, young people who live in the city, and visitors to the city, will 'field test' the trails offered in the software.

There are a number of interrelated research issues and themes resulting from this project. The research group, the *Digital Education Group at Strathclyde* (DEG@S), aims to further develop multimedia or Web-based work in the fields of art, technology and cultural theory. Recent curricular, social and political changes have affected both teachers and those who choose to work in public art. In 1999, for example, Scotland elected its first parliament in almost 300 years, and a consultative document[10] sought views on a Cultural Strategy for Scotland.

The Clydeside and Govan Urban Trail, screenshot from *Scanning the City* [CDROM[. DEG@S, University of Strathclyde, Glasgow, design: Mark Dawes.

During the same period a consultation exercise was carried out on developing a policy for architecture.[11] Both of the consultation documents laid a strong emphasis on education and the role of schools in promoting cultural awareness amongst Scotland's young people.

Scotland's culture will help to broaden horizons and encourage the creative impulse in our schools and colleges. Scotland's culture can provide an opportunity for everyone to be involved in the life of his or her community. Scotland's culture can be the seedbed for new ideas and expressions of creativity that can form the foundations for the development of new artforms and creative industries.[12]

The opportunity to develop an understanding of the built environment should be part of the social and cultural education of all. It is the necessary basis for an active and effective involvement in the decisions and debate that help shape our built environment. Such involvement is an essential part of social participation and inclusion.[13]

In 1998, Her Majesty's Inspectors of Schools in Scotland published *Effective Learning and Teaching in Art and Design*.[14] Whilst recognizing the variety and quality of work in art and design in many schools, the document urged a more adventurous approach to the range of subject matter being offered for study. The report proposed that more use could be made of artists, art galleries and public and community art in helping young people to understand the very significant role played by artists and designers in society. The report also recognized the growing role played by information technology in education:

A good number of departments use slides, videos, films and computer-generated images effectively as an integral part of teaching critical and historical studies and as a stimulus for expressive and design studies.[15]

The work of Adams,[16-17] and Harding[18] on public art and built-environment education, together with that of Swift and Steers[19] in mainstream art education, inform and underpin research through critical examination of the formal sector in art, design and environment education. *Scanning the City* seeks to present public art and urban design in a manner that is accessible to young people and will encourage them to think about the multitude of ways that artists interact with the built environment. In addition, the software has been designed in a non-prescriptive way that will allow teachers to interpret the themes and projects in the manner best suited to their own professional context.

Collaborative projects on the theme of art and the built environment, such as that conducted by Coutts and Dawes[20] in Scotland, explore the interface between the informal and formal sectors in art and environment education. However, learning and teaching in the informal sector has not, as yet, been subject to the kind of rigorous analysis and testing seen in the formal sector. Public art practice often crosses the boundaries between these sectors of education, suggesting the need for more formal research into this interface.

VIDEO: What Is Public Art & Urban Design ?

In this video, Ricardo Marini, David Harding & Eileen Adams discuss public art & urban design.

95

CARD
TEXT
MENU

STOP

Expert Witnesses, screenshot from *Scanning the City* [CDROM]. DEG@S, University of Strathclyde, Glasgow, design: Mark Dawes.

The National Curriculum in England and Wales,[21] the National Guidelines for Expressive Arts 5–14[22] and the HMI[23] in Scotland promote rigorous planning and review by practitioners. A central theme in each curriculum is the aspiration to integrate what Robinson referred to as 'Doing and Making' with 'Reflecting and Responding'.[24]

During the study several 'expert witnesses', artists, planners and academics, were interviewed and a number of case studies in the form of commentaries and videos were included to illuminate practice in the field. Promoting discussion and debate of traditional and innovative public art practice in schools and other, more informal, educational situations is a prime objective of *Scanning the City*.

> *The teacher should encourage greater independence in studying artists and designers, and offer pupils a wider range of sources and reference material from which to choose. Studies should include some consideration of social, environmental and economic factors.*[25]

Content, structure and interface

In Scotland, as in many countries throughout the world, the curriculum in schools has been subject to review. In Scottish art and design education, students and teachers are obliged to engage in 'Critical Activity' or 'Evaluating and Appreciating'. It is this writer's view that the role of artists and designers in society, particularly those who choose to work in public art, could usefully be given more prominence in the art curriculum and elsewhere at a number of levels. The electronic text addresses this issue by linking the discursive content with activities designed to stimulate debate. However, the writer does not underestimate the pressures on teachers to accommodate an increasing range of demands. In an occasional paper for the Scottish Consultative Council for the Curriculum, Tombs wrote of the problems and potential of the built environment as a learning resource across the curriculum:

> *It is easy to dismiss the challenge of ... our built environment as impossibly wide-ranging, and therefore ... adding yet another burden to an already overcrowded curriculum. A greater understanding of the built environment need not be regarded as a stand-alone element of the curriculum. Rather, it is a theme that can connect with other subject areas. The buildings and the built environment that surrounds us should be seen as a readily accessible resource that can assist in the study of history, geography, modern studies, science and technology, religious and moral education, the expressive arts, maths and languages.*[26]

Users have reported that the CD-ROM has a broad appeal in terms of being visually rich with appropriate text. *Scanning the City* features over 700 high-quality photographs, approximately one hour of video, several 'QuickTime Virtual Reality' experiences and short essays on public art. The software sets out to enthuse children and adults through an examination of the City of Glasgow as a site of world-class architecture and public art and urban design.

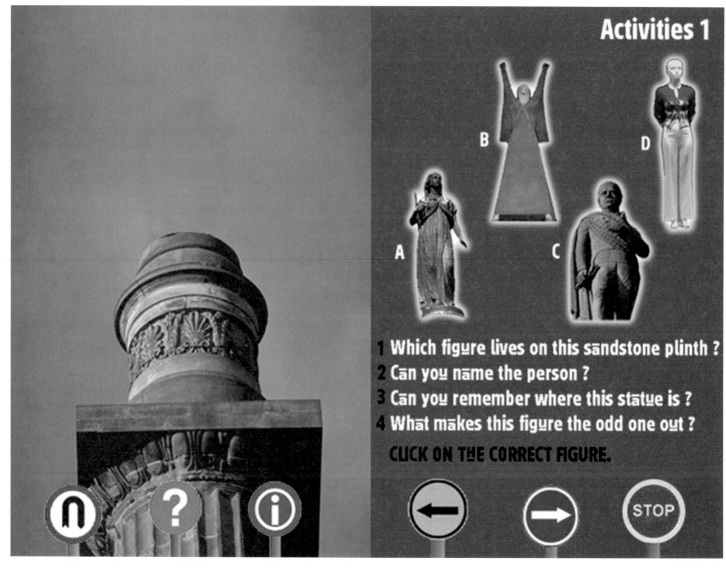

Activities Screen, screenshot from *Scanning the City* [CDROM]. DEG@S, University of Strathclyde, Glasgow, design: Mark Dawes.

The publication contains four interactive sections: the Urban Trails; the Public Art Catalogue; the Forum; and Activities for the Classroom. It includes 'traditional forms' such as public monuments, but also explores new practices such as temporary interventions, street performances and young people working with artists to make public artworks.

Contrasts are evident between the urban trails, for instance, in the 'Woodlands' and the 'Merchant City' trails. In the mainly residential area of Woodlands, Karina Young worked with young children on the 'Bollards' project. In the Merchant City area, by contrast, Shona Kinloch, Alexander Stoddart and Jack Sloan contributed to the redevelopment of the Italian Centre in the commercial heart of the city in partnership with architects and city planners.

Using the CD-ROM

Scanning the City is intended for use by students in schools with a minimum of teacher assistance. The navigation of the CD-ROM has been designed principally with a 10–14 age group in mind, because this is the age group that crosses the two main stages of schooling in Scotland, Primary (ages 5–12) and Secondary (ages 12–18). *Scanning the City* illustrates, as a possible model for replication in other cities, the range of interactive possibilities available by taking a virtual tour of one's own city.

The CD-ROM allows the user to simulate a walk through parts of the city, following the 'Urban Trails'. A map of the trail, once explored on screen, can be printed out and the user is then able to 'field test' the trail. The software does not seek to replace the experience of looking at public art on site. Rather, it aims to raise awareness, encourage debate and deepen understanding and appreciation of public art through virtual and, hopefully, actual contact.

In the 'Public Art Catalogue' public art is presented in the form of case studies. This section of *Scanning the City* enables the user to explore the ways artists impact on the built environment through succinct, informative video sequences and texts about artists and public art projects. This approach was felt to be most appropriate given the age group aimed at, although a wider audience including community groups, postgraduate and undergraduate students have begun to use the software for a variety of purposes beyond the original remit of the commission. The 'Public Art Catalogue' section of the software contains 38 such case studies ranging from large-scale graffiti and mosaic works to temporary projected interventions.

Many artists have used architectural or industrial 'markers' to make a statement about the city's industrial past. One example of an artist drawing on the city's industrial heritage and making such a statement is the Straw Locomotive by George Wyllie. In this sense, *Scanning the City* is a historical document, as the Straw Locomotive no longer exists. On the other hand, Andrew Scott's *Heavy Horse* at the entrance to Glasgow's business park in the East of the city is another, more permanent, example, which reflects the city's industrial heritage.

Bollards Project, screenshot from *Scanning the City* [CDROM]. DEG@S, University of Strathclyde, Glasgow, design: Mark Dawes.

The Merchant City Urban Trail, screenshot from *Scanning the City* [CDROM]. DEG@S, University of Strathclyde, Glasgow, design: Mark Dawes.

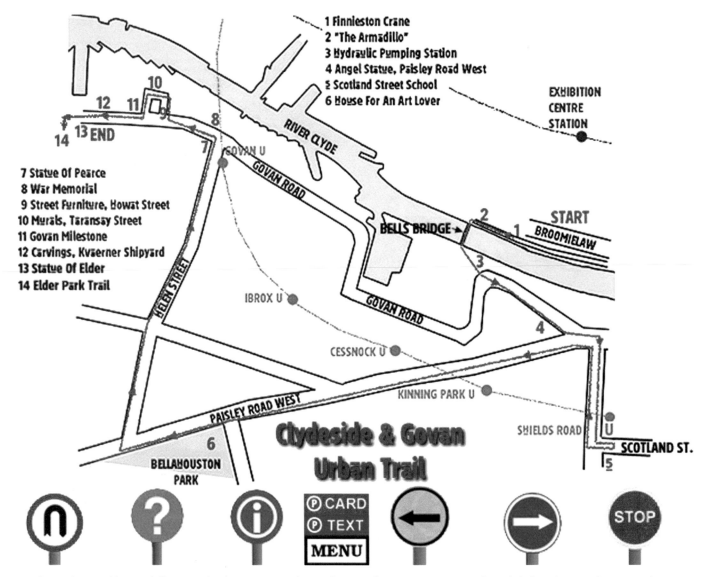

1 Finnieston Crane
2 "The Armadillo"
3 Hydraulic Pumping Station
4 Angel Statue, Paisley Road West
5 Scotland Street School
6 House For An Art Lover

7 Statue Of Pearce
8 War Memorial
9 Street Furniture, Howat Street
10 Murals, Taransay Street
11 Govan Milestone
12 Carvings, Kvaerner Shipyard
13 Statue Of Elder
14 Elder Park Trail

EXHIBITION CENTRE STATION

RIVER CLYDE

GOVAN U

GOVAN ROAD

BELLS BRIDGE →

START
BROOMIELAW

GOVAN ROAD

IBROX U

HELEN STREET

CESSNOCK U

KINNING PARK U

PAISLEY ROAD WEST

SHIELDS ROAD

SCOTLAND ST.

Clydeside & Govan Urban Trail

6

BELLAHOUSTON PARK

END

CARD
TEXT
MENU

STOP

Map of an *Urban Trail* (Garnethill), screenshot from *Scanning the City* [CDROM]. DEG@S, University of Strathclyde, Glasgow, design: Mark Dawes.

Conclusion

The current political impulse towards social inclusion creates the need for the next generation of citizens to be aware of how the physical shape of their city conditions their lives and opens up a dialogue between the artist, the artisan, the contractor, the critic and the citizen. This project is one attempt to synthesize the needs of those involved in designing public art and those who will live with the results in order that the school pupils, who will be the citizens of tomorrow, feel able to play a full and vibrant part in the development and care of their city.

This paper has reported on 'work in progress' and the publication of *Scanning the City*. It is hoped that *Scanning the City* will initiate debate and bring about greater understanding in schools and community groups, which will allow the diversity of public art practice in Glasgow to be more fully documented, and, perhaps, principles of good practice to be extrapolated. In the writer's view, both traditional and digital publications such as CD-ROM or web pages are appropriate media to stimulate discussion on public art, but they are only further tools which, to be really effective, rely on the skills and knowledge of the teacher in the classroom. The CD-ROM is specifically directed at the citizens of tomorrow, and the writer hopes that the design is worthy of interrogation in terms of a wider set of cultural and aesthetic imperatives.

Project team

The Glasgow-based artist and writer Mark Dawes was the researcher for the project. Glen Coutts and Mark Dawes reported on a project to introduce young people in Glasgow schools to public art, and the current paper is one development arising from that project. See Coutts, G. & Dawes, M. [1998]. Drawing in the Artist Outside: Towards 1999, *Journal of Art & Design Education*. Vol. 17. No. 2, pp. 191–196. The CD-ROM *Scanning the City* research and development team: research, authoring and screens designed by Mark Dawes, still photography by Brian Lochrin, video photography by Rob Welsh, sound engineering by Donnie Borland and academic supervision by Paul Dougall and Glen Coutts.

A version of this chapter was published in *The International Journal of Art and Design Education*. Vol. 19. No. 3.

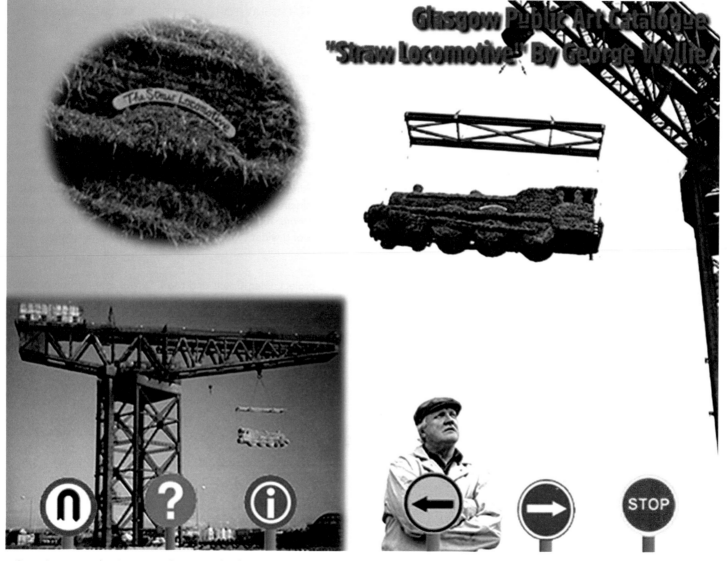

Straw Locomotive by George Wylie, screenshot from *Scanning the City* [CDROM]. DEG@S, University of Strathclyde, Glasgow, design: Mark Dawes.

The Heavy Horse by Andrew Scott. Photograph by Brian Lochrin

Notes

1. Dougall, P., Coutts G. and Dawes, M (1999). *Scanning the City*, Glasgow 1999 and University of Strathclyde (CD-ROM).

2. Harding, D (1997a). The Ill Clad City: Glasgow turns its back on Public Art, *Journal of Art & Design Education*, vol. 16, no. 2, pp. 95–104.

3. Scottish Executive (1999). *Curriculum and Assessment in Scotland, National Guidelines, Expressive Arts; Art and Design*, level F, SEED, Edinburgh, p. 6.

4. Coutts, G., & Dawes, M (1998). Drawing in the Artist Outside: Towards 1999, *Journal of Art & Design Education*, vol. 17, no. 2, p. 192.

5. Coutts, G., Hart, D. A., & Young, M (1998). *Looking at Art*, (CD-ROM), University of Strathclyde, Glasgow.

6. Adams, E., and Ward, C (1982). *Art and the Built Environment: a Teacher's Approach*, Harlow: Longman.

7. Adams, E (1997). *Public Art: People, Projects, Process*. London: London Arts Board.

8. Harding, D., and Buchler, P (Eds.). (1997b). *Decadent; Public Art: Contentious Term and Contested Practice*. Glasgow: Foulis Press.

9. Dougall, P., Coutts, G. & Dawes, M *op. cit.*

10. Scottish Executive (1999a). *A National Cultural Strategy*. Consultation Document. Edinburgh: Scottish Executive.

11. Scottish Executive (1999b). *The Development of a Policy on Architecture for Scotland*. Consultation Document, Edinburgh: Scottish Executive.

12. Scottish Executive (1999a), *op. cit.*, p. 8.

13. Scottish Executive (1999b), *op. cit.*, p. 33.

14. HMI (1998). *Effective Learning and Teaching in Scottish Secondary Schools: Art & Design*. Edinburgh: HMSO.

15. *Ibid.*, p. 18.

16. Adams, E (1997), *op. cit.*, p. 7

17. Adams, E (1999). Site Specific, Streetwise, *The Journal of the National Association of Urban Studies*, vol. 10:1, pp. 31–37.

18. Harding, D. (1997b), *op. cit.*, pp. 9-19.

19. Swift, J. & Steers, J (1999). A Manifesto for Art in Schools, *Journal of Art and Design Education*, vol. 18, no. 1, pp. 7–13.

20. Coutts, G. & Dawes, M *op. cit.*

21. DfE (1995). *The National Curriculum in England and Wales*. London: HMSO.

22. Scottish Office Education and Industry Department (1992). *Curriculum and Assessment in Scotland: National Guidelines: Expressive Arts, 5–14: Art and Design*, Edinburgh: HMSO.

23. HMI (1998), *op. cit.*

24. Robinson, K *et al.* (1990). *The Arts 5–16: A Curriculum Framework*, London: Oliver and Boyd.

25. Scottish Office Education and Industry Department, *op. cit.*, p. 25.

26. Tombs, S (2000). *Tracing the Past, Chasing the Future*, Perspectives Six, an Occasional Paper, Scottish Consultative Committee on the Curriculum, p. 7.

Author's note

Since the paper was written, the Digital Education Group at Strathclyde have continued to research and develop materials that focus on community and public art. See, for example, www. strath.ac.uk/degas.

Notes on Contributors

Eileen Adams's consultancy work links art, design, environment and education, and is underpinned by a wealth of experience as a teacher, lecturer, researcher and writer, both in the UK and worldwide. She was Director of the Schools Council *Art and the Built Environment* Project and of the research project *Learning through Landscapes*. Eileen is Director of *Power Drawing*, the professional development programme of *The Campaign for Drawing*. Current consultancies include an evaluation of the Partnership Programme for the Solent Centre for Architecture and Design and the preparation of an education strategy for SAFLE, a new organization that integrates art and environment. She is a visiting academic at Middlesex University, a commissioner for the Design Commission for Wales, a member of CIWEM's Art and Environment Network and an adviser to the Centre for Drawing at Wimbledon College of Art.

Julie K. Austin graduated from the Royal Scottish Academy of Music and Drama with a Diploma in Speech and Drama, from Glasgow University with a BA in Dramatic Studies, and from Jordanhill College with a PGCE(S) in Drama. She taught speech and drama in secondary schools for twelve years, for eight of them as Head of Drama. For three years she lectured in acting and drama at Glasgow Arts Centre before joining the University of Strathclyde as a Lecturer in Drama, teaching the initial teacher education courses and the BA Community Arts Degree. She went on to become Course Director for the Community Arts course, a post which she held for nine years.

Sarah Bennett is Principal Lecturer in Fine Art and Coordinator of the MA Fine Art course at the University of Plymouth. She is a working artist and is currently undertaking practice-led site-based doctoral research into the process of redeveloping a former psychiatric hospital into owner-occupier dwellings. She is also the co-editor of *Locality, Regeneration and Divers©ties, Art & Urban Futures*. Vol. 1. (2000).

Peter Boyle is co-director of VERGE Urban Landscape Architecture in Brisbane. Peter and the VERGE team are committed to ecologically, socially and economically sustainable outcomes in the application of landscape architecture to the built environment. Peter's involvement with the *Living City* Project began in 1999. He is current Chair of the Queensland Group of the Australian Institute of Architects' university course accreditation panel and has been a casual member of the teaching staff at the Queensland University of Technology for a number of years.

Tony Chisholm has been involved in art education for 37 years. He has been Head of Art and Design in several comprehensive schools and has worked as a lecturer, senior lecturer and teacher-trainer in both Further and Higher Education. He has performed an advisory role with a number of local education authorities and other organizations. He was made a Companion of the Ruskin Society's Guild of St George and a Fellow of the College of Preceptors in 1996, and a Fellow of the Royal Society of Arts in 1997.

Glen Coutts is a Reader in Art and Design Education in the Department of Sport, Culture and the Arts in the Faculty of Education at the University of Strathclyde. He began his career as a community artist, taught art and design in secondary schools for ten years and was head of department in a large secondary school for five years. His teaching and research have focused on two main areas of art education, initial teacher education and public art, but he is also interested in the role of creativity in formal education and the pedagogic potential of digital media. He is a former chair of the Teacher Education Board and President of the NSEAD.

Mark Dawes is an artist, writer and educator based in Glasgow. He has a BA in Fine Art Photography from Glasgow School of Art and an MA in Fine Art from the University of Ulster. Publications include the CD-ROMs *Images From The Royal Scottish Academy: Scottish Art 1780-Present* (Learning & Teaching Scotland, 2006) and *Scanning The City: A Digital Journey Around Public Art & Urban Design In The City Of Glasgow* (University Of Strathclyde, 1999). He currently works in Adult Literacies.

Mirja Hiltunen (LicArt MEd) is a lecturer in Art Education in the Faculty of Art and Design at the University of Lapland. She has devised a performative art strategy as part of her work in art teacher education and has been leading community-based art workshops and projects in Lapland for over ten years. Her Ph.D. topic is community-based art education in a northern sociocultural environment. Her study combines concrete cultural activities, development of these activities through art education projects, and theoretical examination of the subject area. The site-specificity, performativity and social dimensions of art are of particular interest to her, and she has published numerous papers in this area.

Les Hooper is Head of Art at Kelvin Grove State College in Brisbane, Queensland, an inner-city state college with a reputation for excellence in the arts. In 1999, Les was the project officer in Education Queensland for the 30 World Congress of the International Society for Education through Art (InSEA), and the *Living City* project was first developed as a collaborative undertaking for this event. Les is the current president of the Queensland Art Teachers Association.

Maria Huhmarniemi is a Ph.D. student and temporary lecturer with the Department of Art Education in the Faculty of Art and Design at the University of Lapland in Rovaniemi, Finland. Huhmarniemi has co-authored and co-edited several books and authored articles discussing different forms of art and art education in Finland. She has participated in many art projects and tutored several art workshops in northern

Finland and in the Barents region. Huhmarniemi has also tutored and designed Web-based studies in environmental and community art. In her doctoral thesis, she will investigate how the University's Department of Art Education promotes the development of provincial areas through action research, environmental art and community-based art education.

Timo Jokela is Professor of Art Education in the Faculty of Art and Design at the University of Lapland in Rovaniemi, Finland. He has been head of the department since 1995. His theoretical academic studies focus on the phenomenological relationship between art and nature, environmental art, community art and art education. He is responsible for several international cooperative and regional development projects in this field. Jokela works actively as an environmental artist, often with natural materials such as wood, snow and ice, or taking the local cultural heritage as a starting point. He has exhibited regularly and has realized several environmental art and community projects both in his native Finland and further afield.

Ray McKenzie studied art history and philosophy at the University of Glasgow and is now Senior Lecturer in the Department of Historical and Critical Studies at Glasgow School of Art. His publications include *Public Sculpture of Glasgow*, which was commissioned by Liverpool University Press as part of its 'Public Sculpture of Britain' series, and was joint winner of the Saltire Society's Research Book of the Year award in 2002. He is also co-editor of *The State of the Real* (I B Tauris, 2007), which examines the impact of new technology on contemporary aesthetics, and is currently preparing a book on the public sculpture of south-west Scotland.

After graduating with degrees in botany, **Angus McWilliam** worked in environmental conservation, environmental education and outdoor education. This was followed by twelve years as teacher and head teacher in Special Education before he moved back to Higher Education. He currently heads the Department of Sport Culture and the Arts at Strathclyde University.

Malcolm Miles is Professor of Cultural Theory at the University of Plymouth, author of Urban Utopias (2008), Cities & Cultures (2007) and Urban Avant-Gardes (2004) and co-editor of The City Cultures Reader (2nd edition, 2003). His current research is between critical theory and contemporary art, including reconsideration of Herbert Marcuse's writing from the 1960s and 1970s.

INDEX